PREVIOUSLY...

Jim Hammond is the original Human Torch and fought alongside the INVADERS during World War II. He had been quietly adjusting to life as an android in present-day America until CAPTAIN AMERICA asked him to join the super-spy agency S.H.I.E.L.D. Hammond accepted.

The WINTER SOLDIER (formerly Cap's sidekick, BUCKY) found out their old teammate TORO had been apprehended by German terrorist Kurt Dagmar. In an attempt to rescue Toro, NAMOR, Captain America, Winter Soldier and the Torch battled Dagmar's army of nanovirus-controlled DEATHLOKS. Upon defeating the cyborg soldiers with the help of the new IRON CROSS, they discovered Dagmar was really a Martian spy.

What was the Martian really after? The key may be with Jim Hammond, who has been driven insane by the virus that controlled the Deathloks. And now the dangerous and crazed synthetic man is missing...

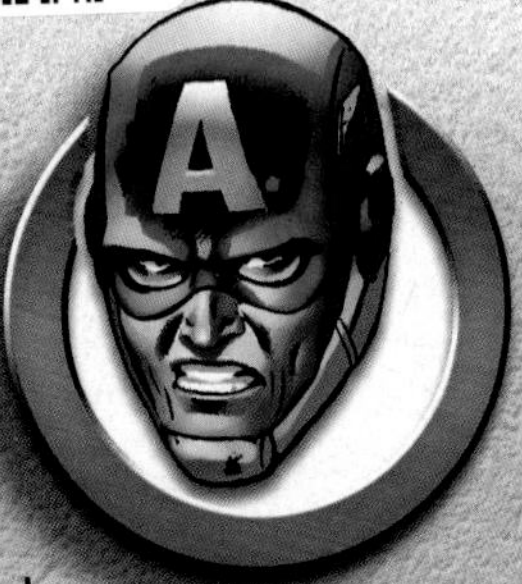

CAPTAIN AMERICA, the super-soldier, living legend, and sentinel of liberty remains the epitome of a national/world hero, with links to both the Avengers and S.H.I.E.L.D. and a continued history of doing good.

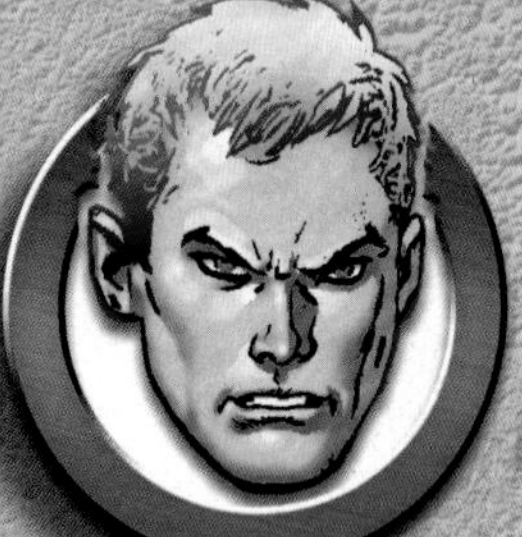

JIM HAMMOND, THE ORIGINAL HUMAN TORCH and the world's first synthetic human, is perhaps the least known of the heroes. Recently a cadre of robots and androids planned to take over Earth, a plan that Jim betrayed and helped defeat for the sake of humanity.

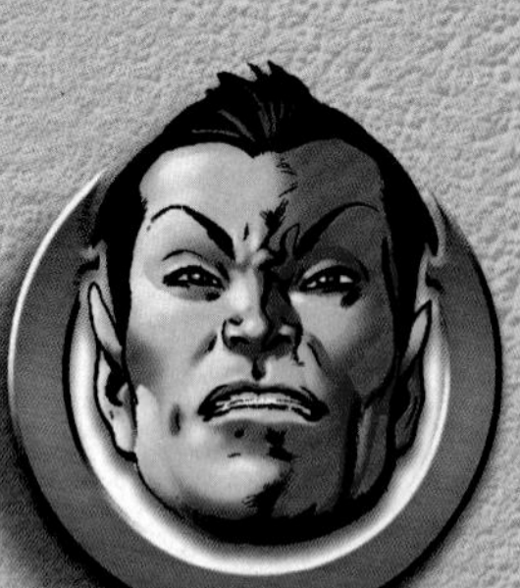

NAMOR, THE SUB-MARINER, aquatic ruler of the undersea kingdom of Atlantis has been a hero too since the war, but at other times, humanity's greatest foe. Currently his place in the world is somewhere between the two.

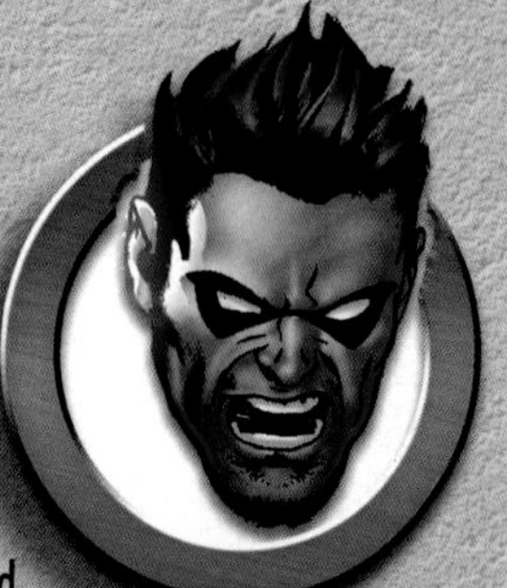

JAMES "BUCKY" BARNES, one-time sidekick of Captain America, was long thought to have died in the closing months of the war. Actually he'd survived and was brainwashed by the Russians into becoming the assassin and super-spy known as the Winter Soldier. He remains a wanted man for his crimes as a Russian killer and was forced to fake his death. The Winter Soldier now lives in the shadows.

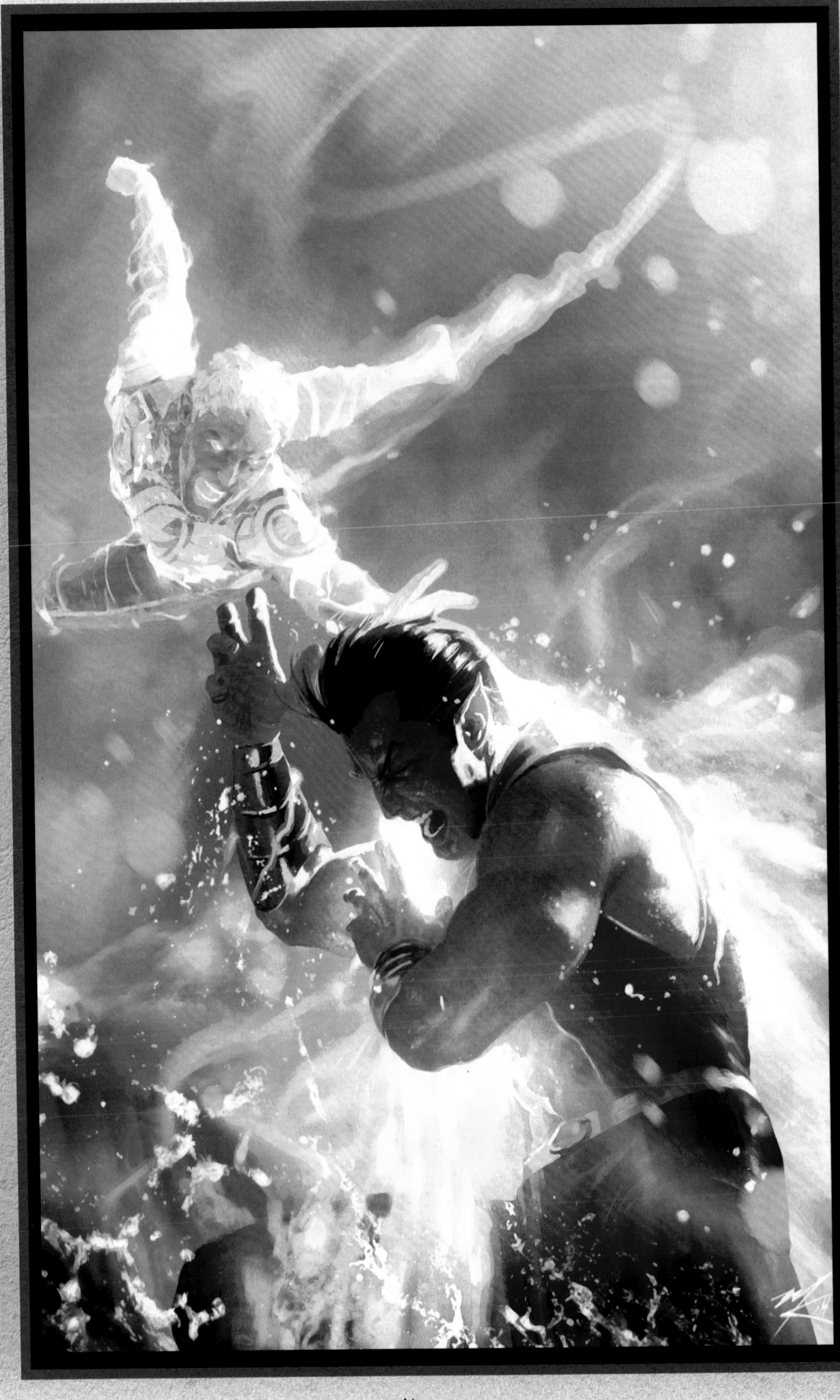

#11

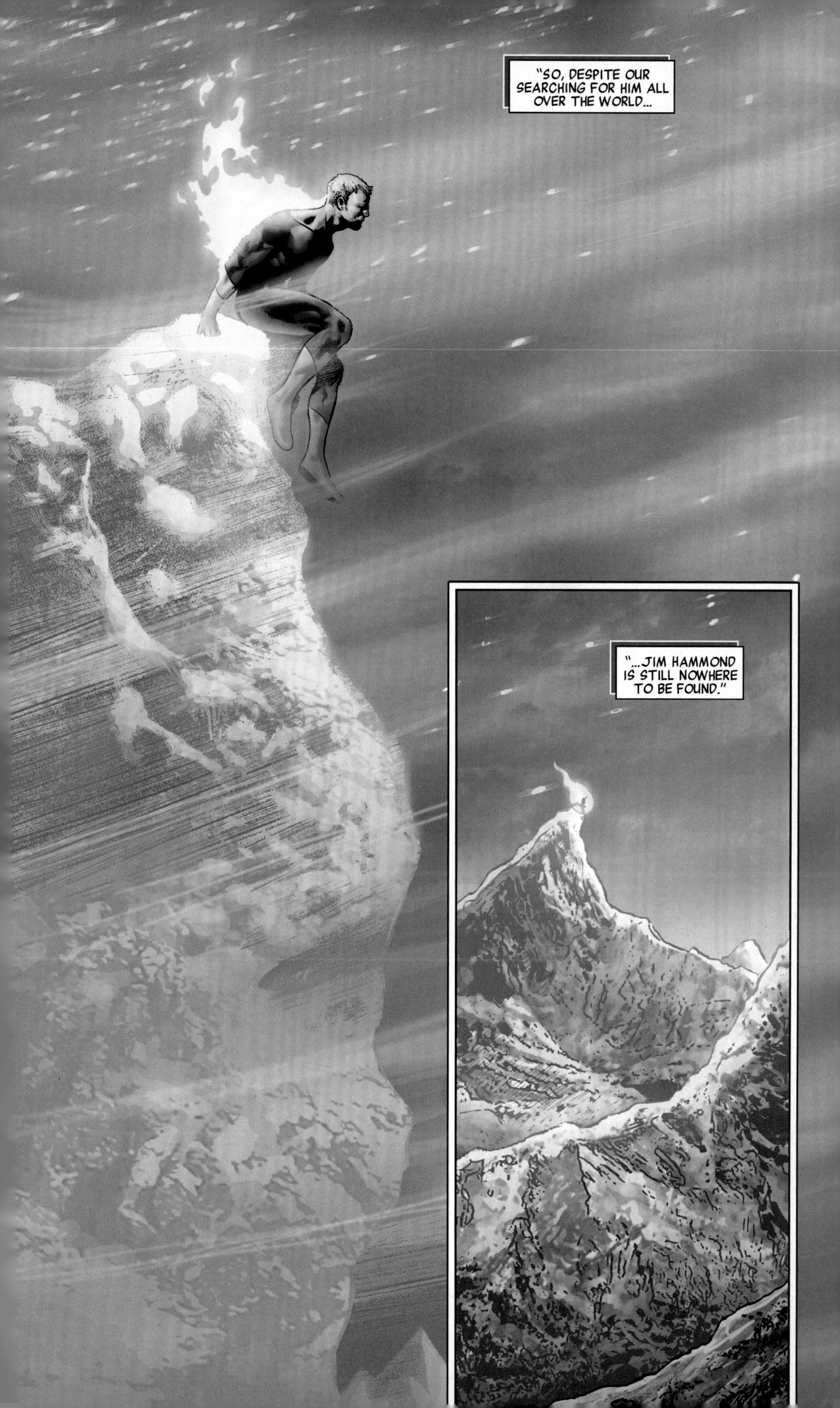
"SO, DESPITE OUR SEARCHING FOR HIM ALL OVER THE WORLD...
"...JIM HAMMOND IS STILL NOWHERE TO BE FOUND."

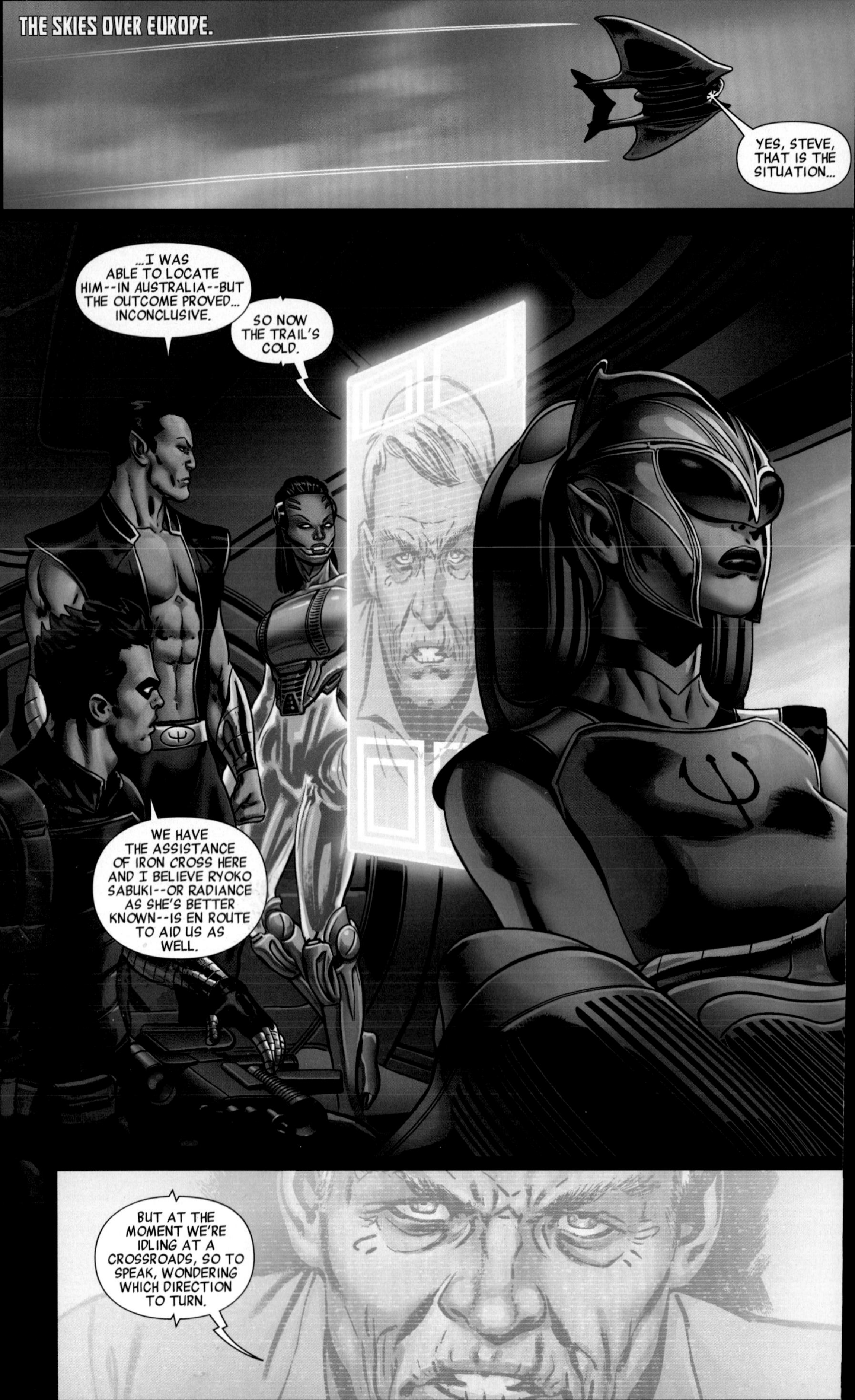
THE SKIES OVER EUROPE.
YES, STEVE, THAT IS THE SITUATION...
...I WAS ABLE TO LOCATE HIM--IN AUSTRALIA--BUT THE OUTCOME PROVED... INCONCLUSIVE.
SO NOW THE TRAIL'S COLD.
WE HAVE THE ASSISTANCE OF IRON CROSS HERE AND I BELIEVE RYOKO SABUKI--OR RADIANCE AS SHE'S BETTER KNOWN--IS EN ROUTE TO AID US AS WELL.
BUT AT THE MOMENT WE'RE IDLING AT A CROSSROADS, SO TO SPEAK, WONDERING WHICH DIRECTION TO TURN.

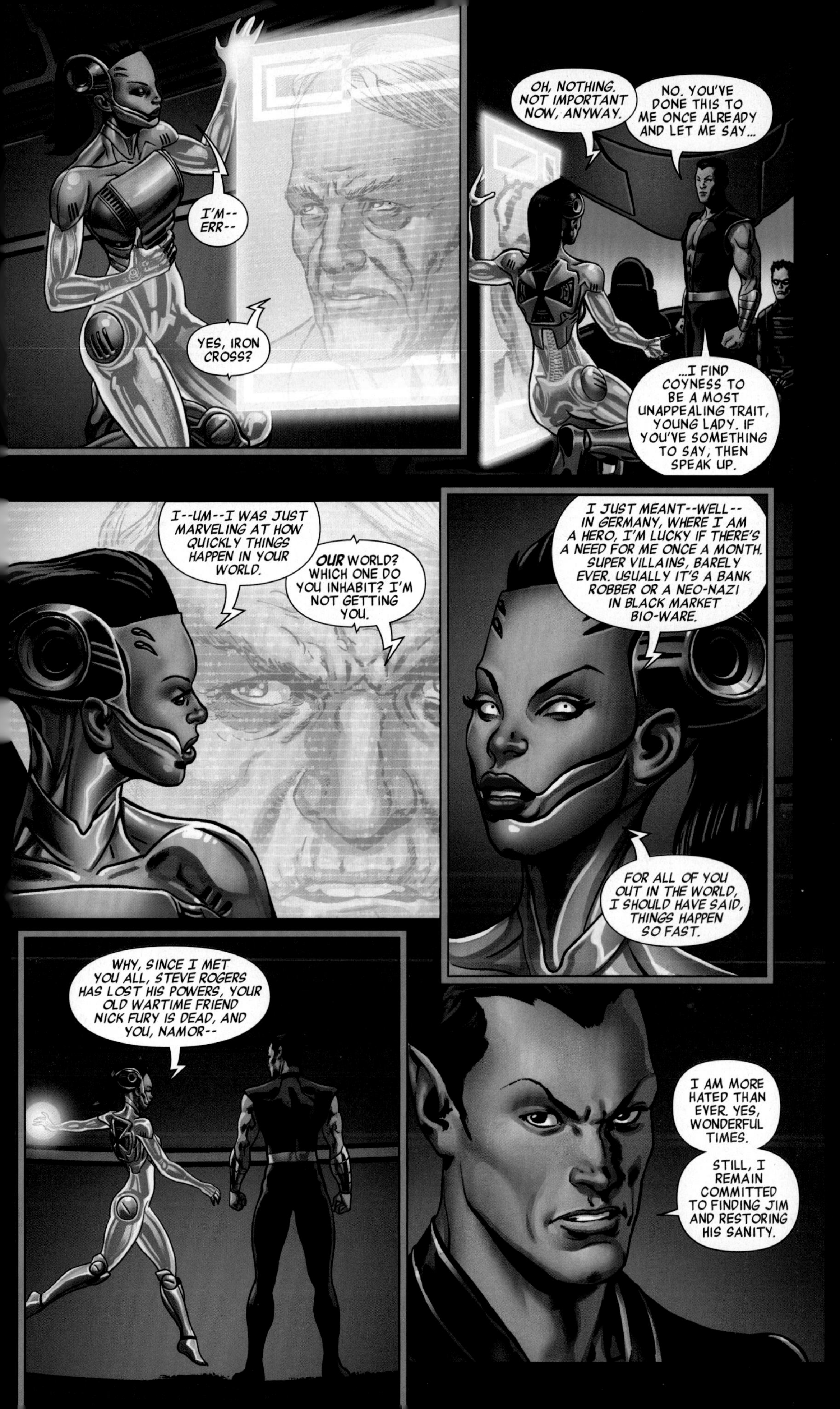
I'M--ERR--
YES, IRON CROSS?
OH, NOTHING. NOT IMPORTANT NOW, ANYWAY.
NO. YOU'VE DONE THIS TO ME ONCE ALREADY AND LET ME SAY...
...I FIND COYNESS TO BE A MOST UNAPPEALING TRAIT, YOUNG LADY. IF YOU'VE SOMETHING TO SAY, THEN SPEAK UP.
I--UM--I WAS JUST MARVELING AT HOW QUICKLY THINGS HAPPEN IN YOUR WORLD.
OUR WORLD? WHICH ONE DO YOU INHABIT? I'M NOT GETTING YOU.
I JUST MEANT--WELL--IN GERMANY, WHERE I AM A HERO, I'M LUCKY IF THERE'S A NEED FOR ME ONCE A MONTH. SUPER VILLAINS, BARELY EVER. USUALLY IT'S A BANK ROBBER OR A NEO-NAZI IN BLACK MARKET BIO-WARE.
FOR ALL OF YOU OUT IN THE WORLD, I SHOULD HAVE SAID, THINGS HAPPEN SO FAST.
WHY, SINCE I MET YOU ALL, STEVE ROGERS HAS LOST HIS POWERS, YOUR OLD WARTIME FRIEND NICK FURY IS DEAD, AND YOU, NAMOR--
I AM MORE HATED THAN EVER. YES, WONDERFUL TIMES.
STILL, I REMAIN COMMITTED TO FINDING JIM AND RESTORING HIS SANITY.

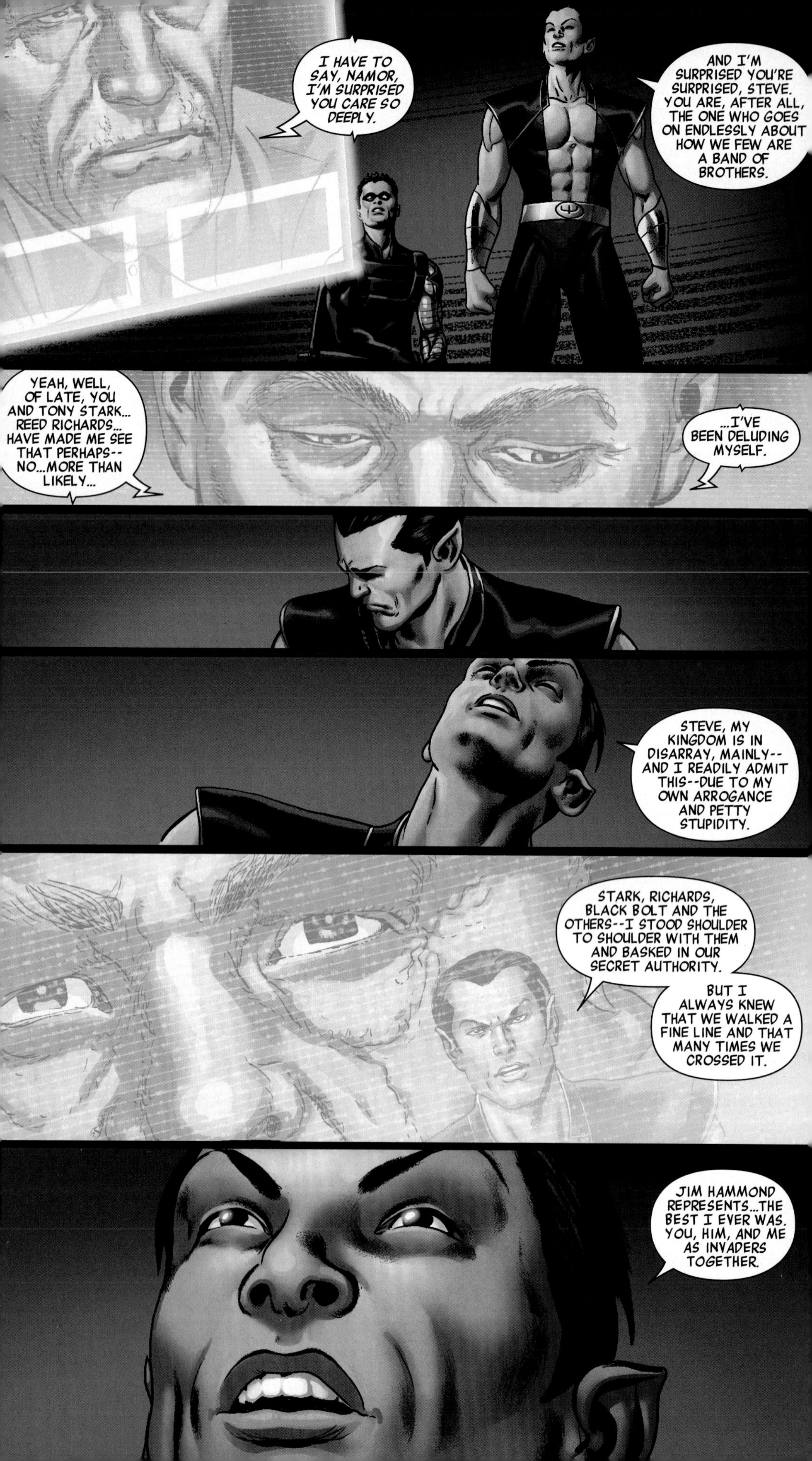
I HAVE TO SAY, NAMOR, I'M SURPRISED YOU CARE SO DEEPLY.
AND I'M SURPRISED YOU'RE SURPRISED, STEVE. YOU ARE, AFTER ALL, THE ONE WHO GOES ON ENDLESSLY ABOUT HOW WE FEW ARE A BAND OF BROTHERS.
YEAH, WELL, OF LATE, YOU AND TONY STARK... REED RICHARDS... HAVE MADE ME SEE THAT PERHAPS-- NO...MORE THAN LIKELY...
...I'VE BEEN DELUDING MYSELF.
STEVE, MY KINGDOM IS IN DISARRAY, MAINLY-- AND I READILY ADMIT THIS--DUE TO MY OWN ARROGANCE AND PETTY STUPIDITY.
STARK, RICHARDS, BLACK BOLT AND THE OTHERS--I STOOD SHOULDER TO SHOULDER WITH THEM AND BASKED IN OUR SECRET AUTHORITY.
BUT I ALWAYS KNEW THAT WE WALKED A FINE LINE AND THAT MANY TIMES WE CROSSED IT.
JIM HAMMOND REPRESENTS...THE BEST I EVER WAS. YOU, HIM, AND ME AS INVADERS TOGETHER.

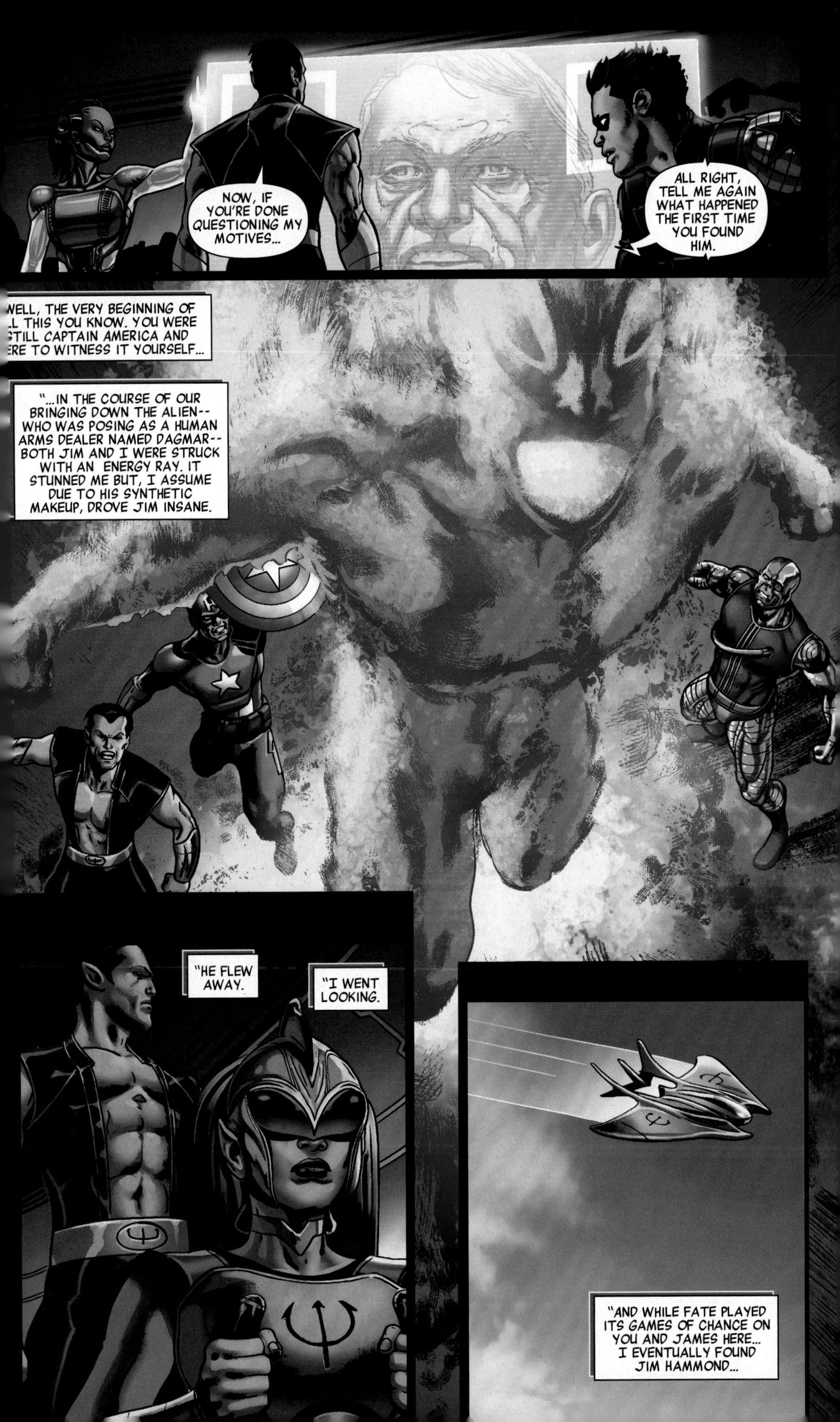
NOW, IF YOU'RE DONE QUESTIONING MY MOTIVES...
ALL RIGHT, TELL ME AGAIN WHAT HAPPENED THE FIRST TIME YOU FOUND HIM.
WELL, THE VERY BEGINNING OF ALL THIS YOU KNOW. YOU WERE STILL CAPTAIN AMERICA AND HERE TO WITNESS IT YOURSELF...
"...IN THE COURSE OF OUR BRINGING DOWN THE ALIEN-- WHO WAS POSING AS A HUMAN ARMS DEALER NAMED DAGMAR-- BOTH JIM AND I WERE STRUCK WITH AN ENERGY RAY. IT STUNNED ME BUT, I ASSUME DUE TO HIS SYNTHETIC MAKEUP, DROVE JIM INSANE.
"HE FLEW AWAY.
"I WENT LOOKING.
"AND WHILE FATE PLAYED ITS GAMES OF CHANCE ON YOU AND JAMES HERE... I EVENTUALLY FOUND JIM HAMMOND...

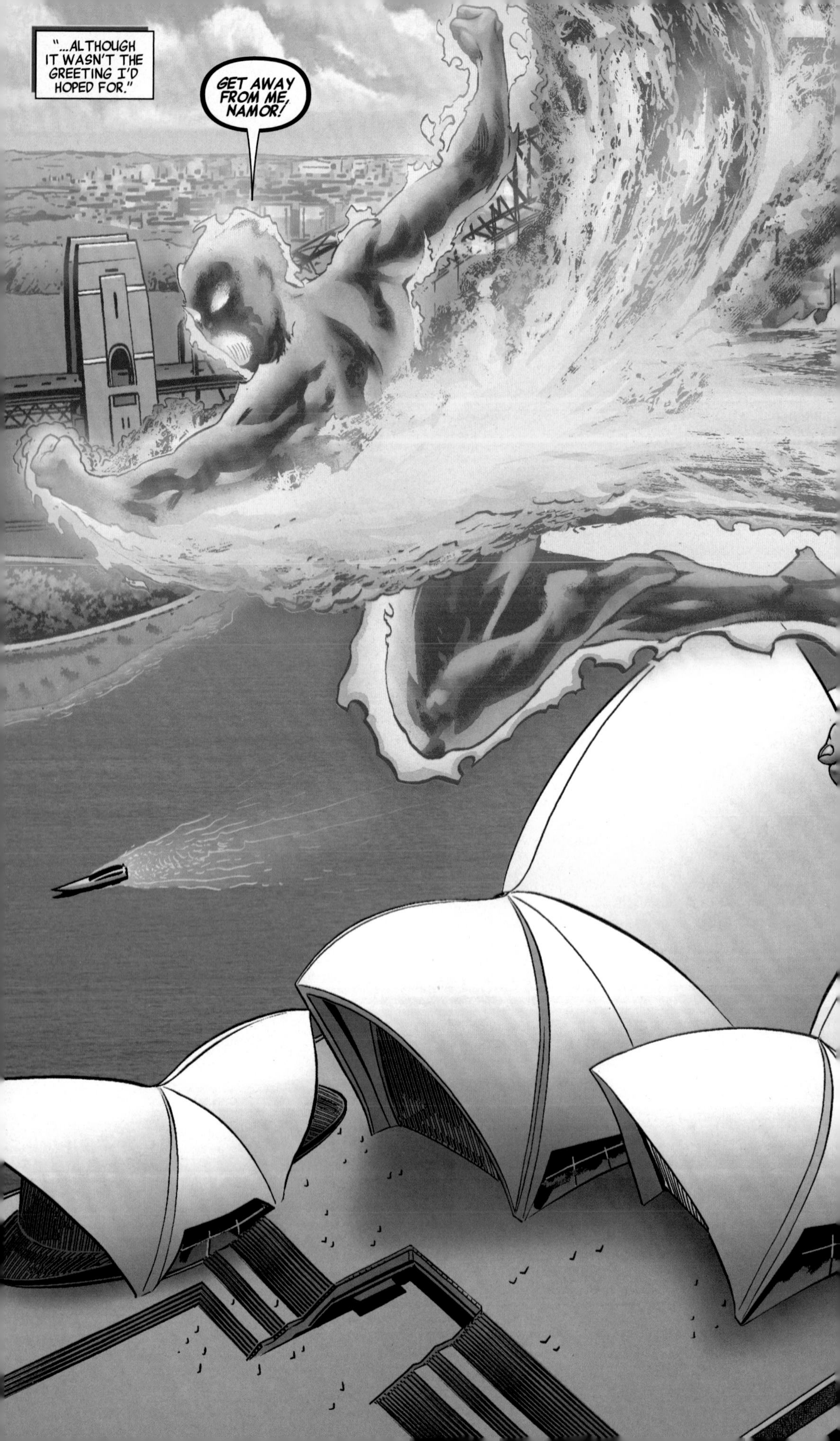
"...ALTHOUGH IT WASN'T THE GREETING I'D HOPED FOR."
GET AWAY FROM ME, NAMOR!

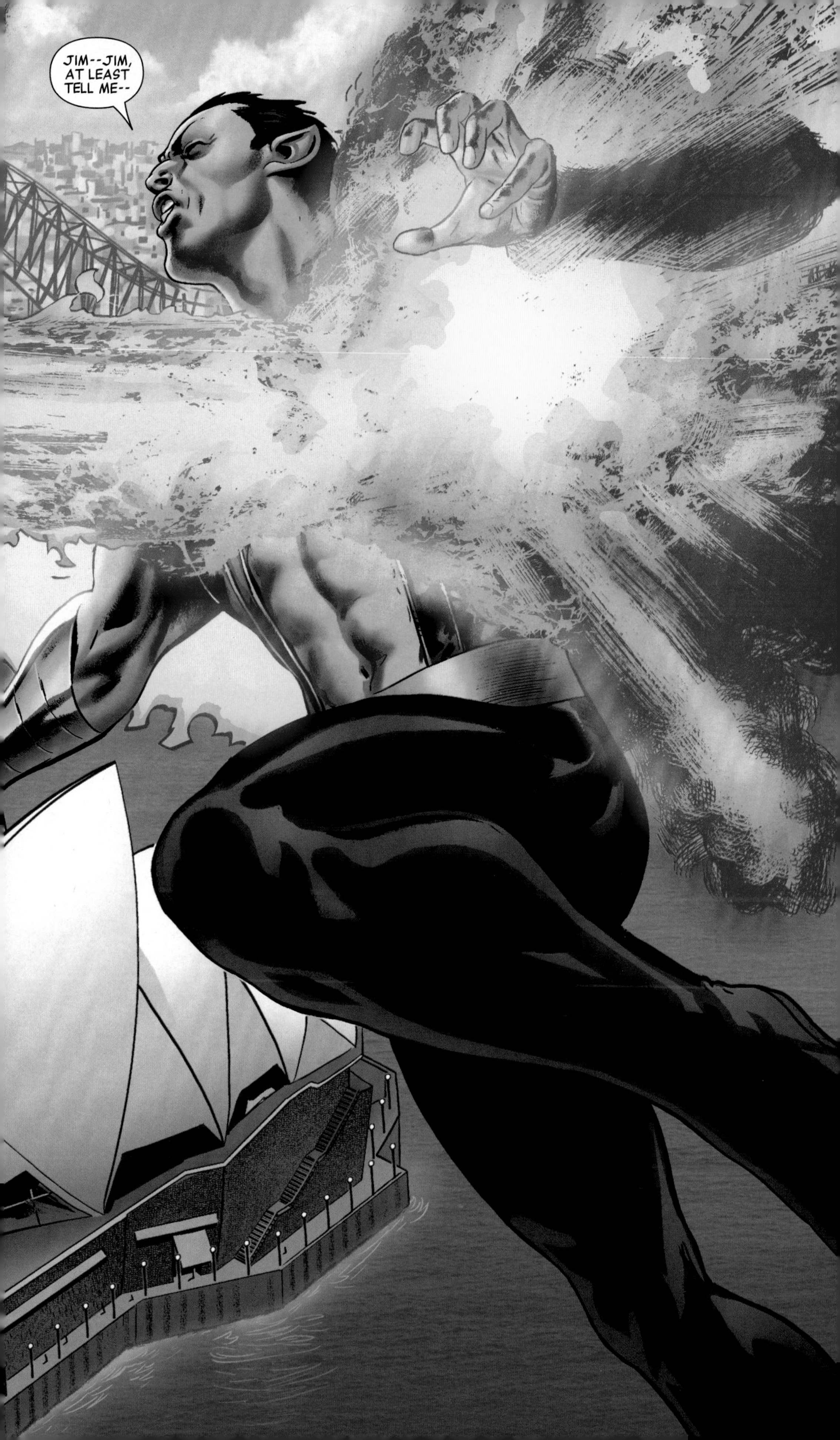
JIM--JIM, AT LEAST TELL ME--

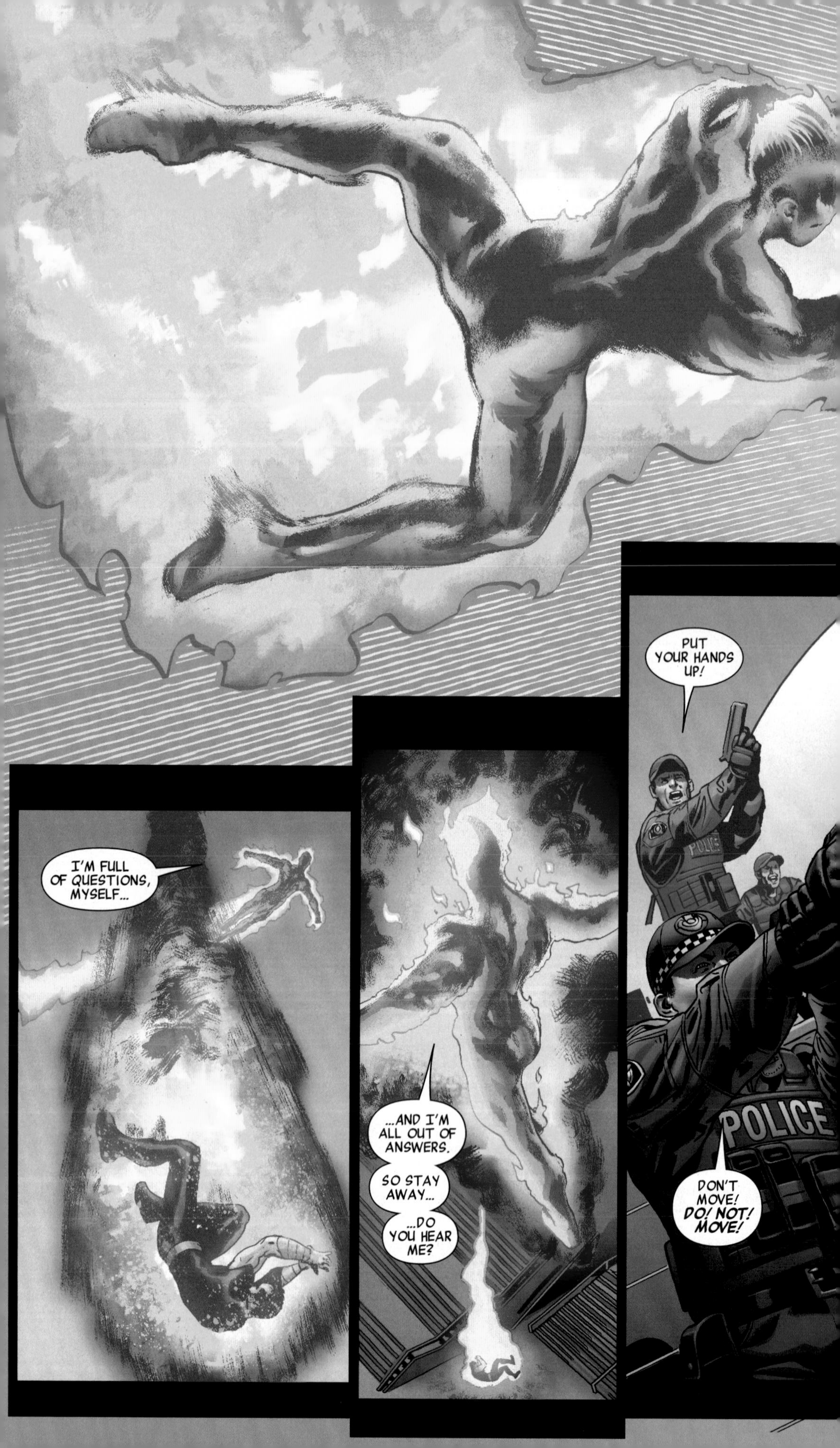
I'M FULL OF QUESTIONS, MYSELF...
...AND I'M ALL OUT OF ANSWERS.
SO STAY AWAY...
...DO YOU HEAR ME?
PUT YOUR HANDS UP!
POLICE
POLICE
DON'T MOVE! DO! NOT! MOVE!

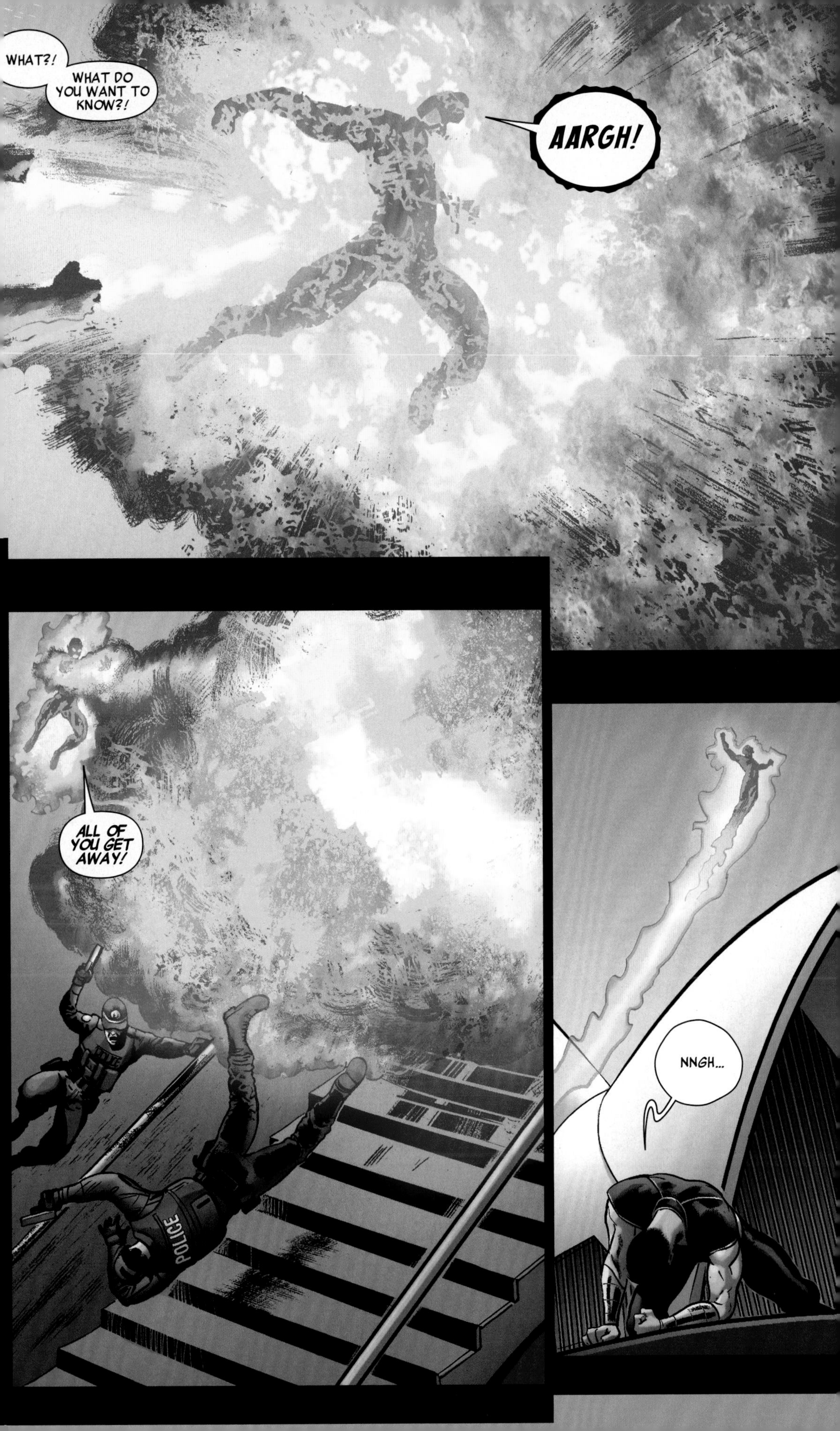
WHAT?!
WHAT DO YOU WANT TO KNOW?!
AARGH!
ALL OF YOU GET AWAY!
NNGH...

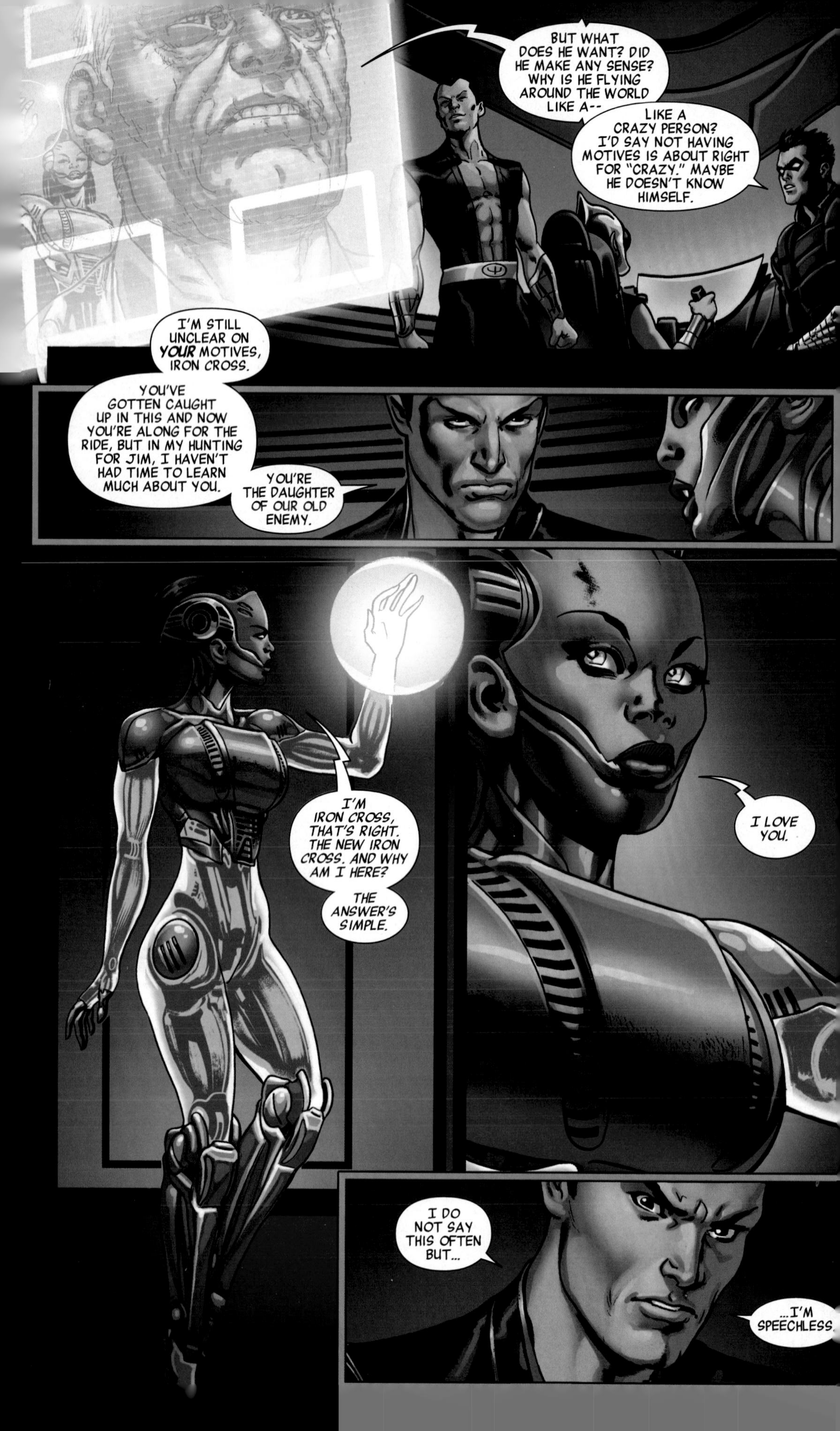
BUT WHAT DOES HE WANT? DID HE MAKE ANY SENSE? WHY IS HE FLYING AROUND THE WORLD LIKE A--
LIKE A CRAZY PERSON? I'D SAY NOT HAVING MOTIVES IS ABOUT RIGHT FOR "CRAZY." MAYBE HE DOESN'T KNOW HIMSELF.
I'M STILL UNCLEAR ON YOUR MOTIVES, IRON CROSS.
YOU'VE GOTTEN CAUGHT UP IN THIS AND NOW YOU'RE ALONG FOR THE RIDE, BUT IN MY HUNTING FOR JIM, I HAVEN'T HAD TIME TO LEARN MUCH ABOUT YOU.
YOU'RE THE DAUGHTER OF OUR OLD ENEMY.
I'M IRON CROSS, THAT'S RIGHT. THE NEW IRON CROSS. AND WHY AM I HERE?
THE ANSWER'S SIMPLE.
I LOVE YOU.
I DO NOT SAY THIS OFTEN BUT...
...I'M SPEECHLESS.

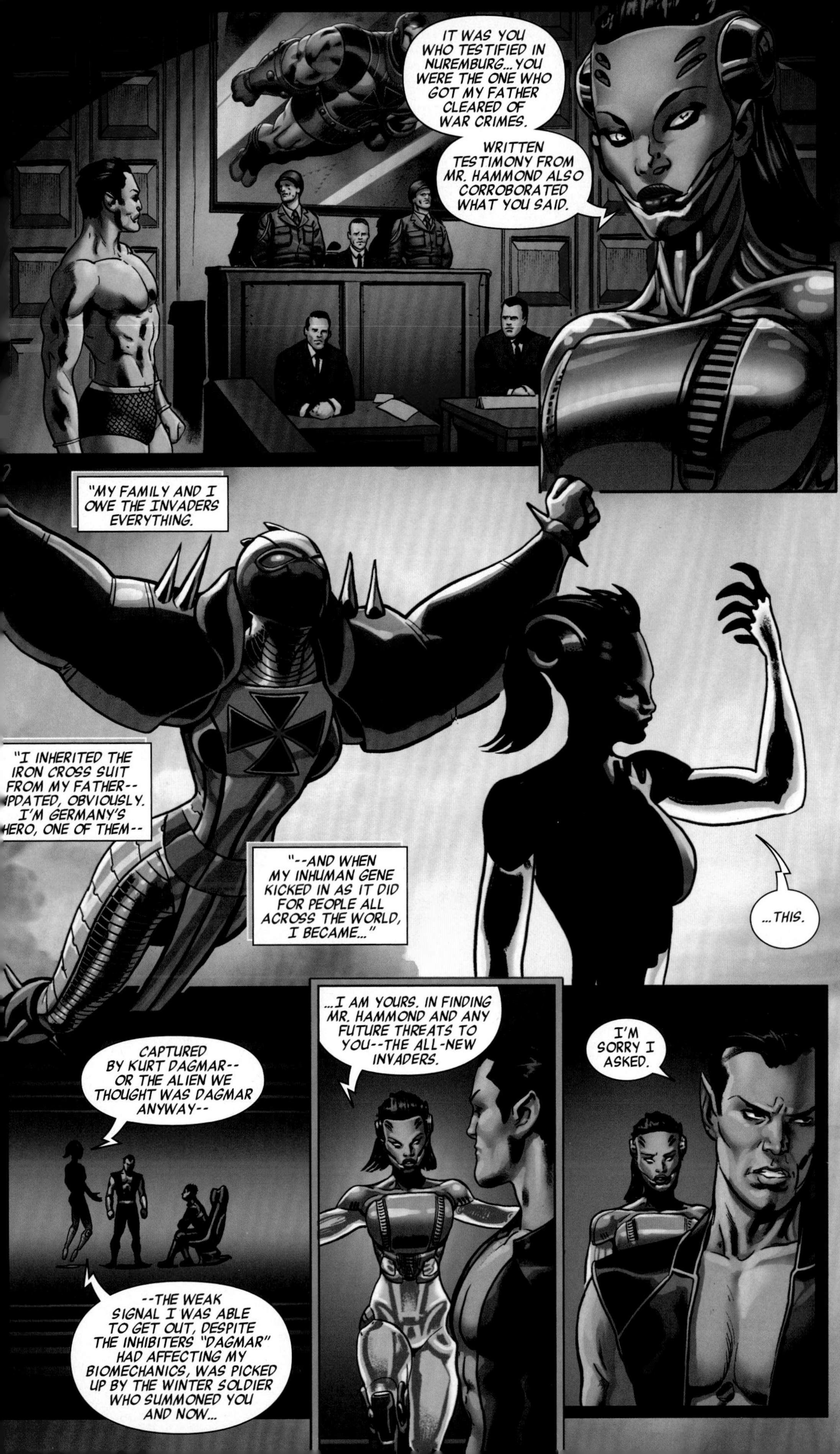
IT WAS YOU WHO TESTIFIED IN NUREMBURG...YOU WERE THE ONE WHO GOT MY FATHER CLEARED OF WAR CRIMES.
WRITTEN TESTIMONY FROM MR. HAMMOND ALSO CORROBORATED WHAT YOU SAID.
"MY FAMILY AND I OWE THE INVADERS EVERYTHING.
"I INHERITED THE IRON CROSS SUIT FROM MY FATHER-- UPDATED, OBVIOUSLY. I'M GERMANY'S HERO, ONE OF THEM--
"--AND WHEN MY INHUMAN GENE KICKED IN AS IT DID FOR PEOPLE ALL ACROSS THE WORLD, I BECAME..."
...THIS.
CAPTURED BY KURT DAGMAR-- OR THE ALIEN WE THOUGHT WAS DAGMAR ANYWAY--
--THE WEAK SIGNAL I WAS ABLE TO GET OUT, DESPITE THE INHIBITERS "DAGMAR" HAD AFFECTING MY BIOMECHANICS, WAS PICKED UP BY THE WINTER SOLDIER WHO SUMMONED YOU AND NOW...
...I AM YOURS. IN FINDING MR. HAMMOND AND ANY FUTURE THREATS TO YOU--THE ALL-NEW INVADERS.
I'M SORRY I ASKED.

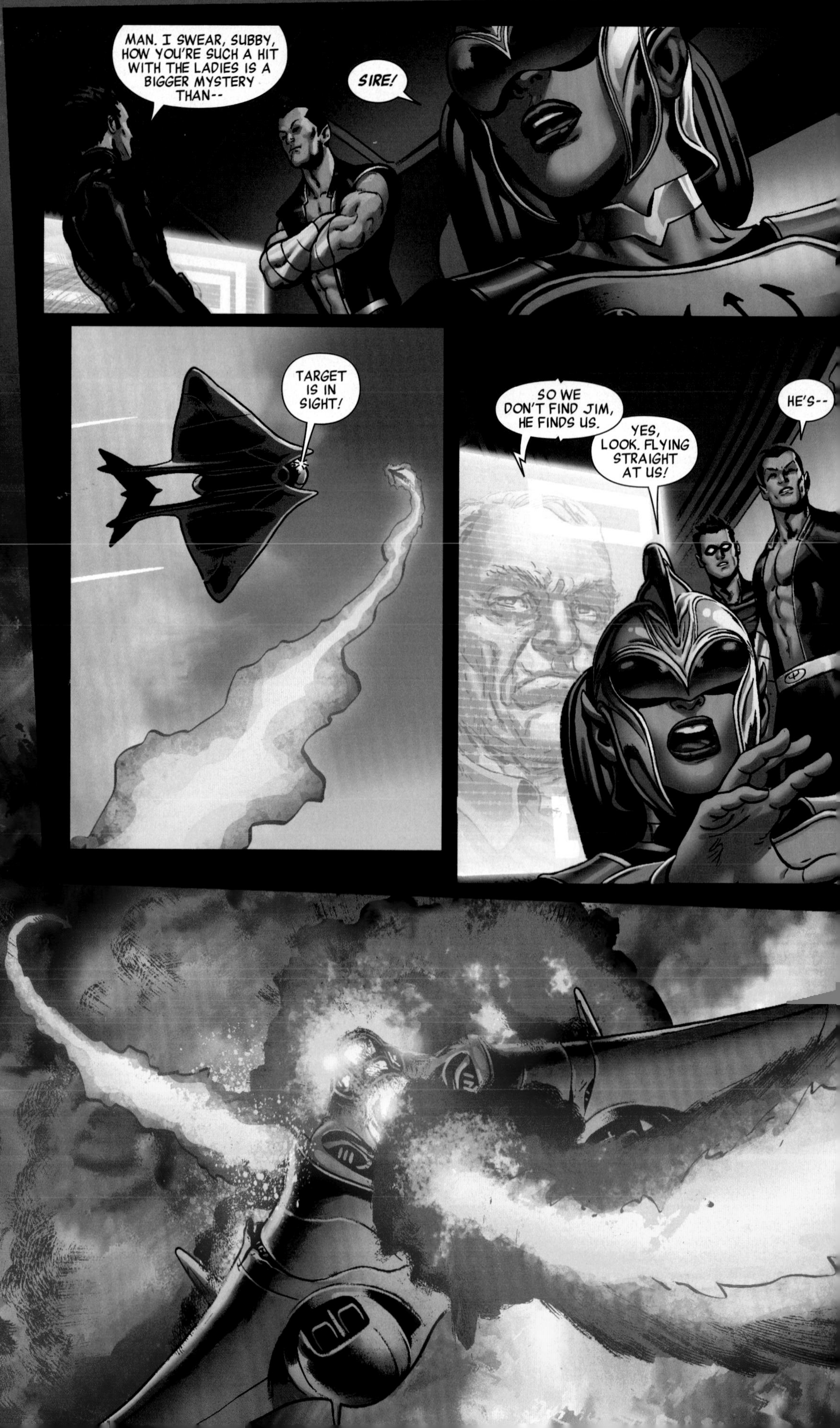
MAN. I SWEAR, SUBBY, HOW YOU'RE SUCH A HIT WITH THE LADIES IS A BIGGER MYSTERY THAN--
SIRE!
TARGET IS IN SIGHT!
SO WE DON'T FIND JIM, HE FINDS US.
YES, LOOK. FLYING STRAIGHT AT US!
HE'S--

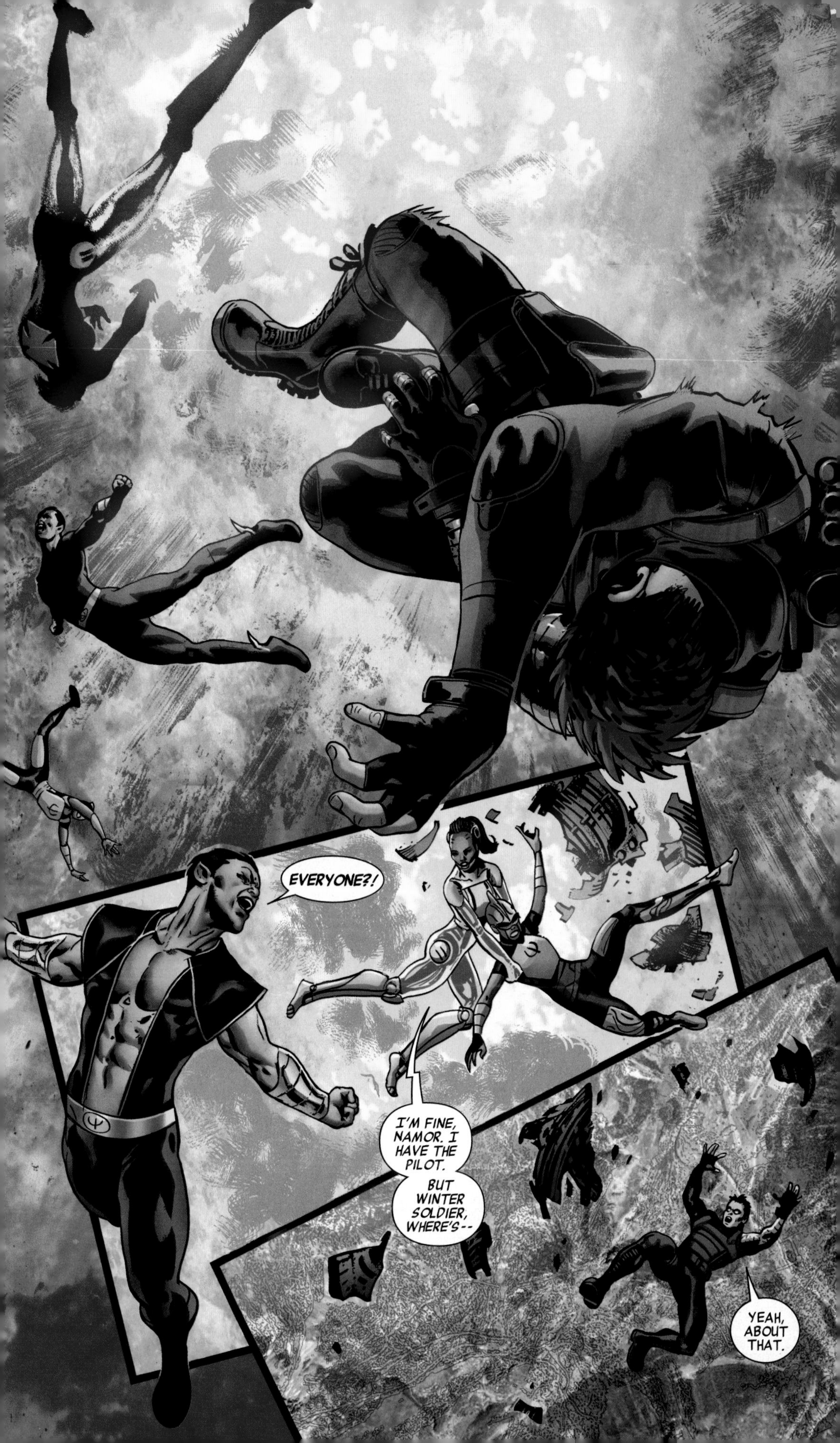
EVERYONE?!
I'M FINE, NAMOR. I HAVE THE PILOT.
BUT WINTER SOLDIER, WHERE'S--
YEAH, ABOUT THAT.

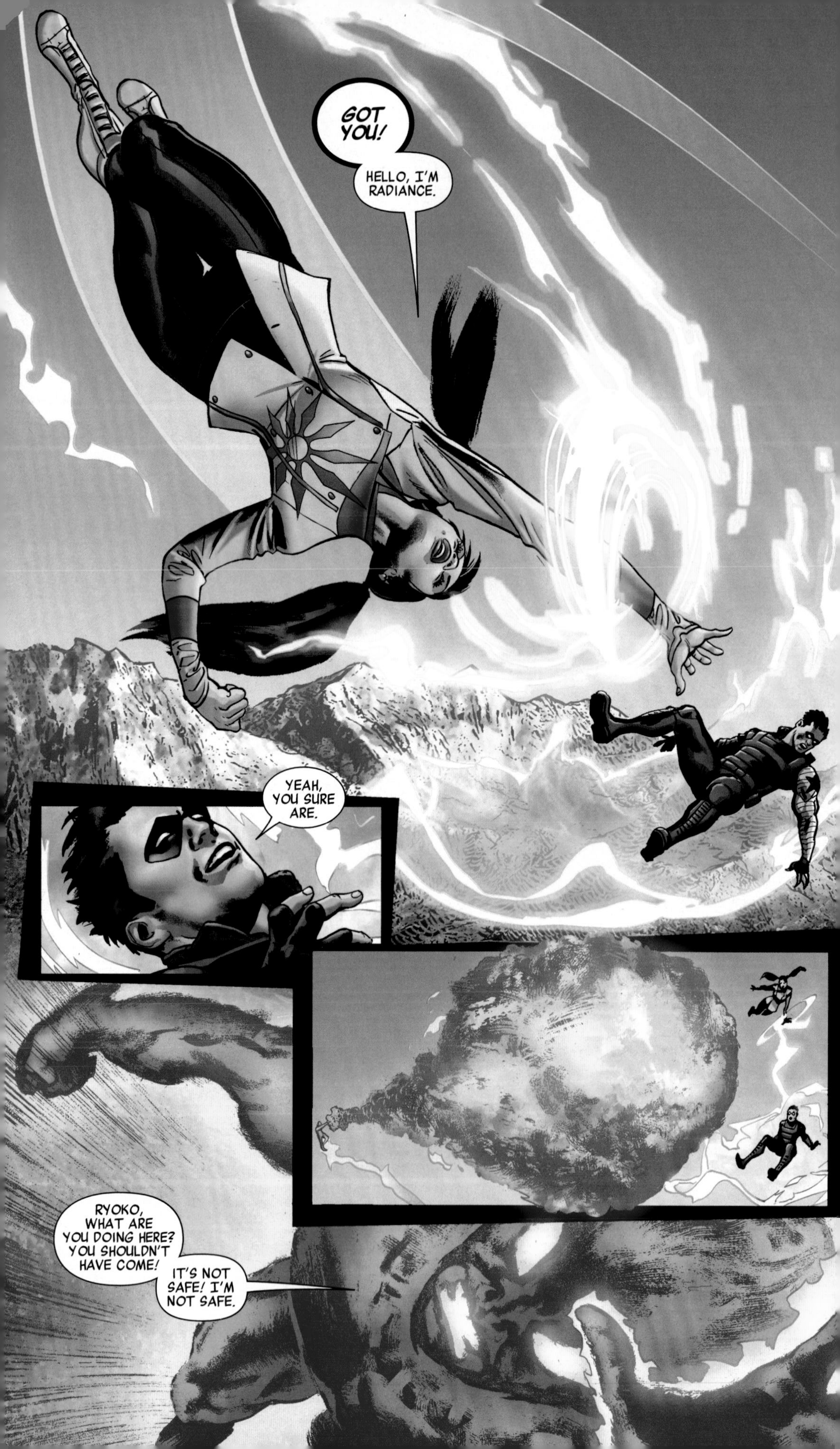
GOT YOU!
HELLO, I'M RADIANCE.
YEAH, YOU SURE ARE.
RYOKO, WHAT ARE YOU DOING HERE? YOU SHOULDN'T HAVE COME!
IT'S NOT SAFE! I'M NOT SAFE.

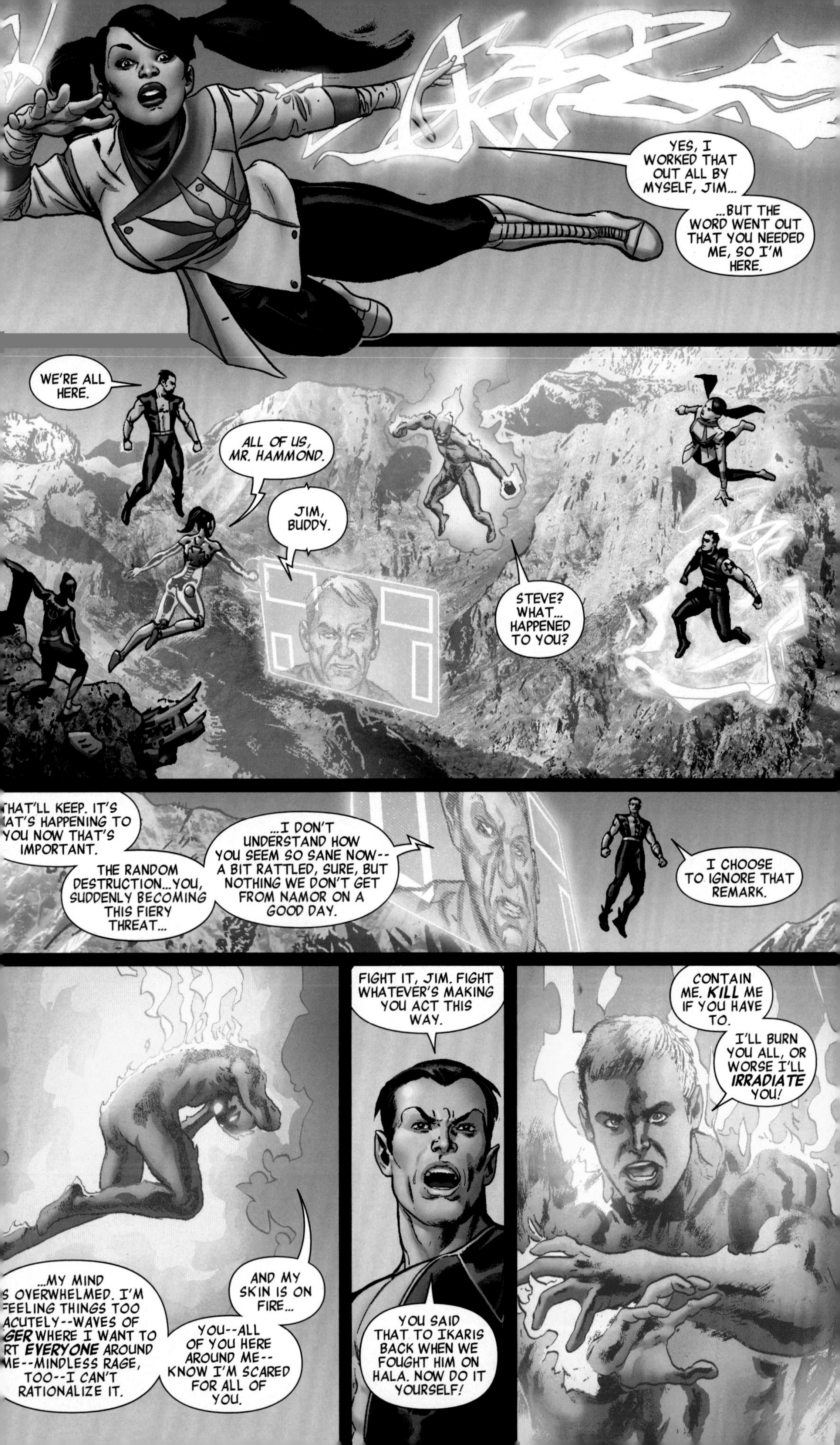
YES, I WORKED THAT OUT ALL BY MYSELF, JIM...
...BUT THE WORD WENT OUT THAT YOU NEEDED ME, SO I'M HERE.
WE'RE ALL HERE.
ALL OF US, MR. HAMMOND.
JIM, BUDDY.
STEVE? WHAT... HAPPENED TO YOU?
HAT'LL KEEP. IT'S AT'S HAPPENING TO YOU NOW THAT'S IMPORTANT.
THE RANDOM DESTRUCTION...YOU, SUDDENLY BECOMING THIS FIERY THREAT...
...I DON'T UNDERSTAND HOW YOU SEEM SO SANE NOW-- A BIT RATTLED, SURE, BUT NOTHING WE DON'T GET FROM NAMOR ON A GOOD DAY.
I CHOOSE TO IGNORE THAT REMARK.
...MY MIND S OVERWHELMED. I'M FEELING THINGS TOO ACUTELY--WAVES OF GER WHERE I WANT TO RT EVERYONE AROUND ME--MINDLESS RAGE, TOO--I CAN'T RATIONALIZE IT.
AND MY SKIN IS ON FIRE...
YOU--ALL OF YOU HERE AROUND ME--KNOW I'M SCARED FOR ALL OF YOU.
FIGHT IT, JIM. FIGHT WHATEVER'S MAKING YOU ACT THIS WAY.
YOU SAID THAT TO IKARIS BACK WHEN WE FOUGHT HIM ON HALA. NOW DO IT YOURSELF!
CONTAIN ME. KILL ME IF YOU HAVE TO.
I'LL BURN YOU ALL, OR WORSE I'LL IRRADIATE YOU!

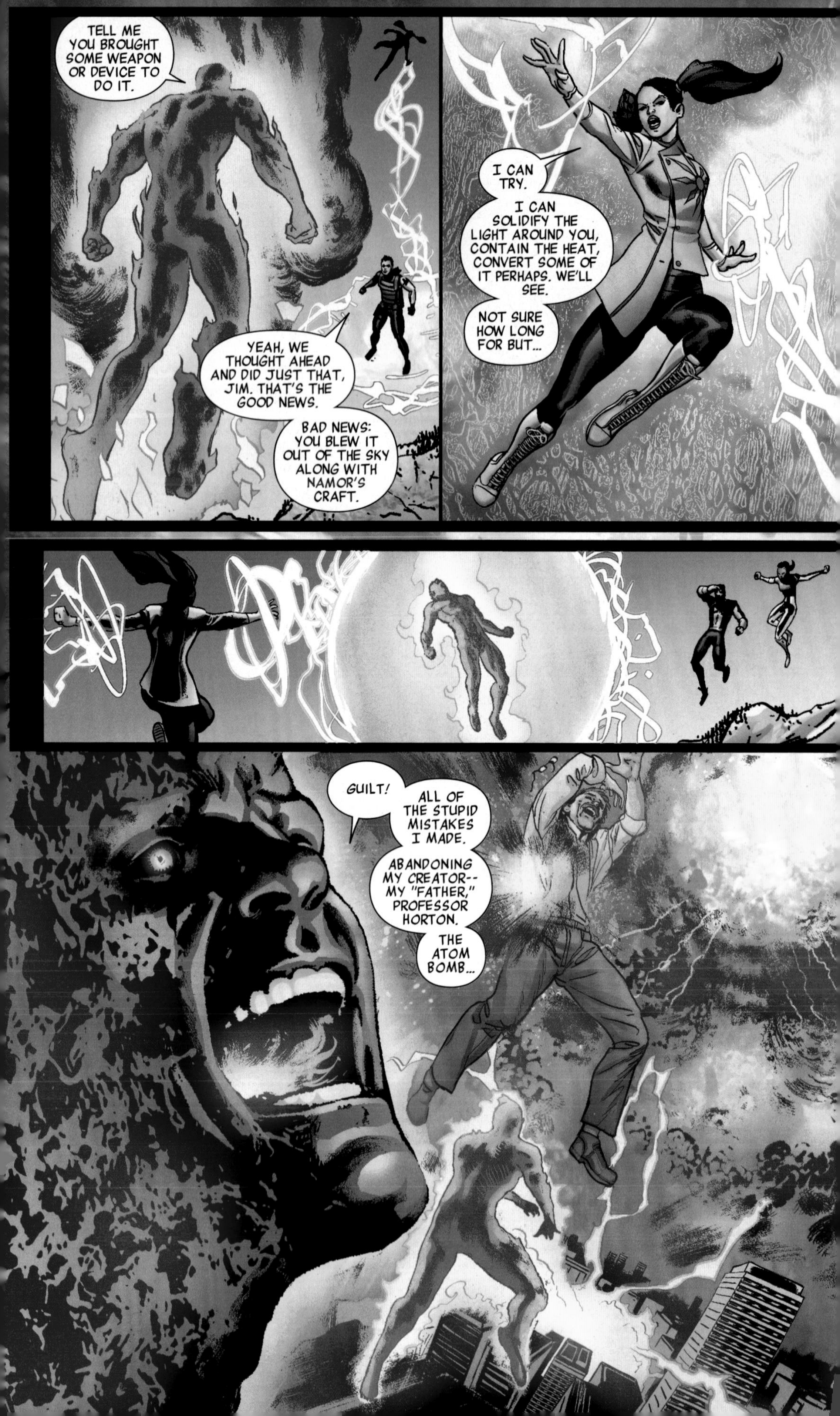
TELL ME YOU BROUGHT SOME WEAPON OR DEVICE TO DO IT.
YEAH, WE THOUGHT AHEAD AND DID JUST THAT, JIM. THAT'S THE GOOD NEWS.
BAD NEWS: YOU BLEW IT OUT OF THE SKY ALONG WITH NAMOR'S CRAFT.
I CAN TRY.
I CAN SOLIDIFY THE LIGHT AROUND YOU, CONTAIN THE HEAT, CONVERT SOME OF IT PERHAPS. WE'LL SEE.
NOT SURE HOW LONG FOR BUT...
GUILT!
ALL OF THE STUPID MISTAKES I MADE.
ABANDONING MY CREATOR-- MY "FATHER," PROFESSOR HORTON.
THE ATOM BOMB...

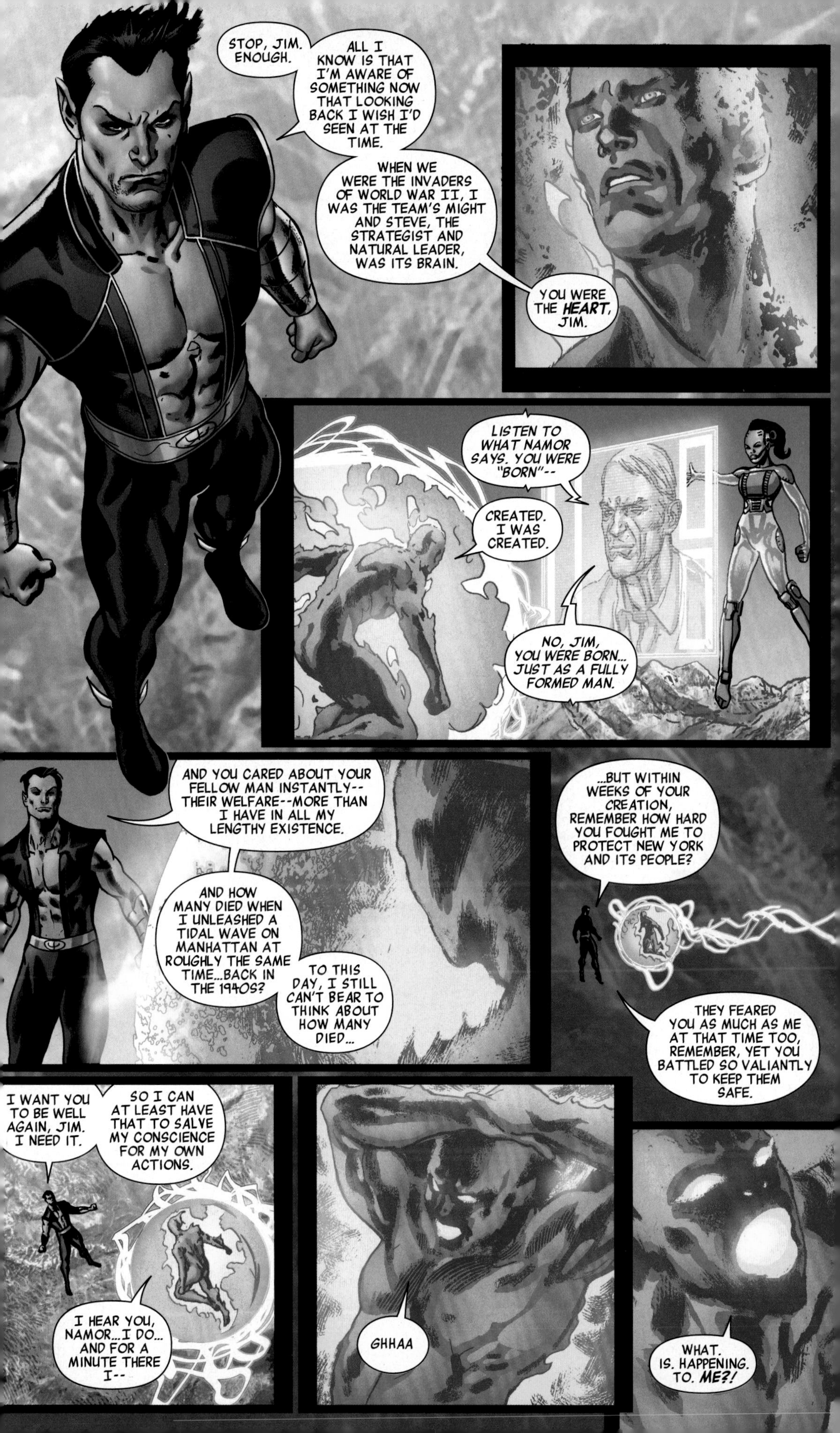
STOP, JIM. ENOUGH.
ALL I KNOW IS THAT I'M AWARE OF SOMETHING NOW THAT LOOKING BACK I WISH I'D SEEN AT THE TIME.
WHEN WE WERE THE INVADERS OF WORLD WAR II, I WAS THE TEAM'S MIGHT AND STEVE, THE STRATEGIST AND NATURAL LEADER, WAS ITS BRAIN.
YOU WERE THE HEART, JIM.
LISTEN TO WHAT NAMOR SAYS. YOU WERE "BORN"--
CREATED. I WAS CREATED.
NO, JIM, YOU WERE BORN... JUST AS A FULLY FORMED MAN.
AND YOU CARED ABOUT YOUR FELLOW MAN INSTANTLY-- THEIR WELFARE--MORE THAN I HAVE IN ALL MY LENGTHY EXISTENCE.
AND HOW MANY DIED WHEN I UNLEASHED A TIDAL WAVE ON MANHATTAN AT ROUGHLY THE SAME TIME...BACK IN THE 1940S?
TO THIS DAY, I STILL CAN'T BEAR TO THINK ABOUT HOW MANY DIED...
...BUT WITHIN WEEKS OF YOUR CREATION, REMEMBER HOW HARD YOU FOUGHT ME TO PROTECT NEW YORK AND ITS PEOPLE?
THEY FEARED YOU AS MUCH AS ME AT THAT TIME TOO, REMEMBER, YET YOU BATTLED SO VALIANTLY TO KEEP THEM SAFE.
I WANT YOU TO BE WELL AGAIN, JIM. I NEED IT.
SO I CAN AT LEAST HAVE THAT TO SALVE MY CONSCIENCE FOR MY OWN ACTIONS.
I HEAR YOU, NAMOR...I DO... AND FOR A MINUTE THERE I--
GHHAA
WHAT. IS. HAPPENING. TO. ME?!

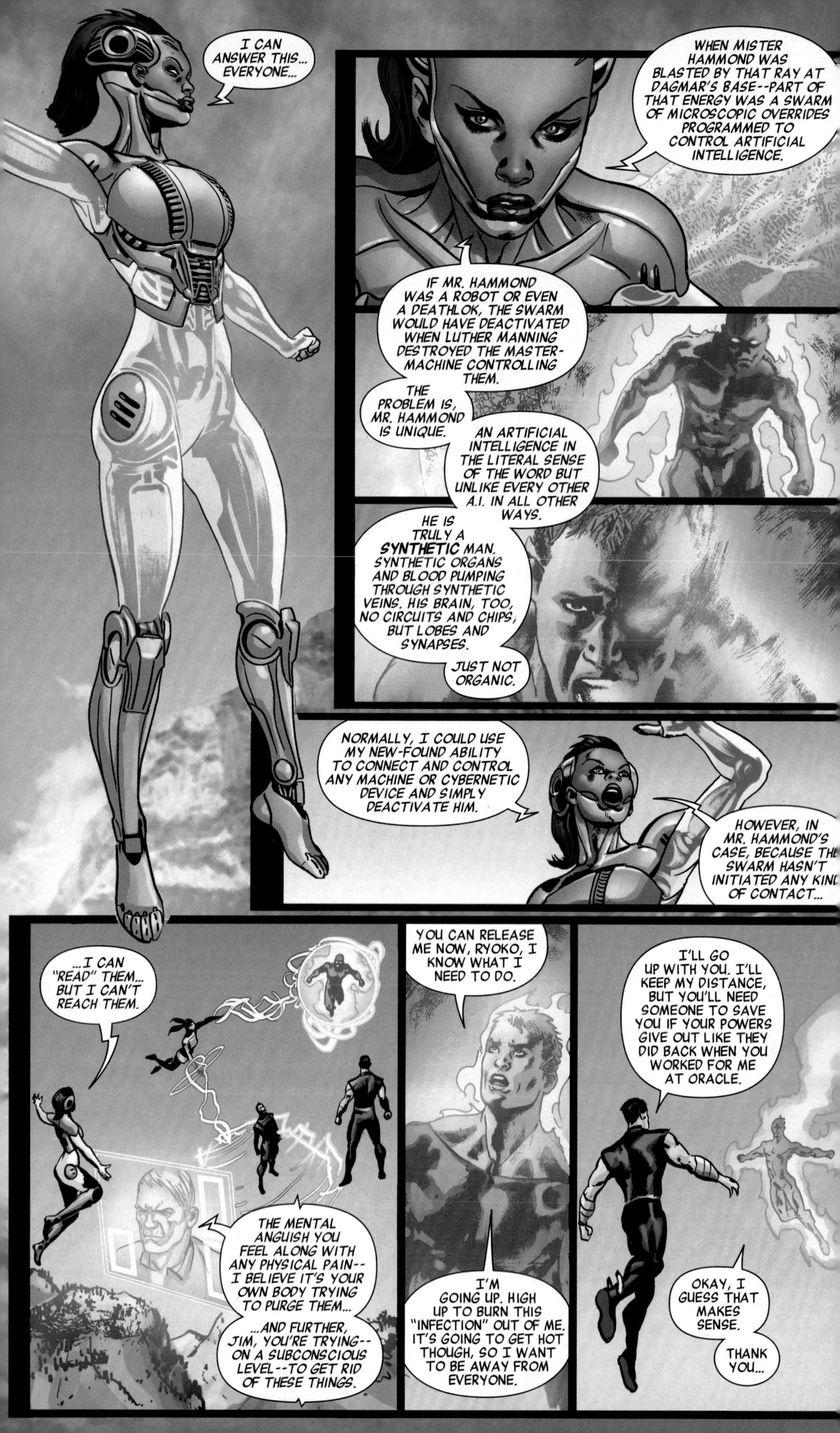
I CAN ANSWER THIS... EVERYONE...
WHEN MISTER HAMMOND WAS BLASTED BY THAT RAY AT DAGMAR'S BASE--PART OF THAT ENERGY WAS A SWARM OF MICROSCOPIC OVERRIDES PROGRAMMED TO CONTROL ARTIFICIAL INTELLIGENCE.
IF MR. HAMMOND WAS A ROBOT OR EVEN A DEATHLOK, THE SWARM WOULD HAVE DEACTIVATED WHEN LUTHER MANNING DESTROYED THE MASTER-MACHINE CONTROLLING THEM.
THE PROBLEM IS, MR. HAMMOND IS UNIQUE.
AN ARTIFICIAL INTELLIGENCE IN THE LITERAL SENSE OF THE WORD BUT UNLIKE EVERY OTHER A.I. IN ALL OTHER WAYS.
HE IS TRULY A **SYNTHETIC** MAN. SYNTHETIC ORGANS AND BLOOD PUMPING THROUGH SYNTHETIC VEINS. HIS BRAIN, TOO, NO CIRCUITS AND CHIPS, BUT LOBES AND SYNAPSES.
JUST NOT ORGANIC.
NORMALLY, I COULD USE MY NEW-FOUND ABILITY TO CONNECT AND CONTROL ANY MACHINE OR CYBERNETIC DEVICE AND SIMPLY DEACTIVATE HIM.
HOWEVER, IN MR. HAMMOND'S CASE, BECAUSE THE SWARM HASN'T INITIATED ANY KIND OF CONTACT...
...I CAN "READ" THEM... BUT I CAN'T REACH THEM.
THE MENTAL ANGUISH YOU FEEL ALONG WITH ANY PHYSICAL PAIN--I BELIEVE IT'S YOUR OWN BODY TRYING TO PURGE THEM...
...AND FURTHER, JIM, YOU'RE TRYING--ON A SUBCONSCIOUS LEVEL--TO GET RID OF THESE THINGS.
YOU CAN RELEASE ME NOW, RYOKO, I KNOW WHAT I NEED TO DO.
I'M GOING UP. HIGH UP TO BURN THIS "INFECTION" OUT OF ME. IT'S GOING TO GET HOT THOUGH, SO I WANT TO BE AWAY FROM EVERYONE.
I'LL GO UP WITH YOU. I'LL KEEP MY DISTANCE, BUT YOU'LL NEED SOMEONE TO SAVE YOU IF YOUR POWERS GIVE OUT LIKE THEY DID BACK WHEN YOU WORKED FOR ME AT ORACLE.
OKAY, I GUESS THAT MAKES SENSE.
THANK YOU...

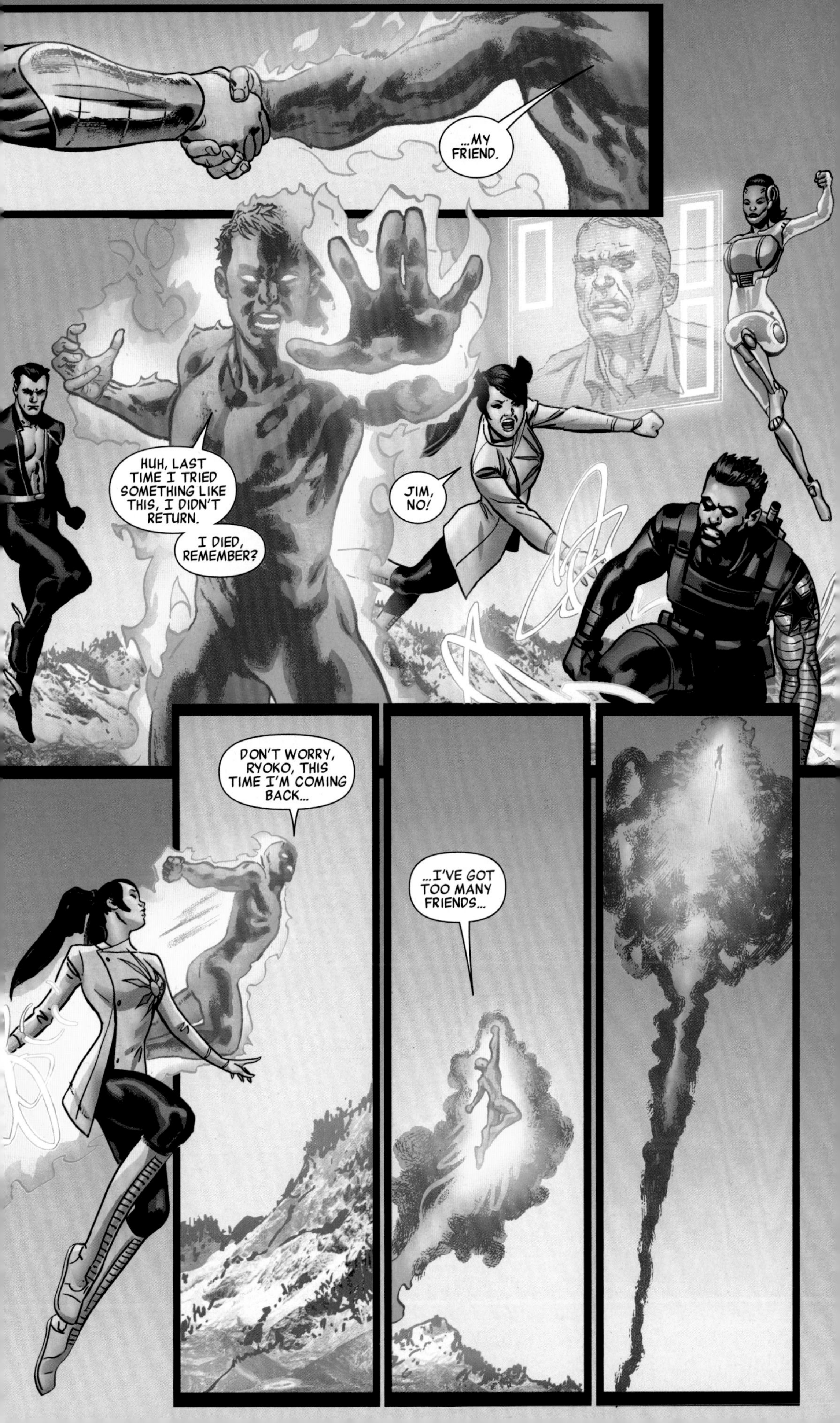
...MY FRIEND.
HUH, LAST TIME I TRIED SOMETHING LIKE THIS, I DIDN'T RETURN.
I DIED, REMEMBER?
JIM, NO!
DON'T WORRY, RYOKO, THIS TIME I'M COMING BACK...
...I'VE GOT TOO MANY FRIENDS...

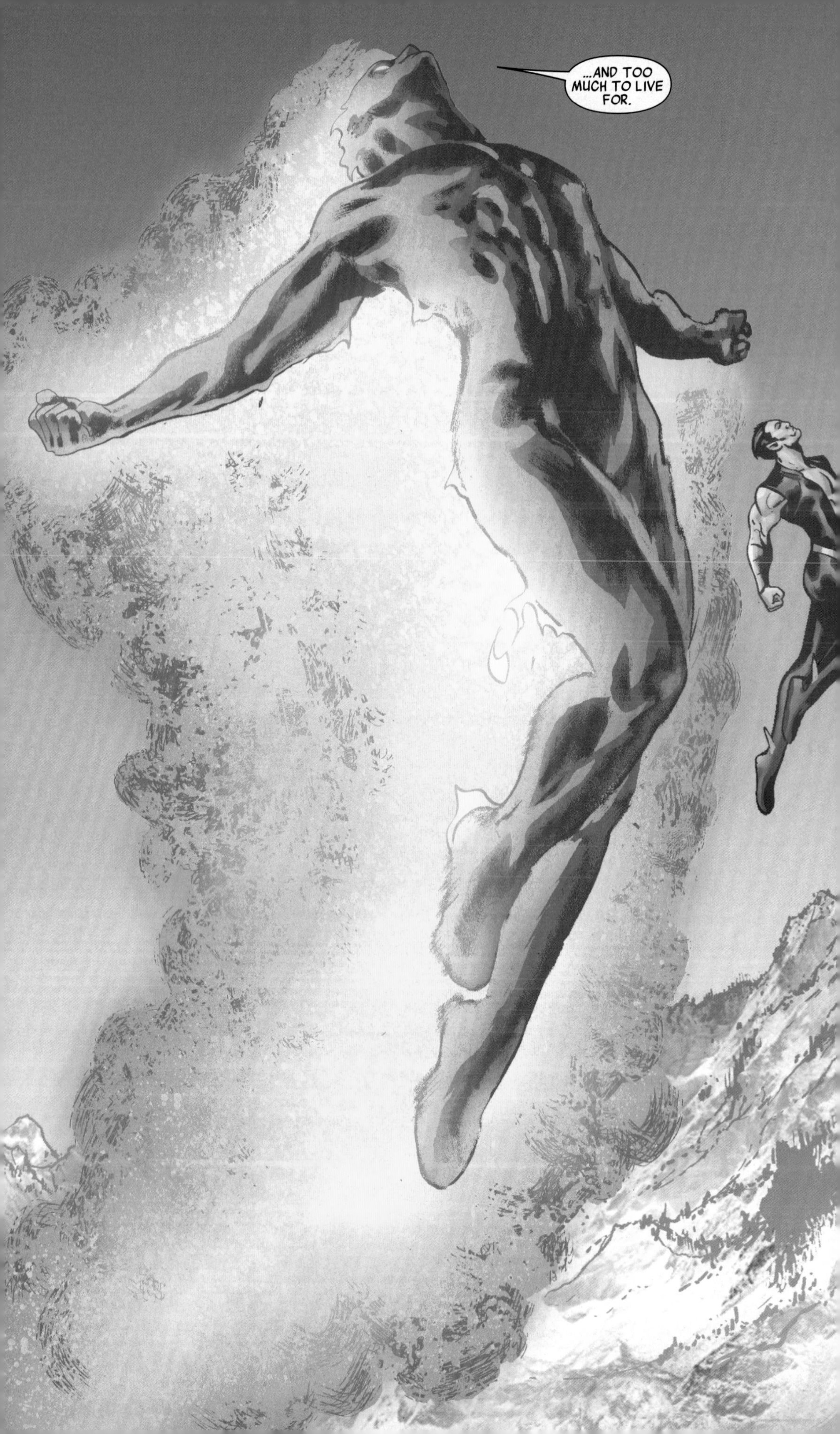
...AND TOO MUCH TO LIVE FOR.

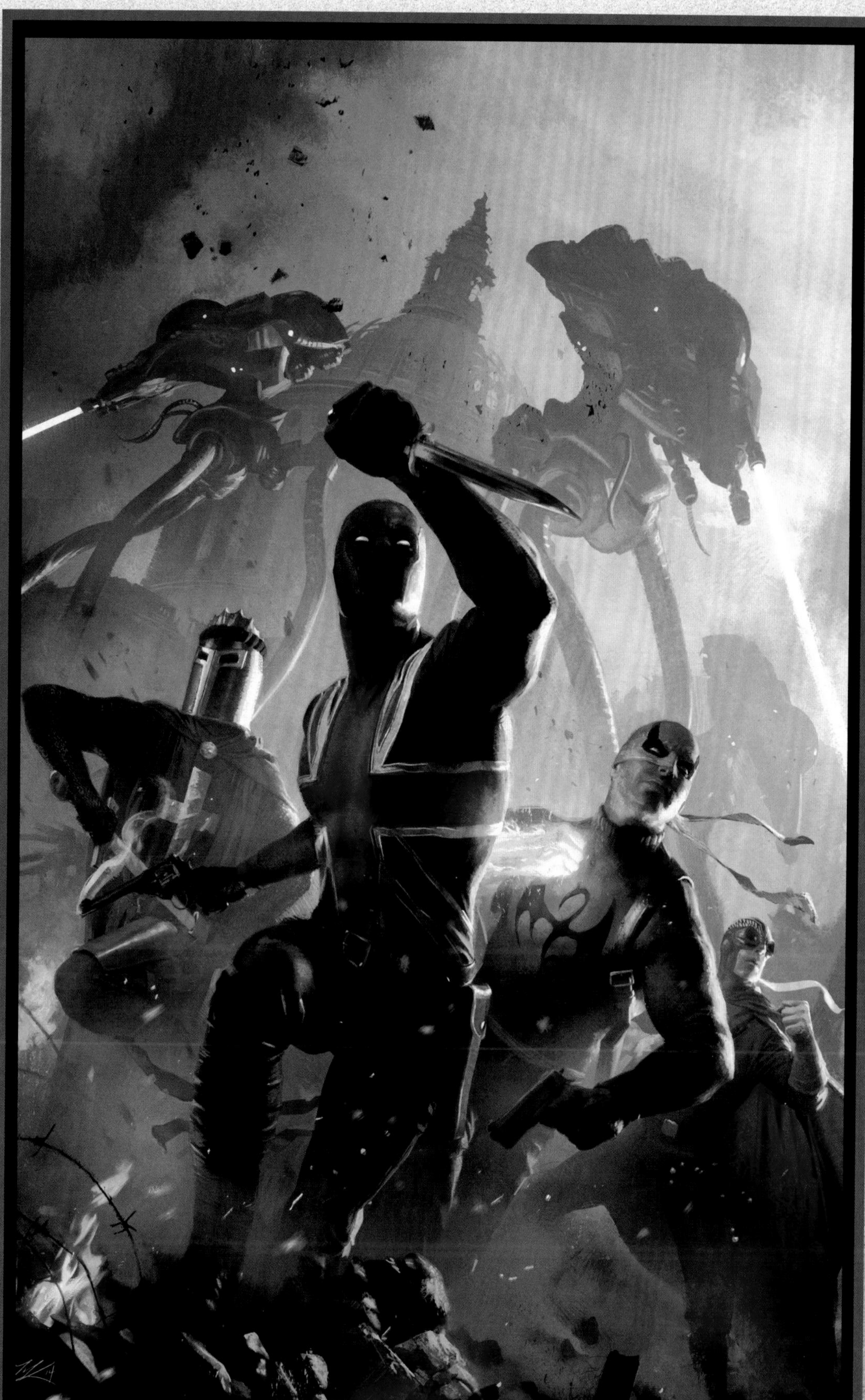

#12

It seems like a dream now, as I recollect that day and the *horrors* that unfolded then.

Or like the ravings of a madman...

...His mind areel with visions nonsensical and untoward.

But no, this was *true*.

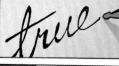

true

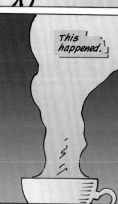

This happened.

They came out of the mist at 6:07 on a bruised and brooding Thursday morning.

October, 1917.

LUM'ME, BUT THAT'S A *BIG'UN*.

YES, NED, OF THAT I ADAMANTLY CONCUR.

ÇA NE SERA PAS UNE VICTOIRE FACILE. NON, LOIN DE LÀ.

NOT SURE WHAT ANY OF YOU JUST SAID, BUT THIS DON'T SEEM THE TIME FOR CHIT-CHAT ANYWAY.

SIR STEEL.

UNION JACK.

THE CRIMSON CAVALIER.

IRON FIST

Except this *wasn't* the filthy Hun who my team and I--Union Jack-- were seeing make their advance...

...*Nor* were these the wastelands of Mons or Flanders...

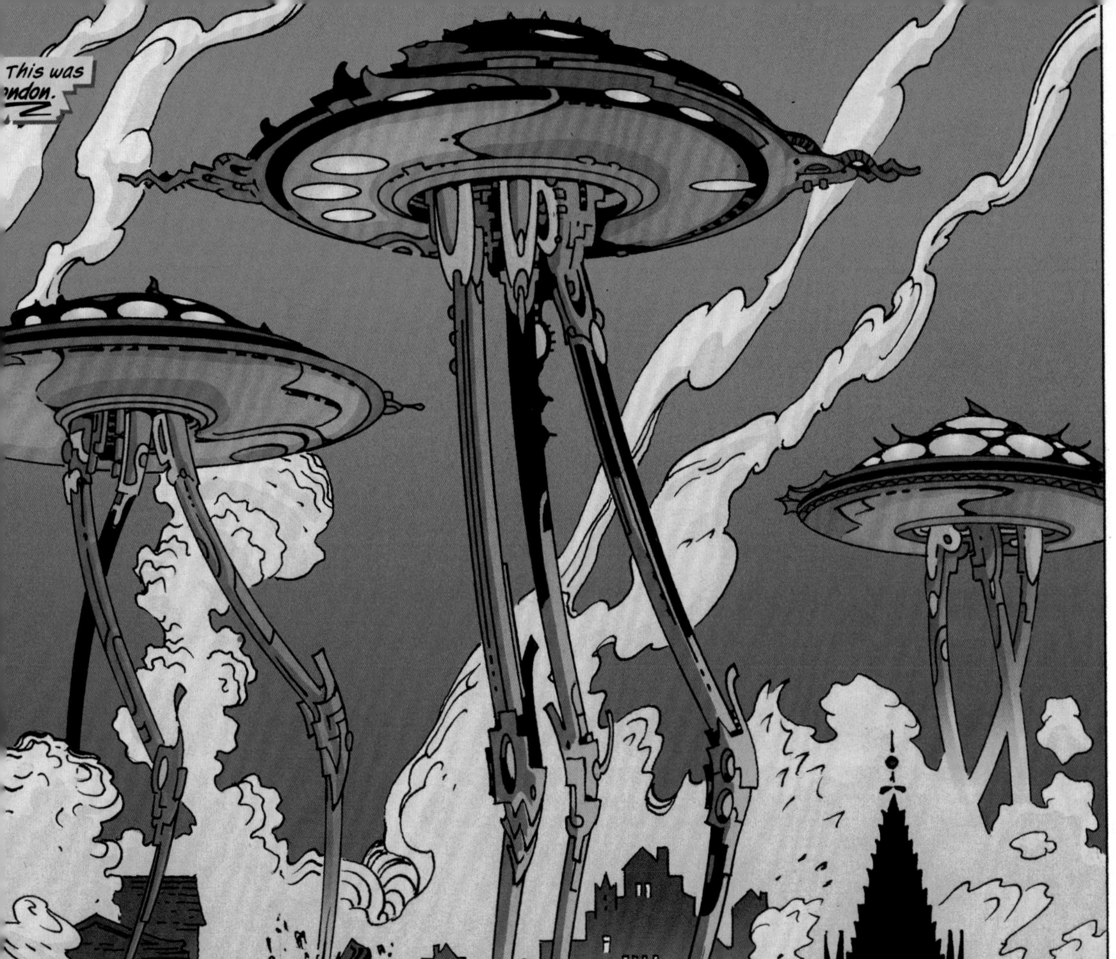
This was
ondon.

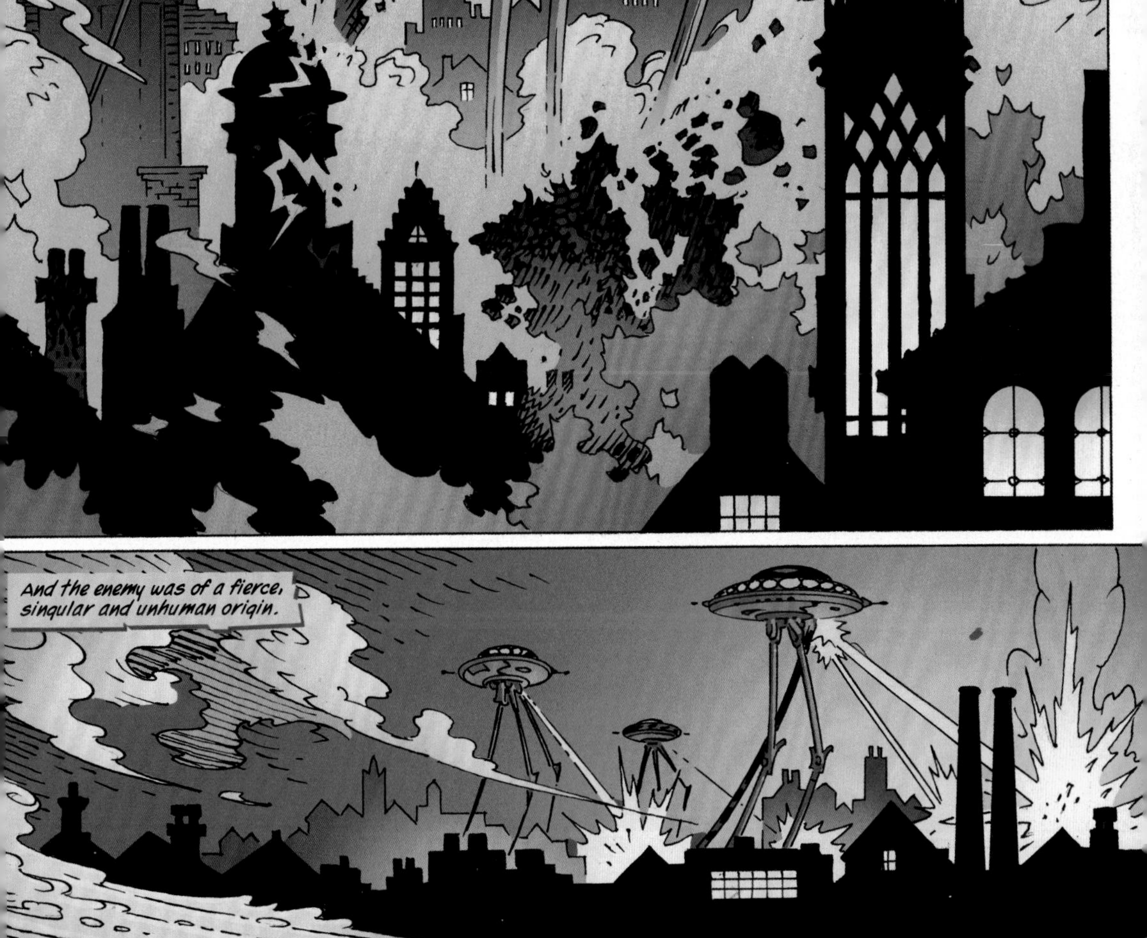
And the enemy was of a fierce, singular and unhuman origin.

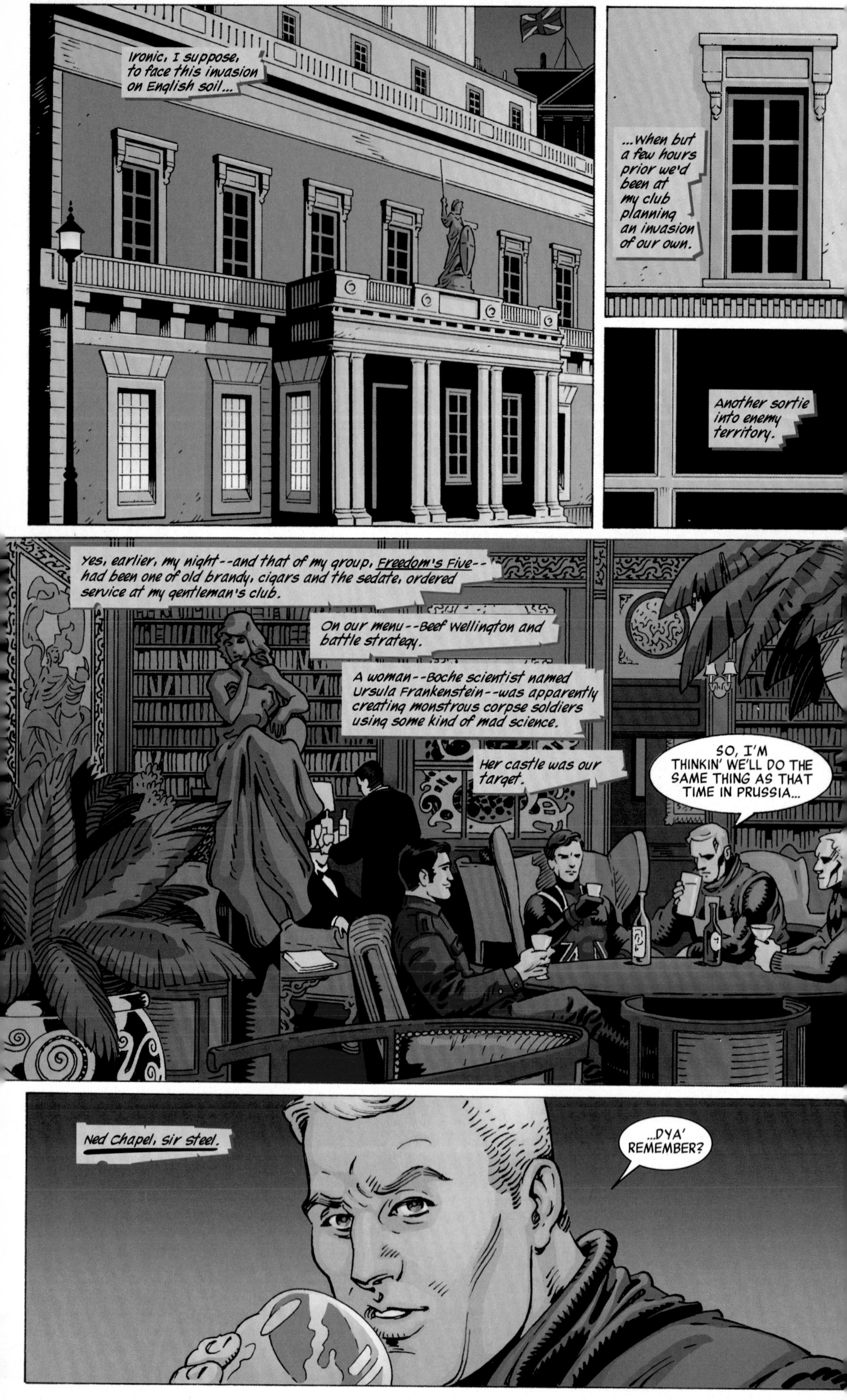

Ironic, I suppose, to face this invasion on English soil...
...when but a few hours prior we'd been at my club planning an invasion of our own.
Another sortie into enemy territory.
Yes, earlier, my night--and that of my group, Freedom's Five--had been one of old brandy, cigars and the sedate, ordered service at my gentleman's club.
On our menu--Beef Wellington and battle strategy.
A woman--Boche scientist named Ursula Frankenstein--was apparently creating monstrous corpse soldiers using some kind of mad science.
Her castle was our target.
SO, I'M THINKIN' WE'LL DO THE SAME THING AS THAT TIME IN PRUSSIA...
Ned Chapel, sir steel.
...DYA' REMEMBER?

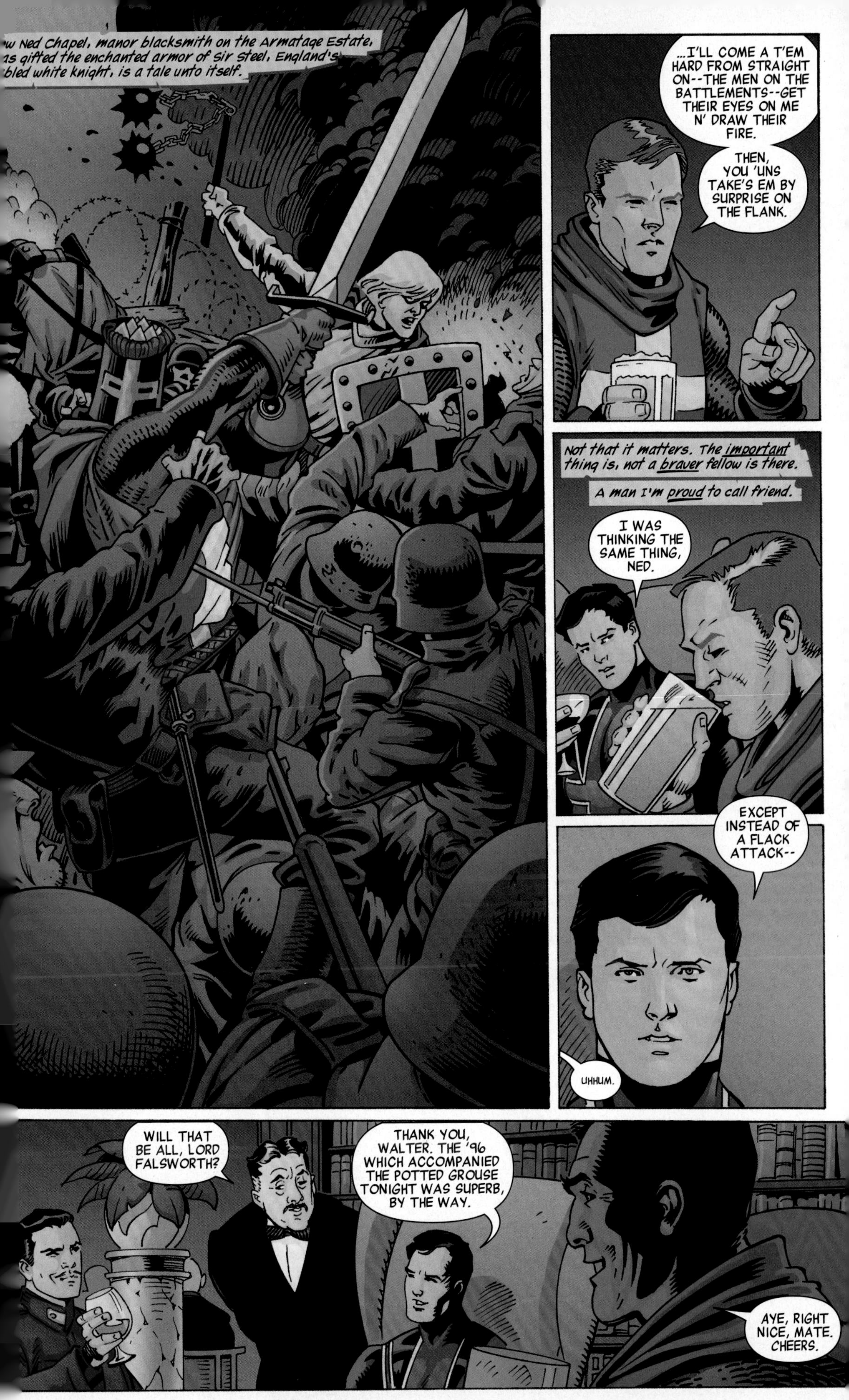

w Ned Chapel, manor blacksmith on the Armatage Estate, as gifted the enchanted armor of Sir Steel, England's bled white knight, is a tale unto itself.
...I'LL COME A T'EM HARD FROM STRAIGHT ON--THE MEN ON THE BATTLEMENTS--GET THEIR EYES ON ME N' DRAW THEIR FIRE.
THEN, YOU 'UNS TAKE'S EM BY SURPRISE ON THE FLANK.
Not that it matters. The important thing is, not a braver fellow is there.
A man I'm proud to call friend.
I WAS THINKING THE SAME THING, NED.
EXCEPT INSTEAD OF A FLACK ATTACK--
UHHUM.
WILL THAT BE ALL, LORD FALSWORTH?
THANK YOU, WALTER. THE '96 WHICH ACCOMPANIED THE POTTED GROUSE TONIGHT WAS SUPERB, BY THE WAY.
AYE, RIGHT NICE, MATE. CHEERS.

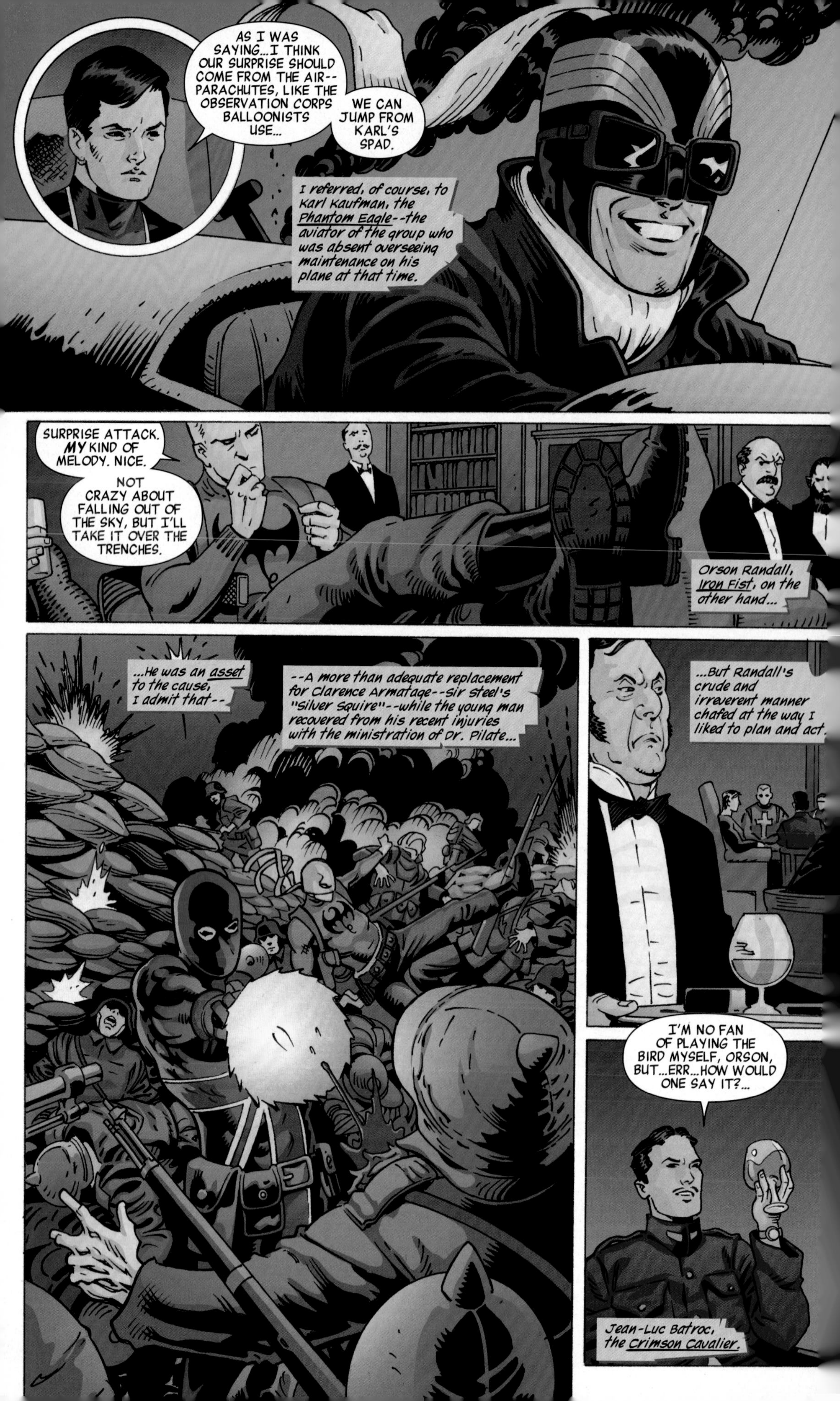

AS I WAS SAYING...I THINK OUR SURPRISE SHOULD COME FROM THE AIR--PARACHUTES, LIKE THE OBSERVATION CORPS BALLOONISTS USE...
WE CAN JUMP FROM KARL'S SPAD.
I referred, of course, to Karl Kaufman, the Phantom Eagle--the aviator of the group who was absent overseeing maintenance on his plane at that time.
SURPRISE ATTACK. MY KIND OF MELODY. NICE.
NOT CRAZY ABOUT FALLING OUT OF THE SKY, BUT I'LL TAKE IT OVER THE TRENCHES.
Orson Randall, Iron Fist, on the other hand...
...He was an asset to the cause, I admit that--
--A more than adequate replacement for Clarence Armatage--Sir Steel's "Silver Squire"--while the young man recovered from his recent injuries with the ministration of Dr. Pilate...
...But Randall's crude and irreverent manner chafed at the way I liked to plan and act.
I'M NO FAN OF PLAYING THE BIRD MYSELF, ORSON, BUT...ERR...HOW WOULD ONE SAY IT?...
Jean-Luc Batroc, the Crimson Cavalier.

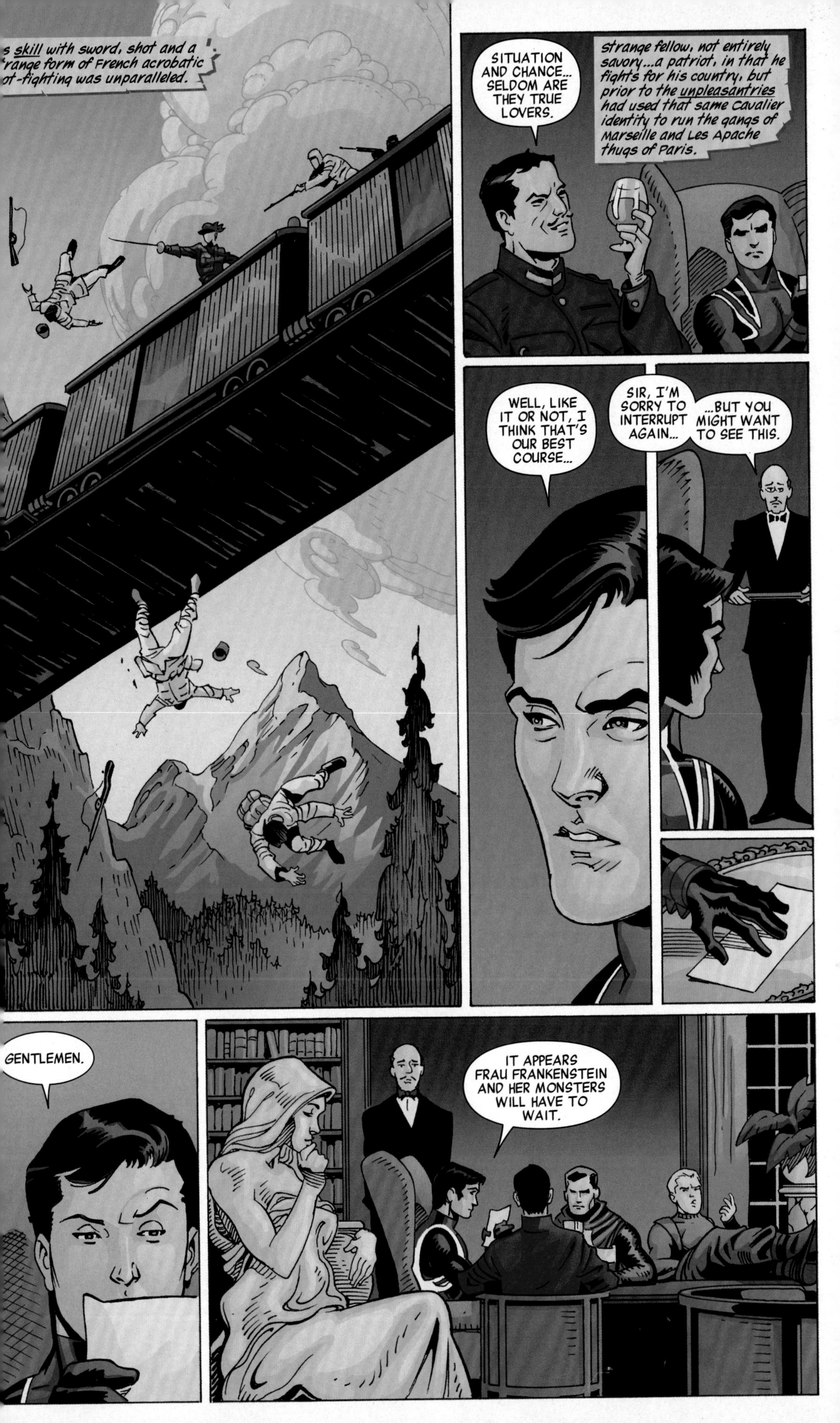

s skill with sword, shot and a
'range form of French acrobatic
ot-fighting was unparalleled.
SITUATION AND CHANCE... SELDOM ARE THEY TRUE LOVERS.
strange fellow, not entirely savory...a patriot, in that he fights for his country, but prior to the unpleasantries had used that same Cavalier identity to run the gangs of Marseille and Les Apache thugs of Paris.
WELL, LIKE IT OR NOT, I THINK THAT'S OUR BEST COURSE...
SIR, I'M SORRY TO INTERRUPT AGAIN...
...BUT YOU MIGHT WANT TO SEE THIS.
GENTLEMEN.
IT APPEARS FRAU FRANKENSTEIN AND HER MONSTERS WILL HAVE TO WAIT.

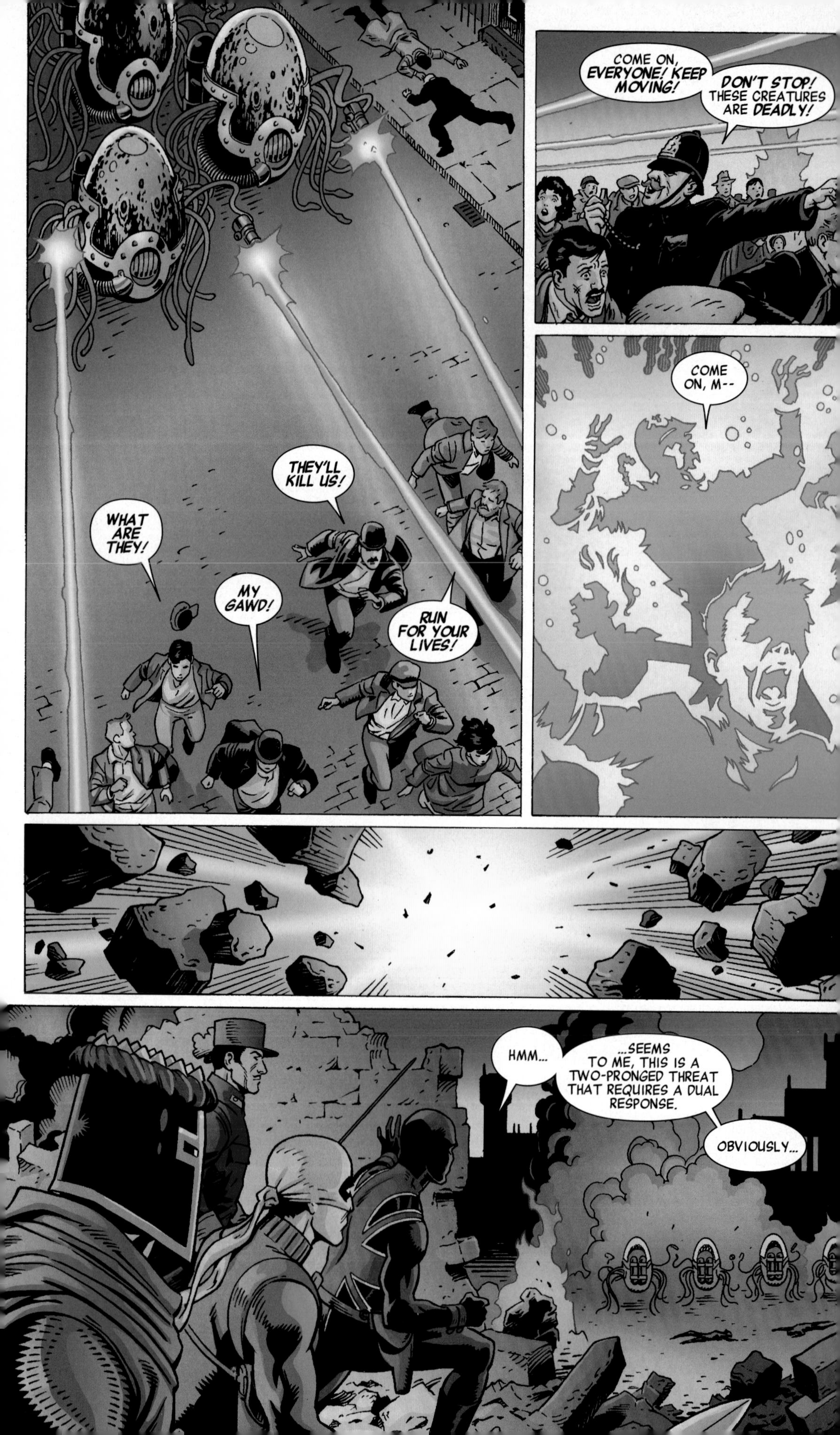
THEY'LL KILL US!
WHAT ARE THEY!
MY GAWD!
RUN FOR YOUR LIVES!
COME ON, EVERYONE! KEEP MOVING!
DON'T STOP! THESE CREATURES ARE DEADLY!
COME ON, M--
HMM...
...SEEMS TO ME, THIS IS A TWO-PRONGED THREAT THAT REQUIRES A DUAL RESPONSE.
OBVIOUSLY...

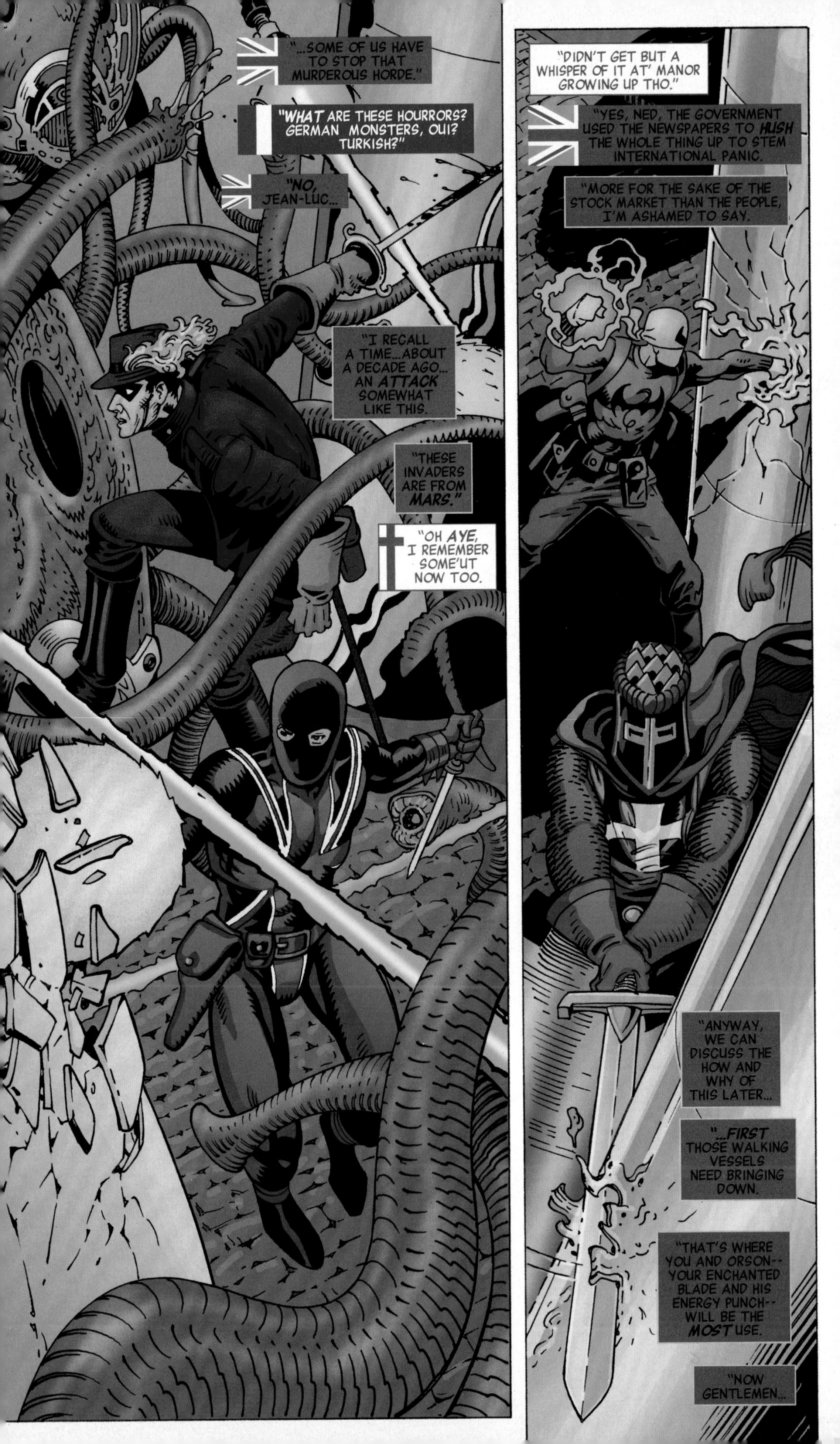
"...SOME OF US HAVE TO STOP THAT MURDEROUS HORDE."
"WHAT ARE THESE HOURRORS? GERMAN MONSTERS, OUI? TURKISH?"
"NO, JEAN-LUC...
"I RECALL A TIME...ABOUT A DECADE AGO... AN ATTACK SOMEWHAT LIKE THIS.
"THESE INVADERS ARE FROM MARS."
"OH AYE, I REMEMBER SOME'UT NOW TOO.
"DIDN'T GET BUT A WHISPER OF IT AT' MANOR GROWING UP THO."
"YES, NED, THE GOVERNMENT USED THE NEWSPAPERS TO HUSH THE WHOLE THING UP TO STEM INTERNATIONAL PANIC.
"MORE FOR THE SAKE OF THE STOCK MARKET THAN THE PEOPLE, I'M ASHAMED TO SAY.
"ANYWAY, WE CAN DISCUSS THE HOW AND WHY OF THIS LATER...
"...FIRST THOSE WALKING VESSELS NEED BRINGING DOWN.
"THAT'S WHERE YOU AND ORSON-- YOUR ENCHANTED BLADE AND HIS ENERGY PUNCH-- WILL BE THE MOST USE.
"NOW GENTLEMEN...

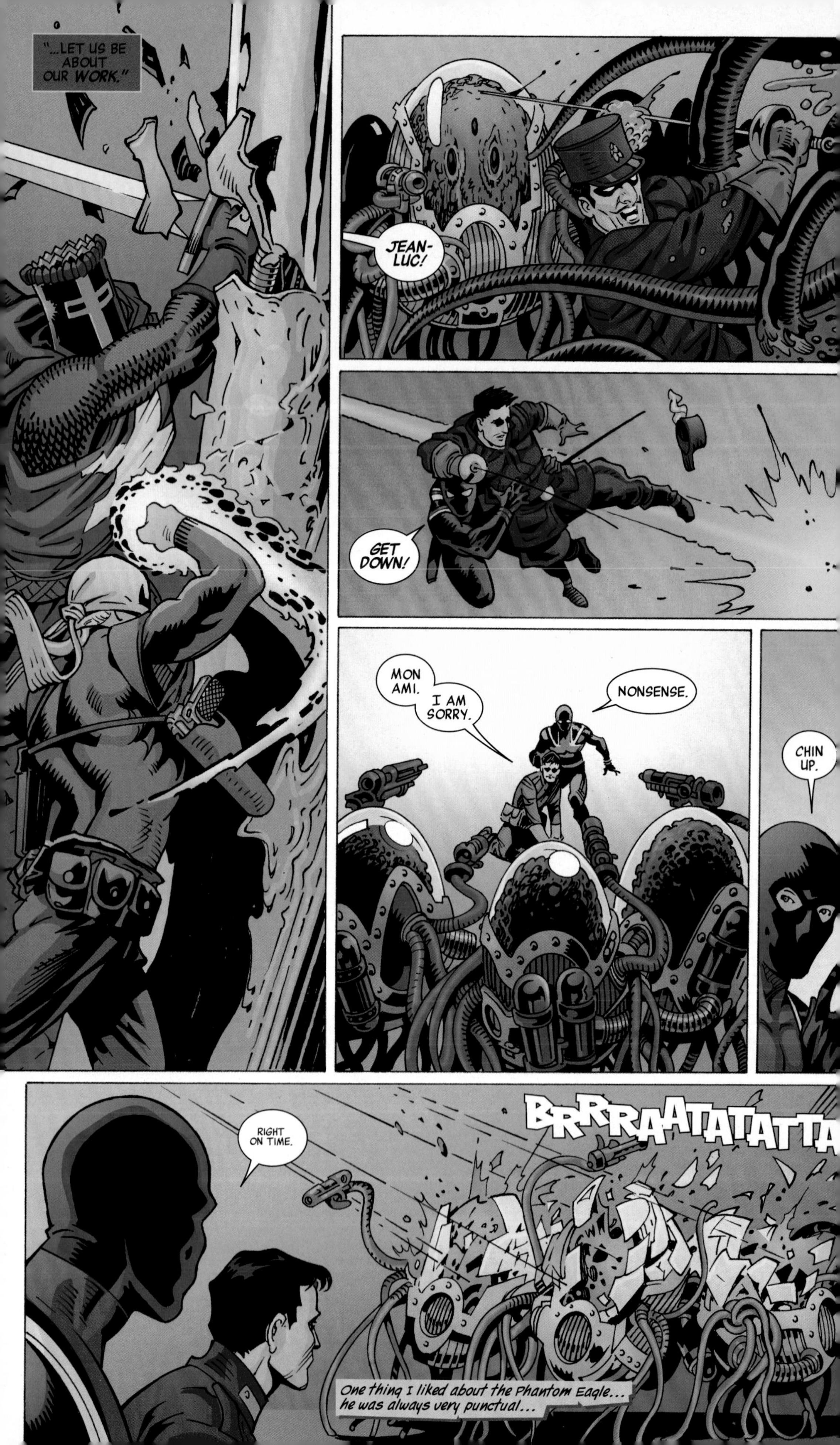
"...LET US BE ABOUT OUR WORK."
JEAN-LUC!
GET DOWN!
MON AMI.
I AM SORRY.
NONSENSE.
CHIN UP.
RIGHT ON TIME.
BRRRAATATATTA
One thing I liked about the Phantom Eagle... he was always very punctual...

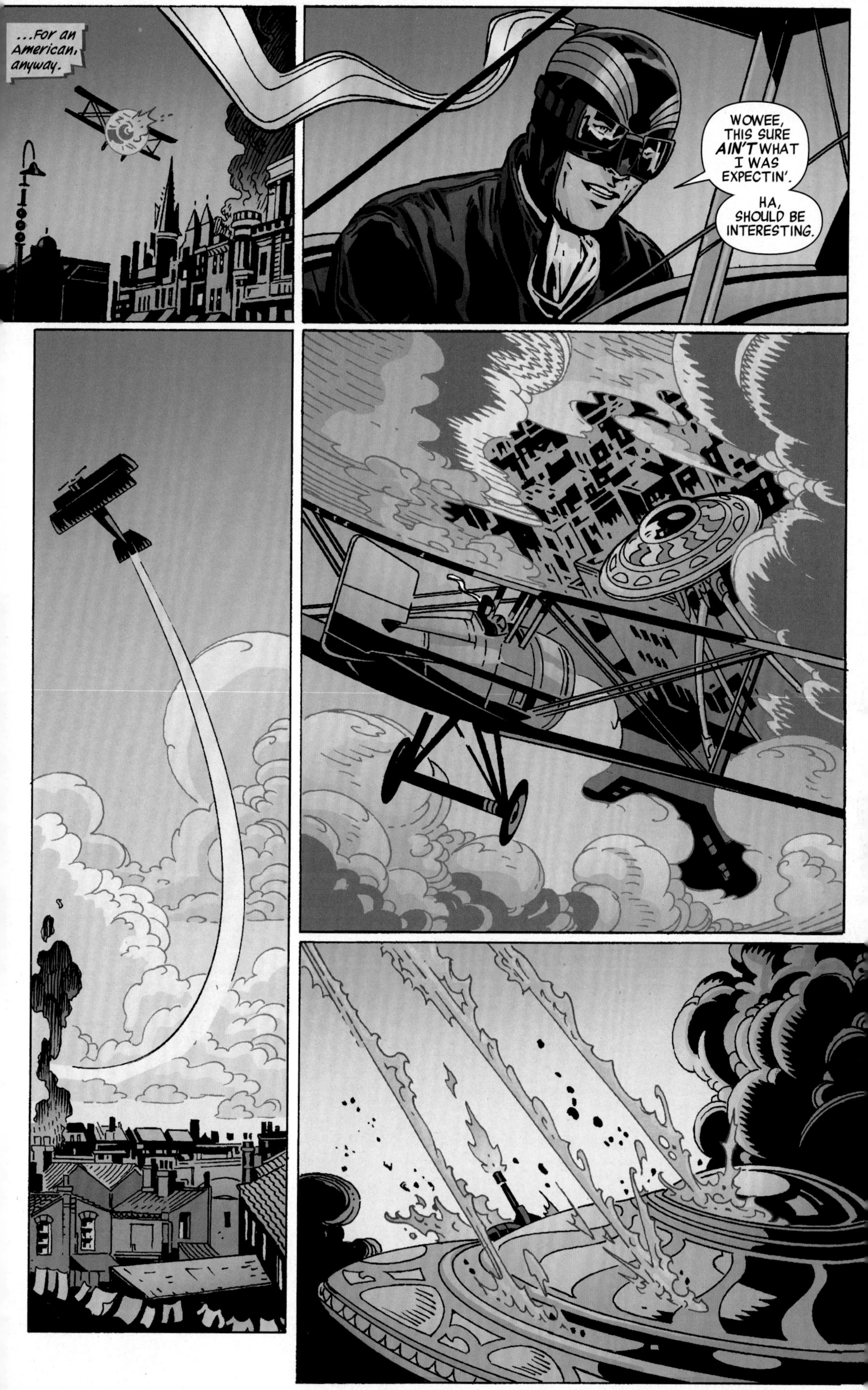
...For an American, anyway.
WOWEE, THIS SURE AIN'T WHAT I WAS EXPECTIN'.
HA, SHOULD BE INTERESTING.

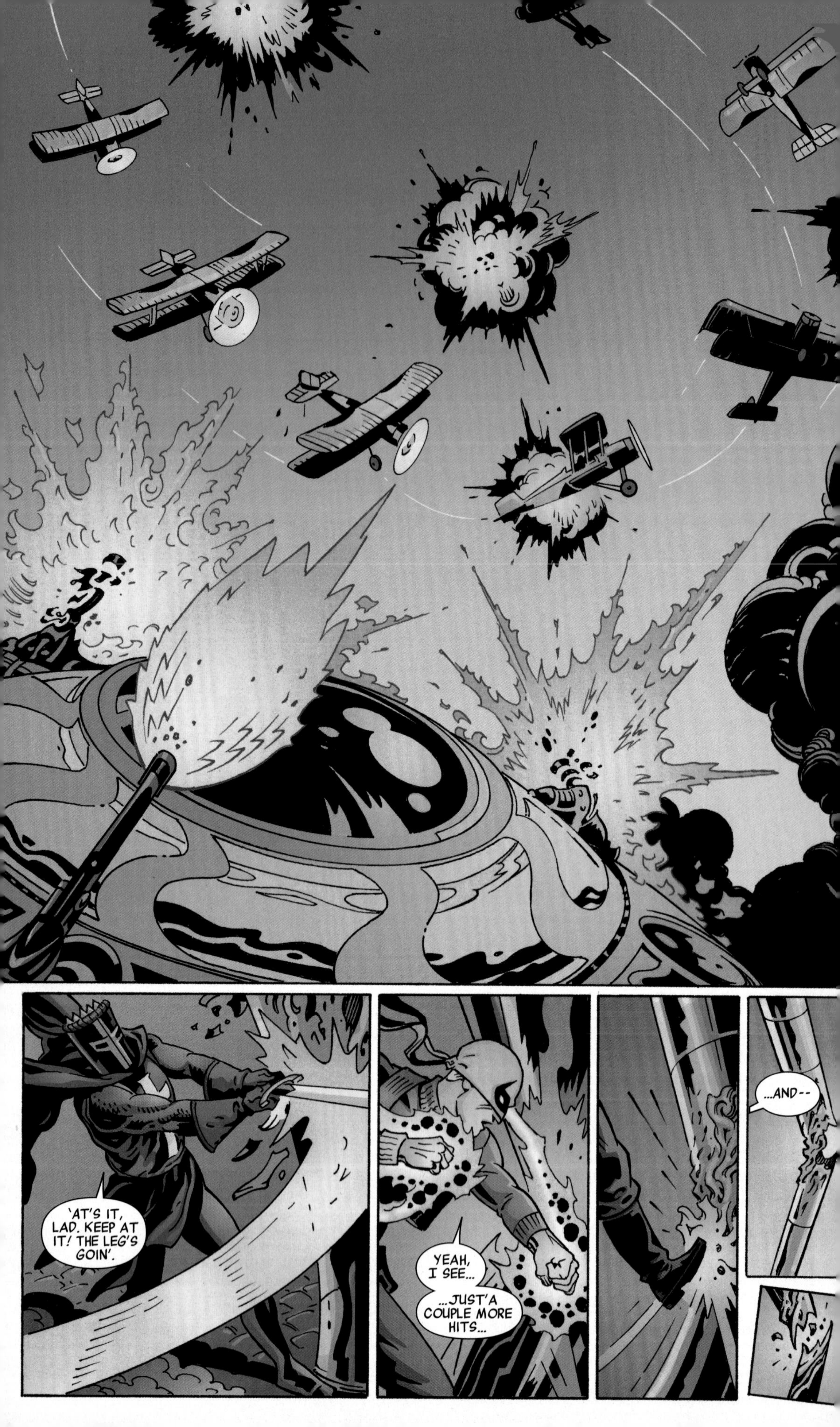
'AT'S IT, LAD. KEEP AT IT! THE LEG'S GOIN'.
YEAH, I SEE...
...JUST'A COUPLE MORE HITS...
...AND--

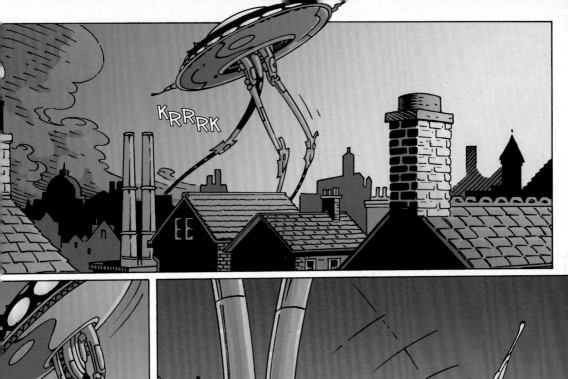

KRRRK

KREEEEK

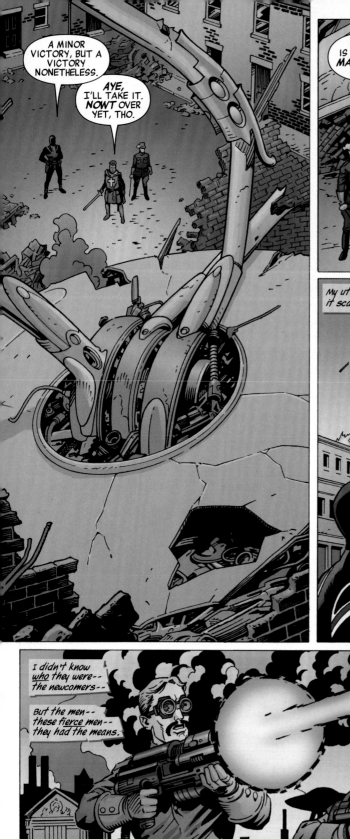

A MINOR VICTORY, BUT A VICTORY NONETHELESS.

AYE, I'LL TAKE IT. NOWT OVER YET, THO.

YES, THIS IS BUT ONE OF MANY WALKING HORRORS.

AND WE'VE BARELY THE MEANS OR MEN TO--

My utterance proved false before it scant left my mouth.

I didn't know who they were-- the newcomers--

But the men-- these fierce men-- they had the means.

Weaponry akin to the martian invaders themselves, as least to my eyes.

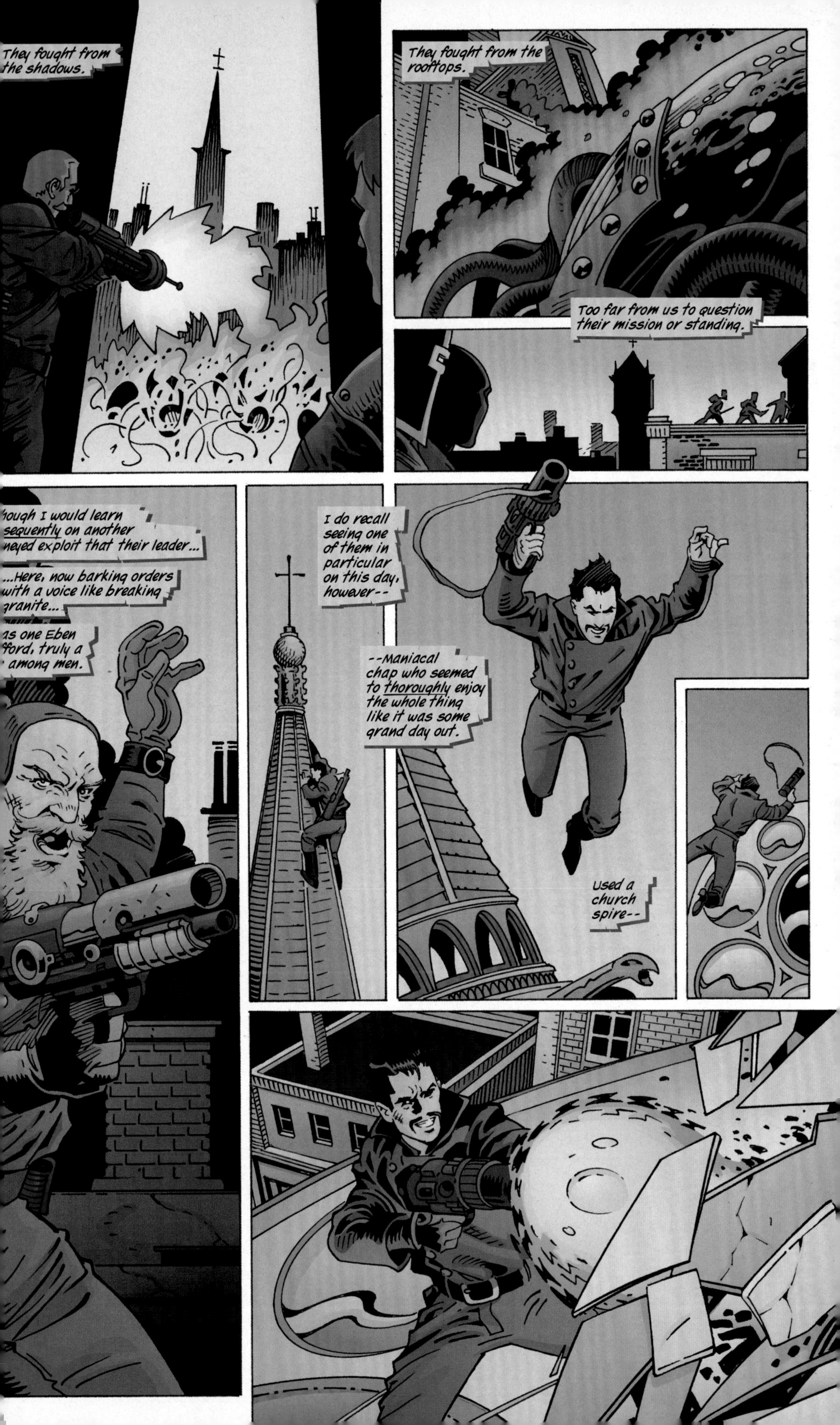

They fought from the shadows.
They fought from the rooftops.
Too far from us to question their mission or standing.
hough I would learn sequently on another neyed exploit that their leader...
...Here, now barking orders with a voice like breaking granite...
as one Eben fford, truly a among men.
I do recall seeing one of them in particular on this day, however--
--Maniacal chap who seemed to thoroughly enjoy the whole thing like it was some grand day out.
Used a church spire--

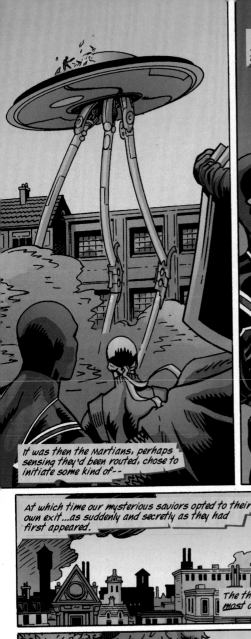

It was then the Martians, perhaps sensing they'd been routed, chose to initiate some kind of--

--Enchantment? I don't know what to call it...

--And vanished before our eyes, taking that one gleefully violent fellow with them back to Mars or Hell or wherever they truly came from.

At which time our mysterious saviors opted to their own exit...as suddenly and secretly as they had first appeared.

The thing I recall most of that moment, then...

Was the silence.

It's 1922 as I write this. Summer. A lovely day, actually.

The "Jazz Age" as it's known, is upon us, which sounds so jolly, despite it comprising lost men of all classes--myself included--left to guess what the "Great" war was all about in the first place.

In the time between...

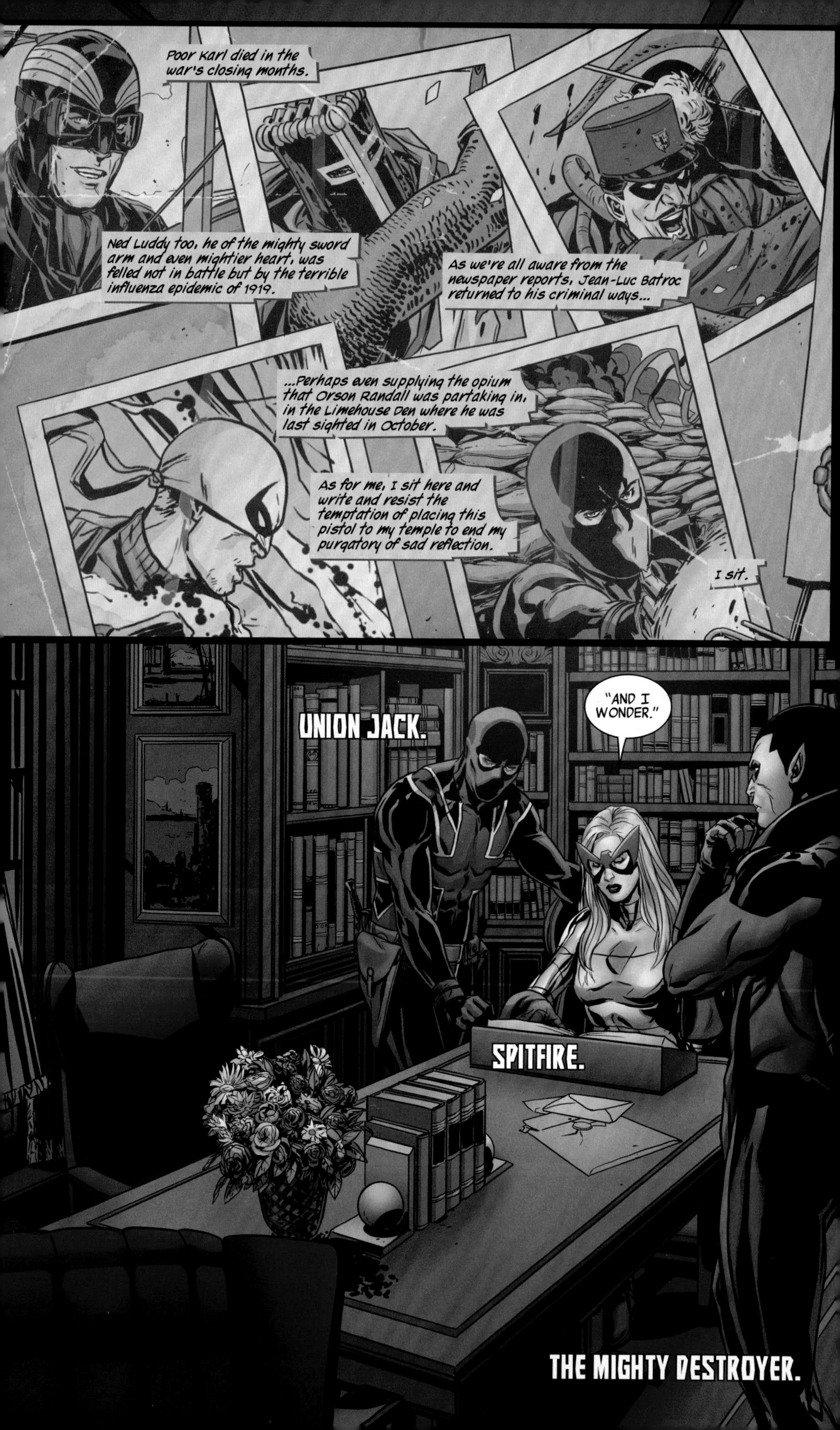
Poor Karl died in the war's closing months.
Ned Luddy too, he of the mighty sword arm and even mightier heart, was felled not in battle but by the terrible influenza epidemic of 1919.
As we're all aware from the newspaper reports, Jean-Luc Batroc returned to his criminal ways...
...Perhaps even supplying the opium that Orson Randall was partaking in, in the Limehouse Den where he was last sighted in October.
As for me, I sit here and write and resist the temptation of placing this pistol to my temple to end my purgatory of sad reflection.
I sit.
"AND I WONDER."
UNION JACK.
SPITFIRE.
THE MIGHTY DESTROYER.

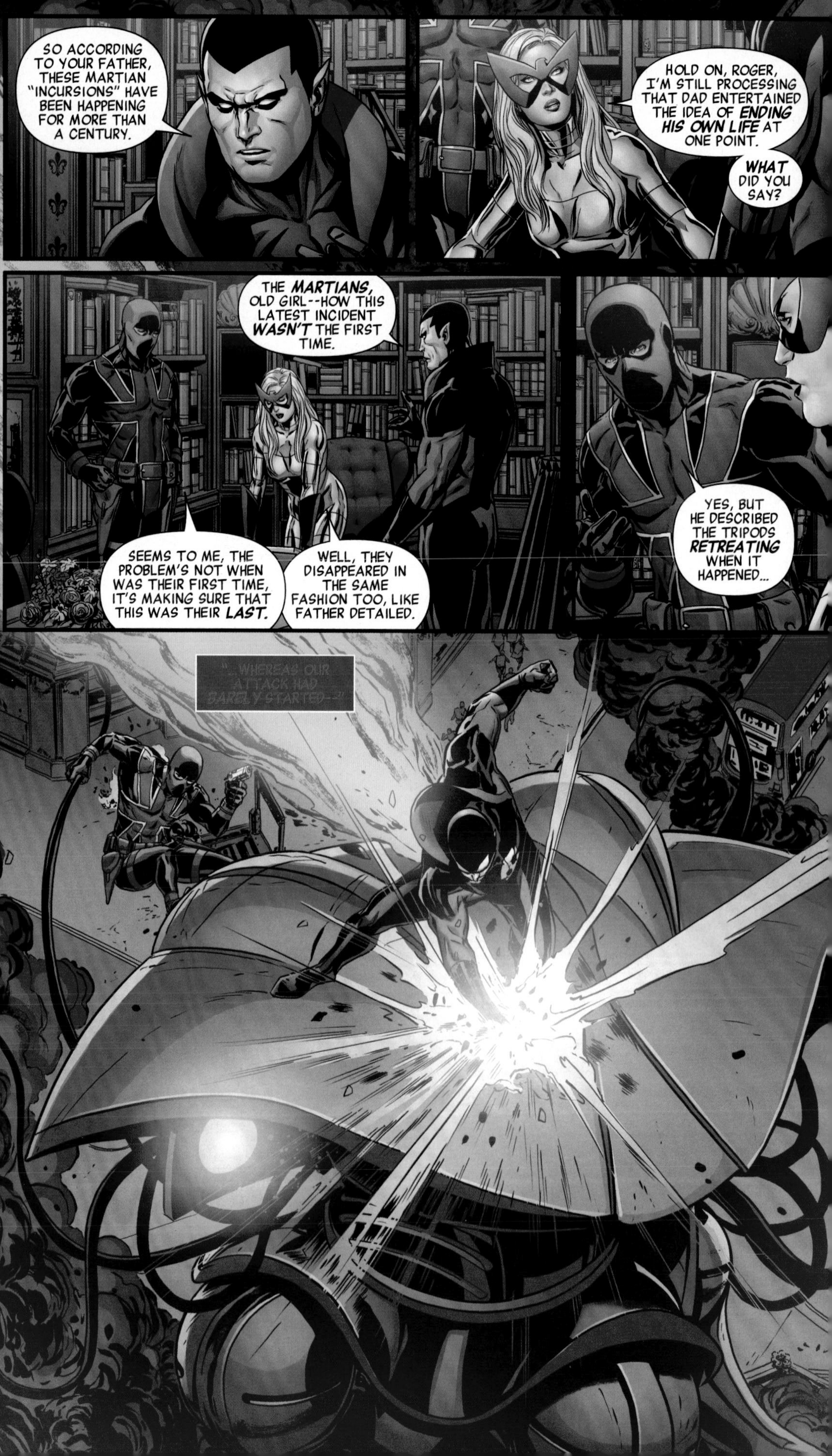
SO ACCORDING TO YOUR FATHER, THESE MARTIAN "INCURSIONS" HAVE BEEN HAPPENING FOR MORE THAN A CENTURY.
HOLD ON, ROGER, I'M STILL PROCESSING THAT DAD ENTERTAINED THE IDEA OF **ENDING HIS OWN LIFE** AT ONE POINT.
WHAT DID YOU SAY?
THE **MARTIANS,** OLD GIRL--HOW THIS LATEST INCIDENT **WASN'T** THE FIRST TIME.
SEEMS TO ME, THE PROBLEM'S NOT WHEN WAS THEIR FIRST TIME, IT'S MAKING SURE THAT THIS WAS THEIR **LAST.**
WELL, THEY DISAPPEARED IN THE SAME FASHION TOO, LIKE FATHER DETAILED.
YES, BUT HE DESCRIBED THE TRIPODS **RETREATING** WHEN IT HAPPENED...
"...WHEREAS OUR ATTACK HAD BARELY STARTED--"

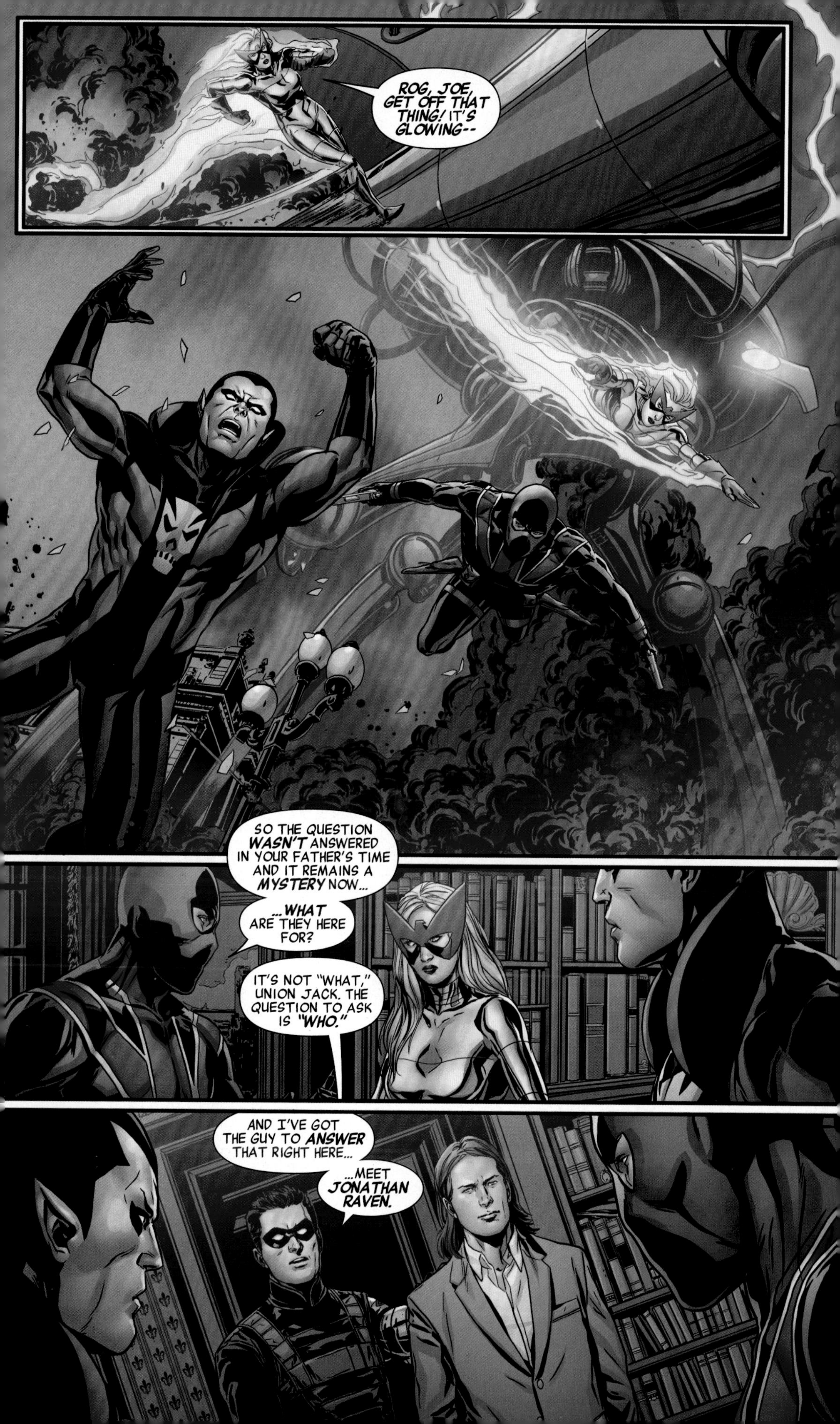
ROG, JOE, GET OFF THAT THING! IT'S GLOWING--
SO THE QUESTION WASN'T ANSWERED IN YOUR FATHER'S TIME AND IT REMAINS A MYSTERY NOW...
...WHAT ARE THEY HERE FOR?
IT'S NOT "WHAT," UNION JACK. THE QUESTION TO ASK IS "WHO."
AND I'VE GOT THE GUY TO ANSWER THAT RIGHT HERE...
...MEET JONATHAN RAVEN.

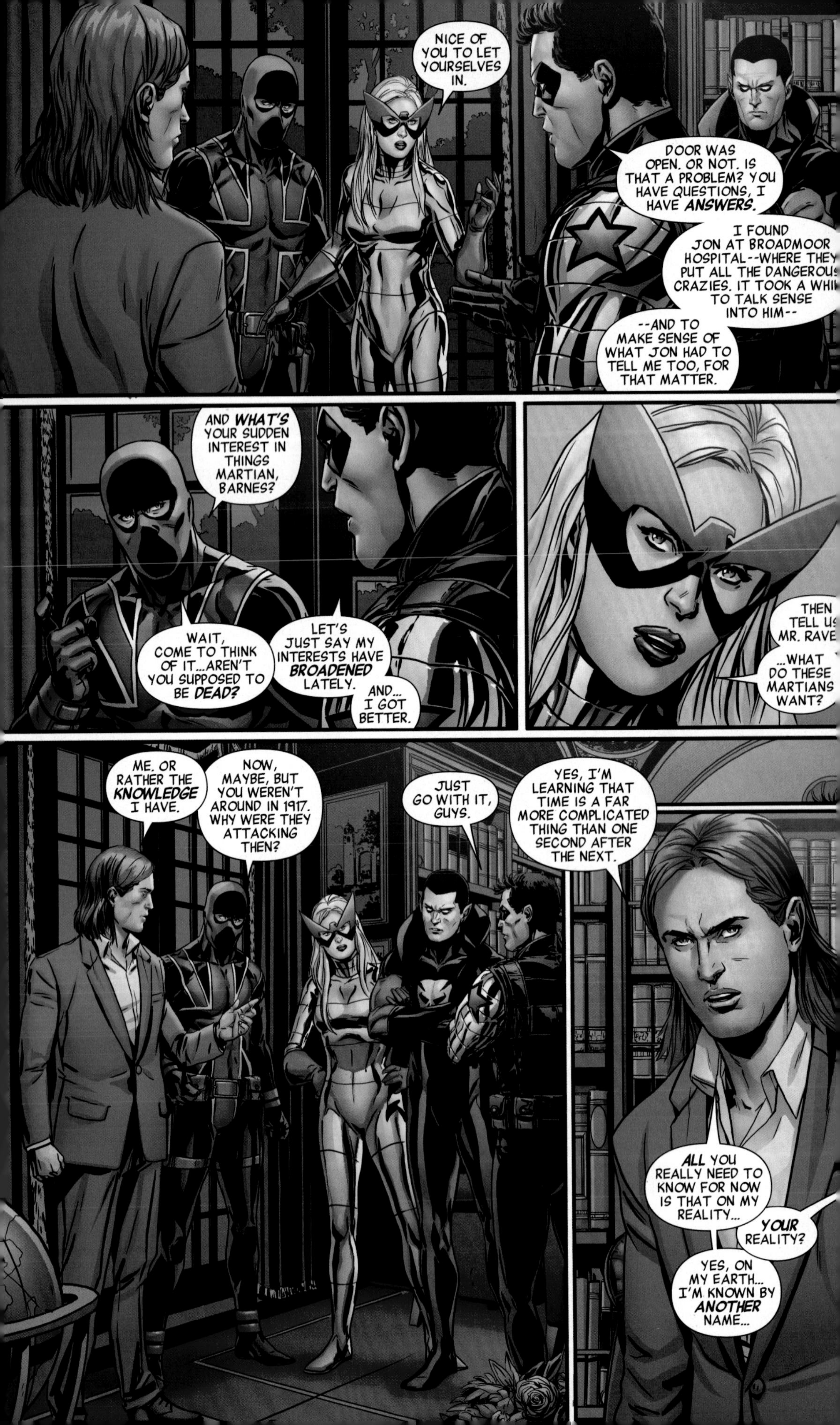
NICE OF YOU TO LET YOURSELVES IN.
DOOR WAS OPEN. OR NOT. IS THAT A PROBLEM? YOU HAVE QUESTIONS, I HAVE ANSWERS.
I FOUND JON AT BROADMOOR HOSPITAL--WHERE THEY PUT ALL THE DANGEROUS CRAZIES. IT TOOK A WHILE TO TALK SENSE INTO HIM--
--AND TO MAKE SENSE OF WHAT JON HAD TO TELL ME TOO, FOR THAT MATTER.
AND WHAT'S YOUR SUDDEN INTEREST IN THINGS MARTIAN, BARNES?
WAIT, COME TO THINK OF IT...AREN'T YOU SUPPOSED TO BE DEAD?
LET'S JUST SAY MY INTERESTS HAVE BROADENED LATELY.
AND... I GOT BETTER.
THEN TELL US MR. RAVE
...WHAT DO THESE MARTIANS WANT?
ME. OR RATHER THE KNOWLEDGE I HAVE.
NOW, MAYBE, BUT YOU WEREN'T AROUND IN 1917. WHY WERE THEY ATTACKING THEN?
JUST GO WITH IT, GUYS.
YES, I'M LEARNING THAT TIME IS A FAR MORE COMPLICATED THING THAN ONE SECOND AFTER THE NEXT.
ALL YOU REALLY NEED TO KNOW FOR NOW IS THAT ON MY REALITY...
YOUR REALITY?
YES, ON MY EARTH... I'M KNOWN BY ANOTHER NAME...

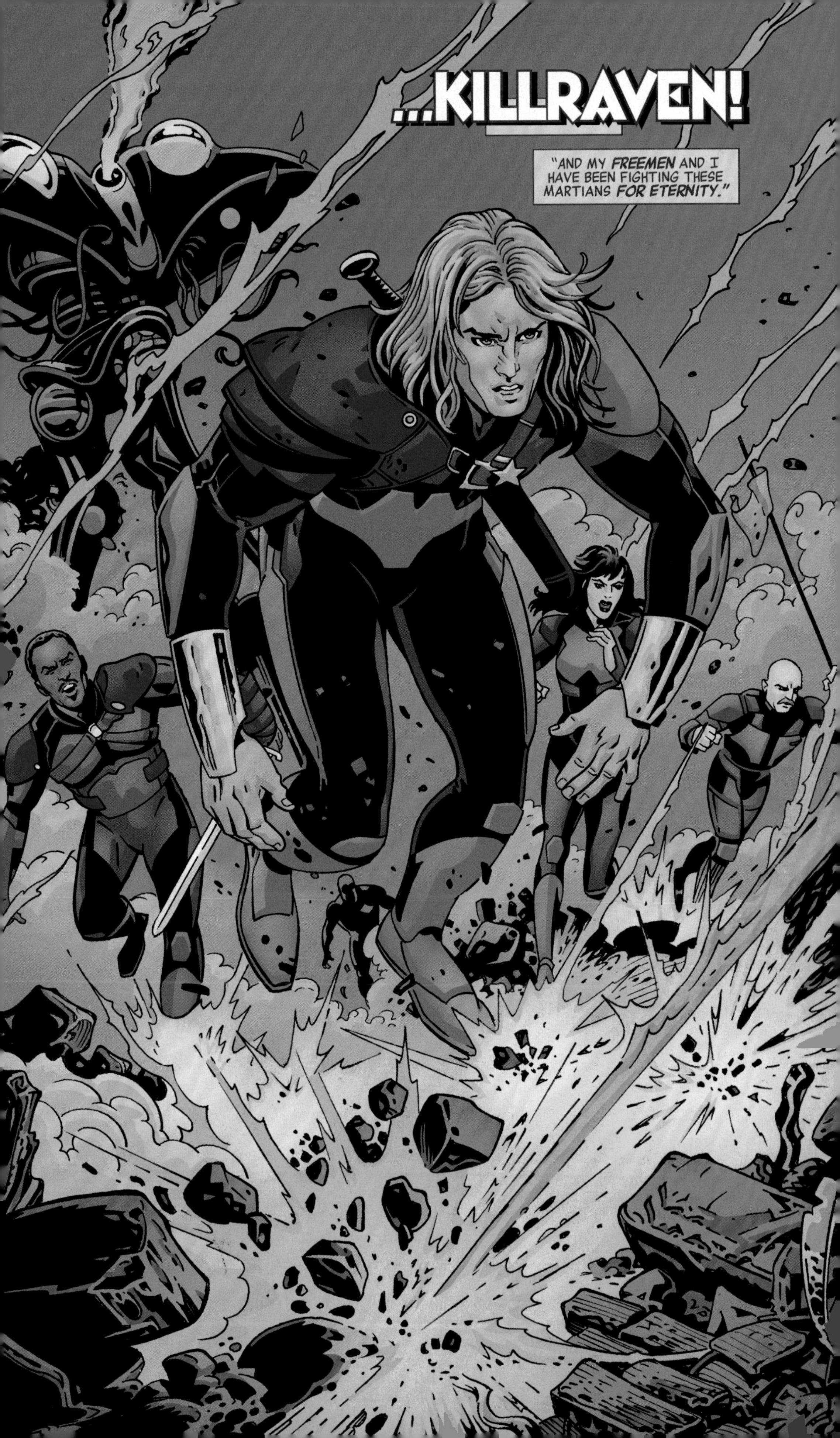
...KILLRAVEN!
"AND MY FREEMEN AND I HAVE BEEN FIGHTING THESE MARTIANS FOR ETERNITY."

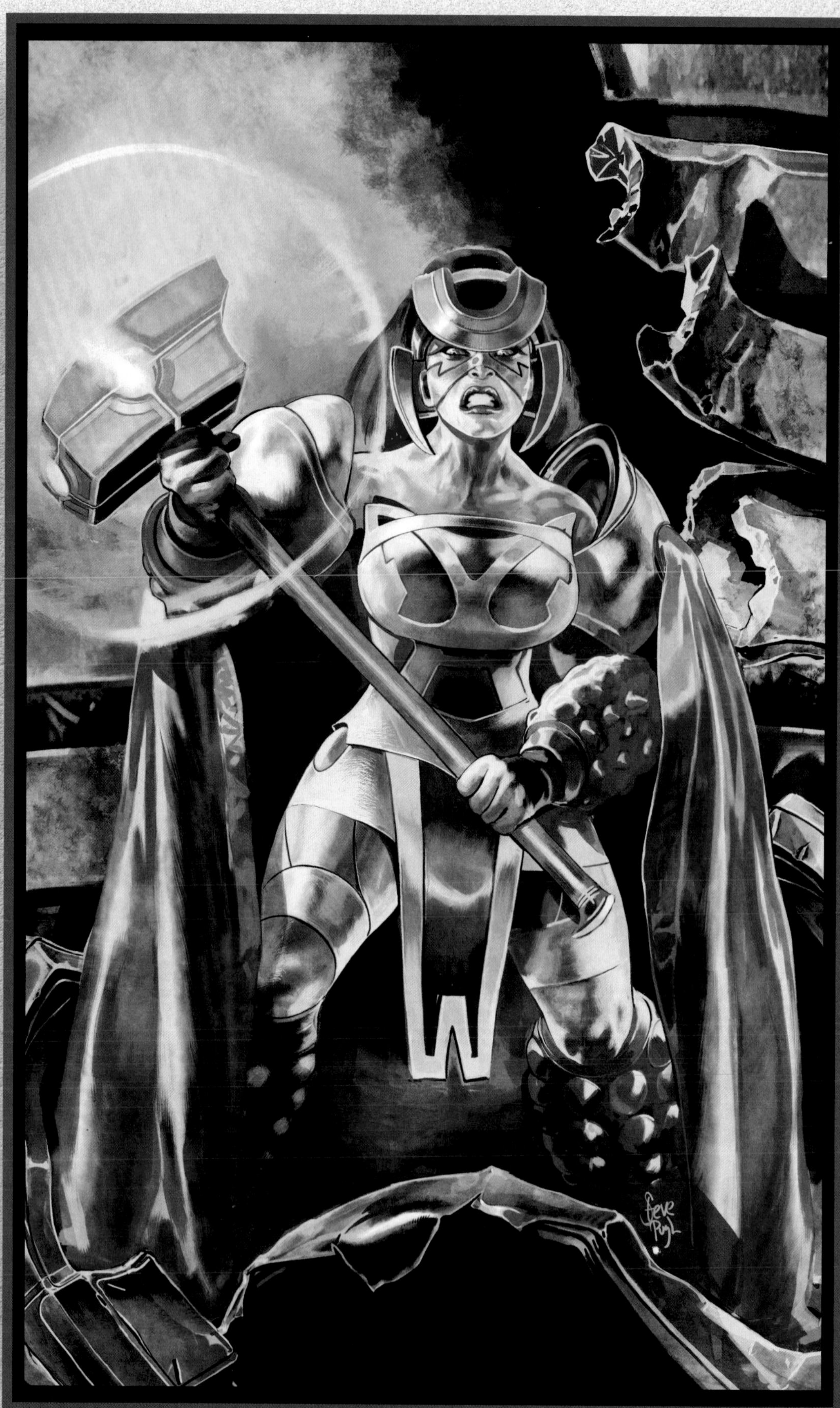
Steve Pugh

#13

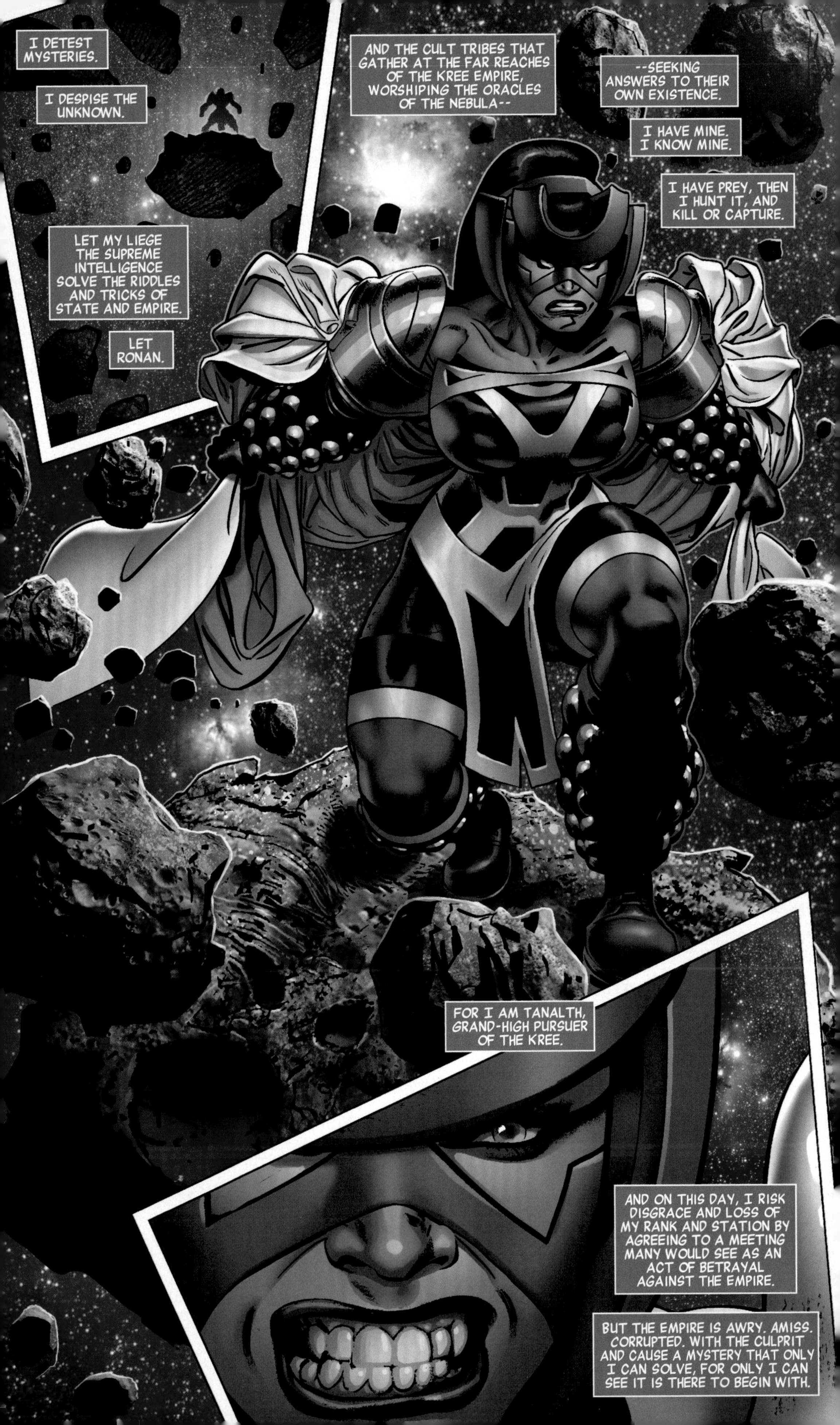
I DETEST MYSTERIES.
I DESPISE THE UNKNOWN.
LET MY LIEGE THE SUPREME INTELLIGENCE SOLVE THE RIDDLES AND TRICKS OF STATE AND EMPIRE.
LET RONAN.
AND THE CULT TRIBES THAT GATHER AT THE FAR REACHES OF THE KREE EMPIRE, WORSHIPING THE ORACLES OF THE NEBULA--
--SEEKING ANSWERS TO THEIR OWN EXISTENCE.
I HAVE MINE. I KNOW MINE.
I HAVE PREY, THEN I HUNT IT, AND KILL OR CAPTURE.
FOR I AM TANALTH, GRAND-HIGH PURSUER OF THE KREE.
AND ON THIS DAY, I RISK DISGRACE AND LOSS OF MY RANK AND STATION BY AGREEING TO A MEETING MANY WOULD SEE AS AN ACT OF BETRAYAL AGAINST THE EMPIRE.
BUT THE EMPIRE IS AWRY. AMISS. CORRUPTED. WITH THE CULPRIT AND CAUSE A MYSTERY THAT ONLY I CAN SOLVE, FOR ONLY I CAN SEE IT IS THERE TO BEGIN WITH.

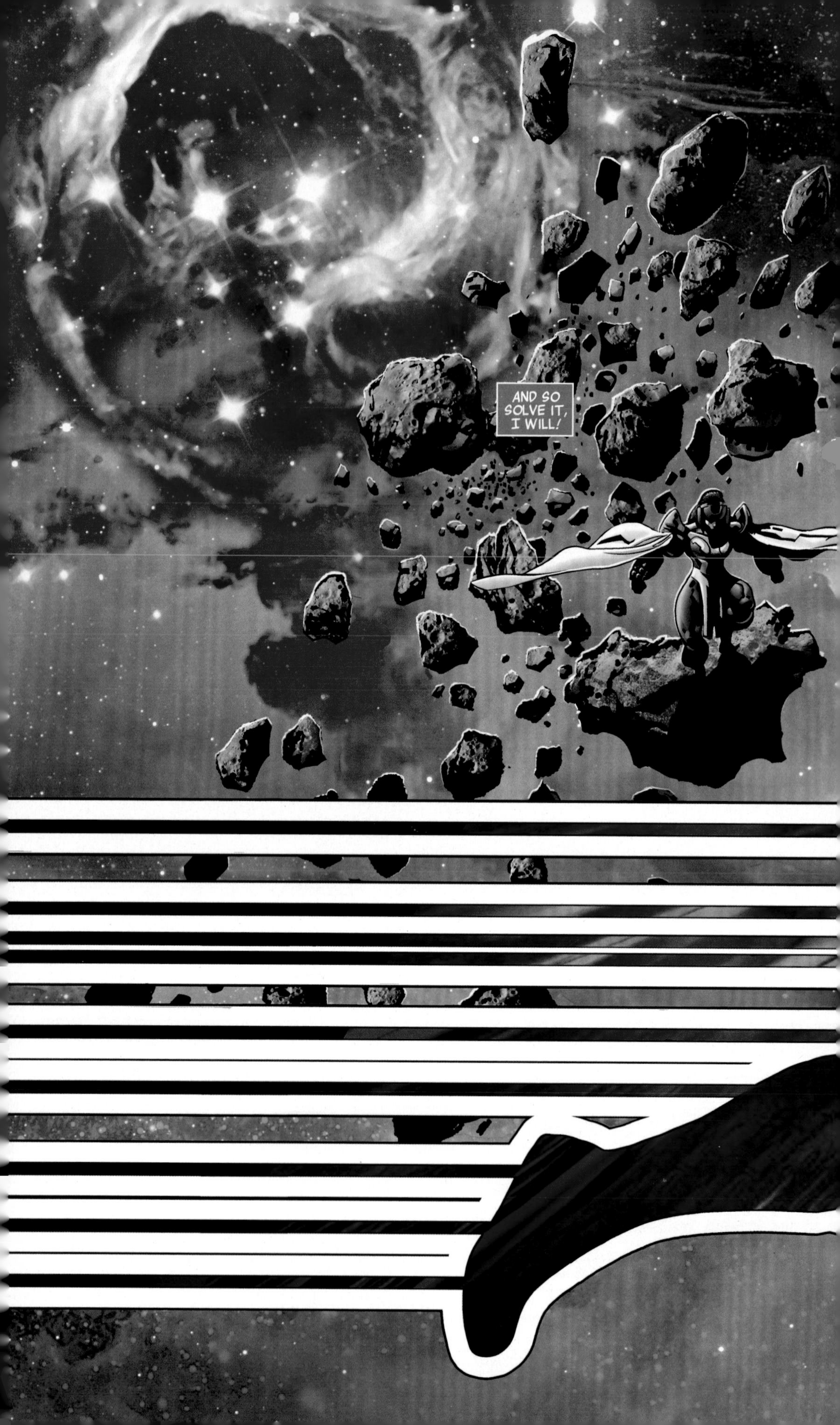
AND SO SOLVE IT, I WILL!

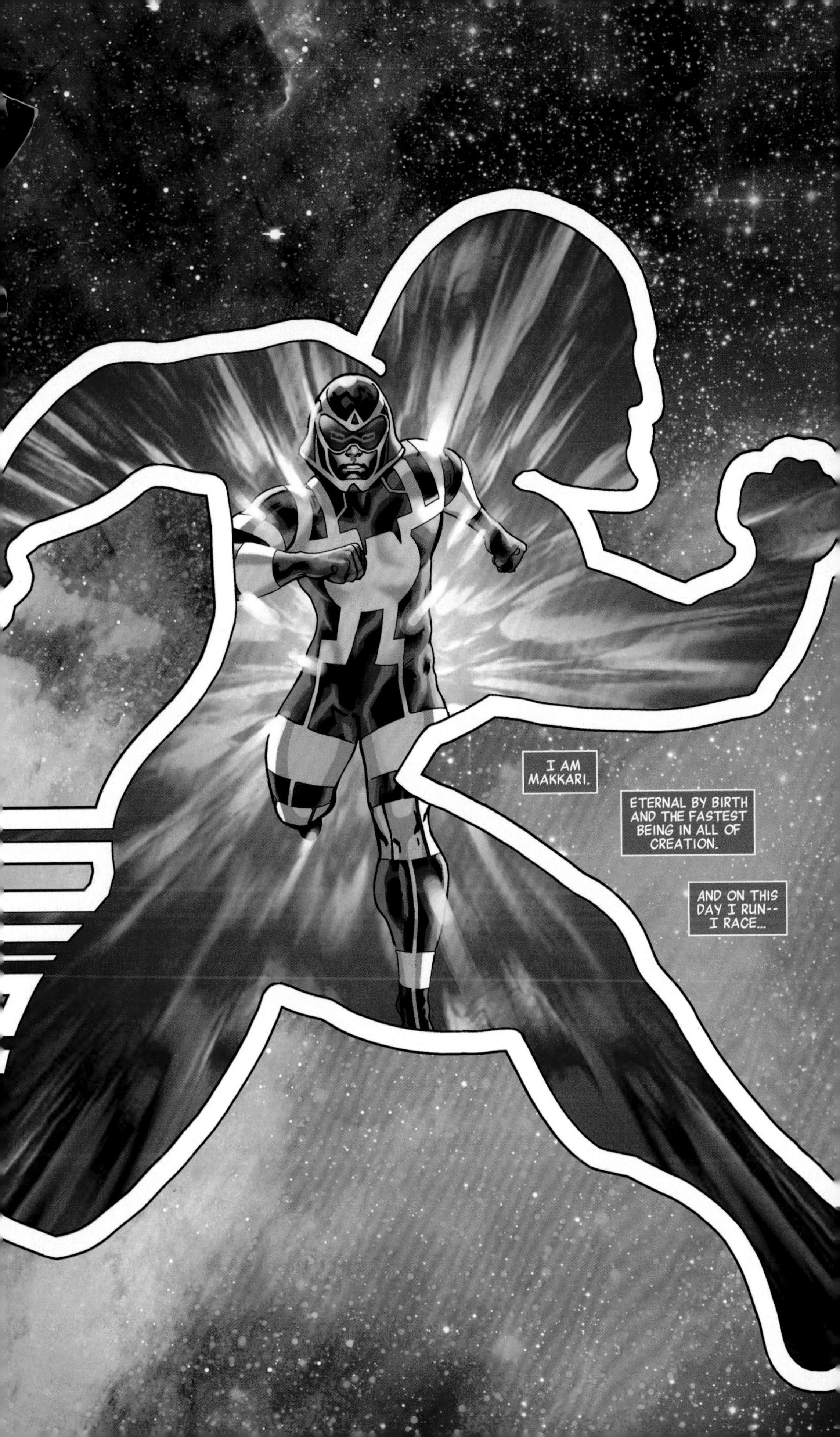
I AM MAKKARI.
ETERNAL BY BIRTH AND THE FASTEST BEING IN ALL OF CREATION.
AND ON THIS DAY I RUN-- I RACE...

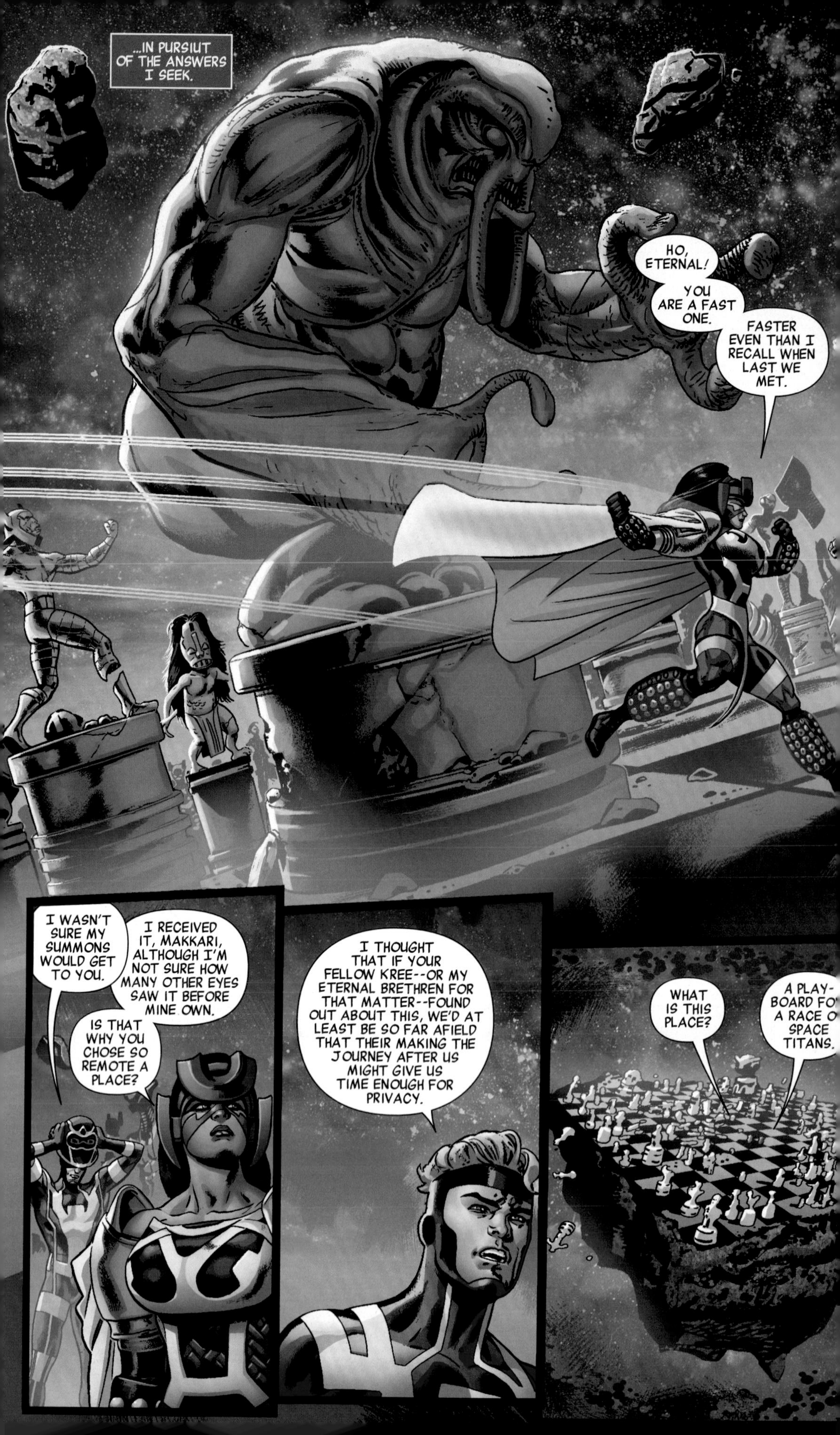
...IN PURSIUT OF THE ANSWERS I SEEK.
HO, ETERNAL!
YOU ARE A FAST ONE.
FASTER EVEN THAN I RECALL WHEN LAST WE MET.
I WASN'T SURE MY SUMMONS WOULD GET TO YOU.
I RECEIVED IT, MAKKARI, ALTHOUGH I'M NOT SURE HOW MANY OTHER EYES SAW IT BEFORE MINE OWN.
IS THAT WHY YOU CHOSE SO REMOTE A PLACE?
I THOUGHT THAT IF YOUR FELLOW KREE--OR MY ETERNAL BRETHREN FOR THAT MATTER--FOUND OUT ABOUT THIS, WE'D AT LEAST BE SO FAR AFIELD THAT THEIR MAKING THE JOURNEY AFTER US MIGHT GIVE US TIME ENOUGH FOR PRIVACY.
WHAT IS THIS PLACE?

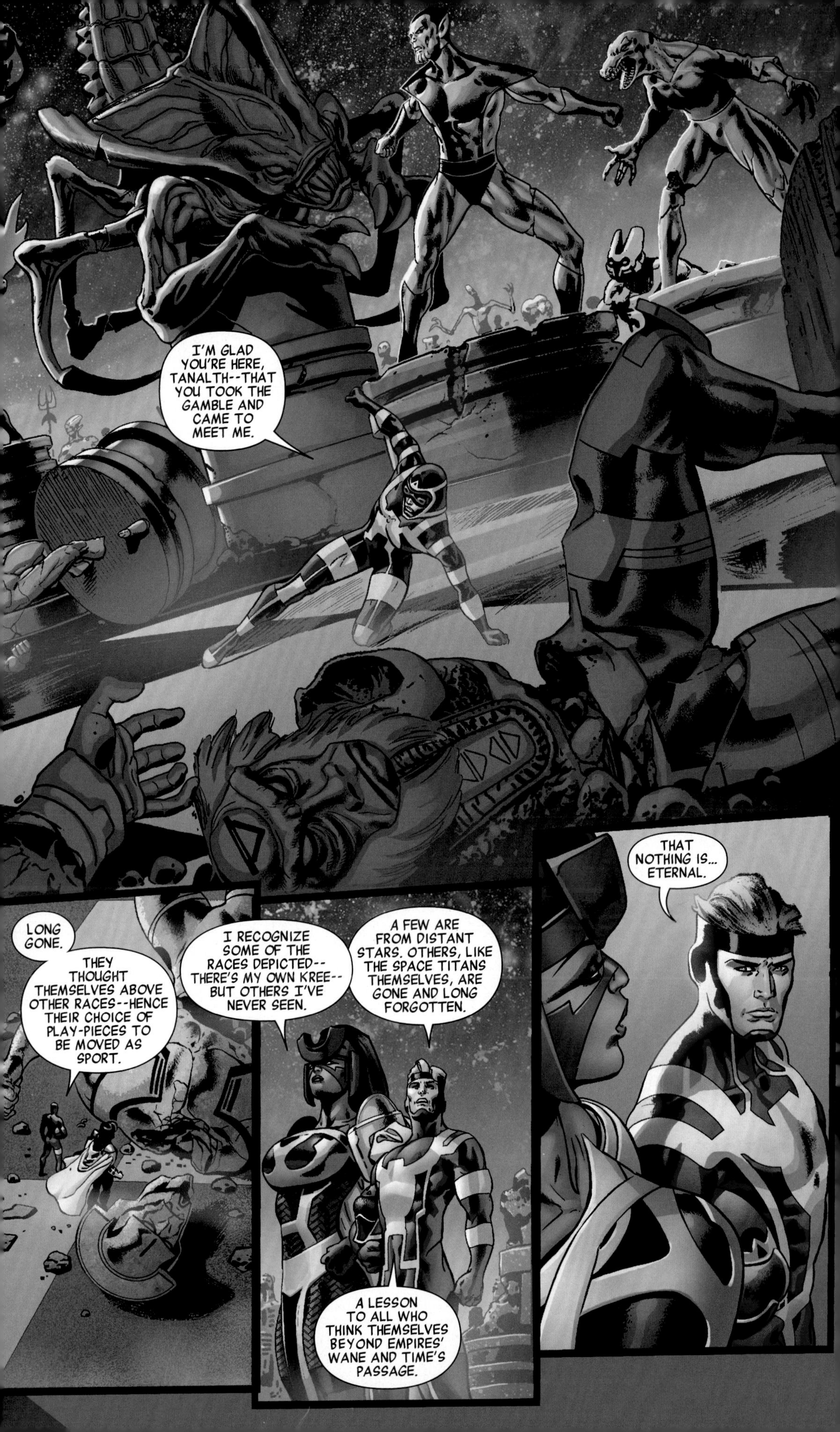
I'M GLAD YOU'RE HERE, TANALTH--THAT YOU TOOK THE GAMBLE AND CAME TO MEET ME.
LONG GONE.
THEY THOUGHT THEMSELVES ABOVE OTHER RACES--HENCE THEIR CHOICE OF PLAY-PIECES TO BE MOVED AS SPORT.
I RECOGNIZE SOME OF THE RACES DEPICTED--THERE'S MY OWN KREE--BUT OTHERS I'VE NEVER SEEN.
A FEW ARE FROM DISTANT STARS. OTHERS, LIKE THE SPACE TITANS THEMSELVES, ARE GONE AND LONG FORGOTTEN.
A LESSON TO ALL WHO THINK THEMSELVES BEYOND EMPIRES' WANE AND TIME'S PASSAGE.
THAT NOTHING IS... ETERNAL.

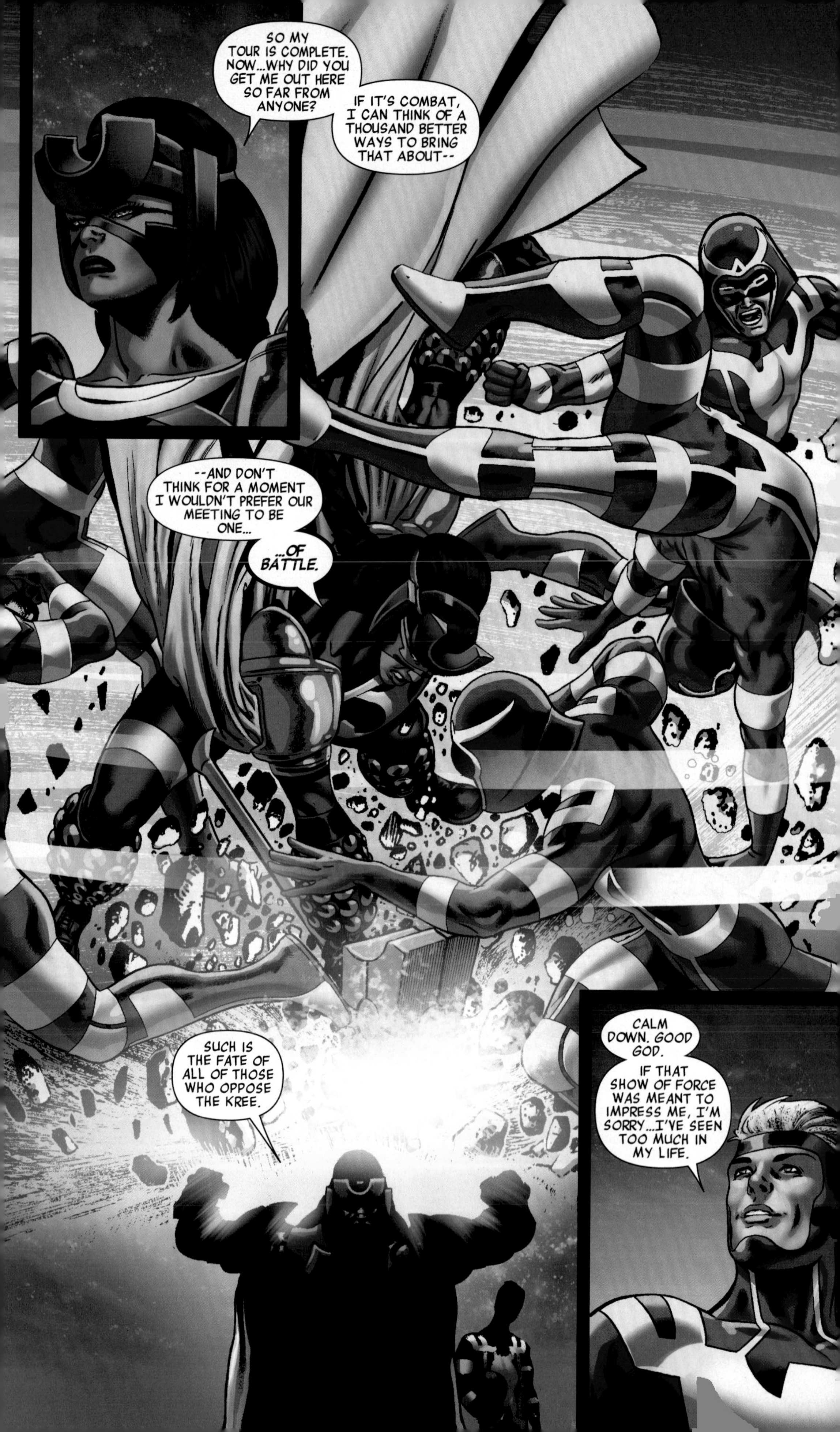
SO MY TOUR IS COMPLETE. NOW...WHY DID YOU GET ME OUT HERE SO FAR FROM ANYONE?
IF IT'S COMBAT, I CAN THINK OF A THOUSAND BETTER WAYS TO BRING THAT ABOUT--
--AND DON'T THINK FOR A MOMENT I WOULDN'T PREFER OUR MEETING TO BE ONE...
...OF BATTLE.
SUCH IS THE FATE OF ALL OF THOSE WHO OPPOSE THE KREE.
CALM DOWN. GOOD GOD.
IF THAT SHOW OF FORCE WAS MEANT TO IMPRESS ME, I'M SORRY...I'VE SEEN TOO MUCH IN MY LIFE.

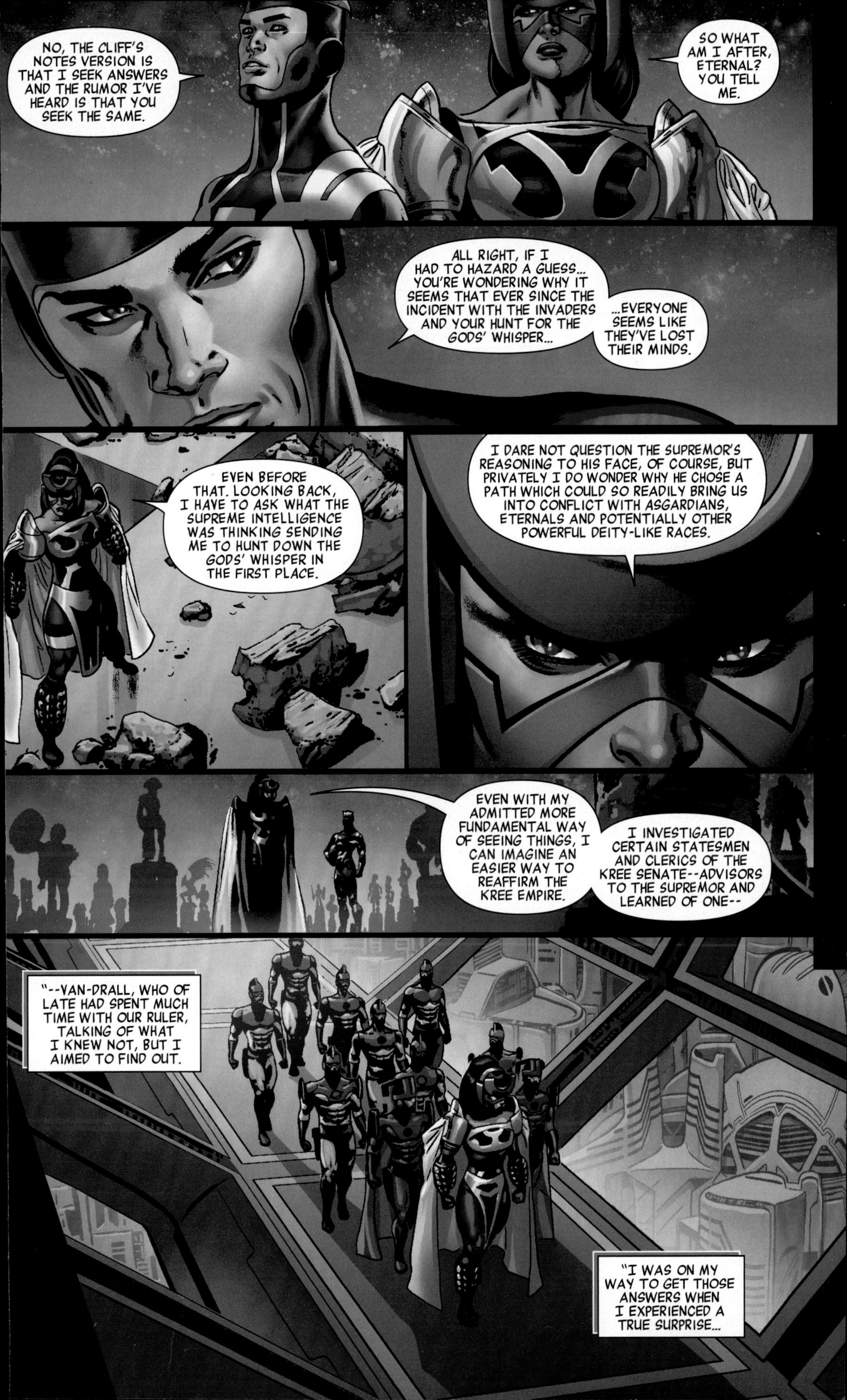
NO, THE CLIFF'S NOTES VERSION IS THAT I SEEK ANSWERS AND THE RUMOR I'VE HEARD IS THAT YOU SEEK THE SAME.
SO WHAT AM I AFTER, ETERNAL? YOU TELL ME.
ALL RIGHT, IF I HAD TO HAZARD A GUESS... YOU'RE WONDERING WHY IT SEEMS THAT EVER SINCE THE INCIDENT WITH THE INVADERS AND YOUR HUNT FOR THE GODS' WHISPER...
...EVERYONE SEEMS LIKE THEY'VE LOST THEIR MINDS.
EVEN BEFORE THAT. LOOKING BACK, I HAVE TO ASK WHAT THE SUPREME INTELLIGENCE WAS THINKING SENDING ME TO HUNT DOWN THE GODS' WHISPER IN THE FIRST PLACE.
I DARE NOT QUESTION THE SUPREMOR'S REASONING TO HIS FACE, OF COURSE, BUT PRIVATELY I DO WONDER WHY HE CHOSE A PATH WHICH COULD SO READILY BRING US INTO CONFLICT WITH ASGARDIANS, ETERNALS AND POTENTIALLY OTHER POWERFUL DEITY-LIKE RACES.
EVEN WITH MY ADMITTED MORE FUNDAMENTAL WAY OF SEEING THINGS, I CAN IMAGINE AN EASIER WAY TO REAFFIRM THE KREE EMPIRE.
I INVESTIGATED CERTAIN STATESMEN AND CLERICS OF THE KREE SENATE--ADVISORS TO THE SUPREMOR AND LEARNED OF ONE--
"--VAN-DRALL, WHO OF LATE HAD SPENT MUCH TIME WITH OUR RULER, TALKING OF WHAT I KNEW NOT, BUT I AIMED TO FIND OUT.
"I WAS ON MY WAY TO GET THOSE ANSWERS WHEN I EXPERIENCED A TRUE SURPRISE...

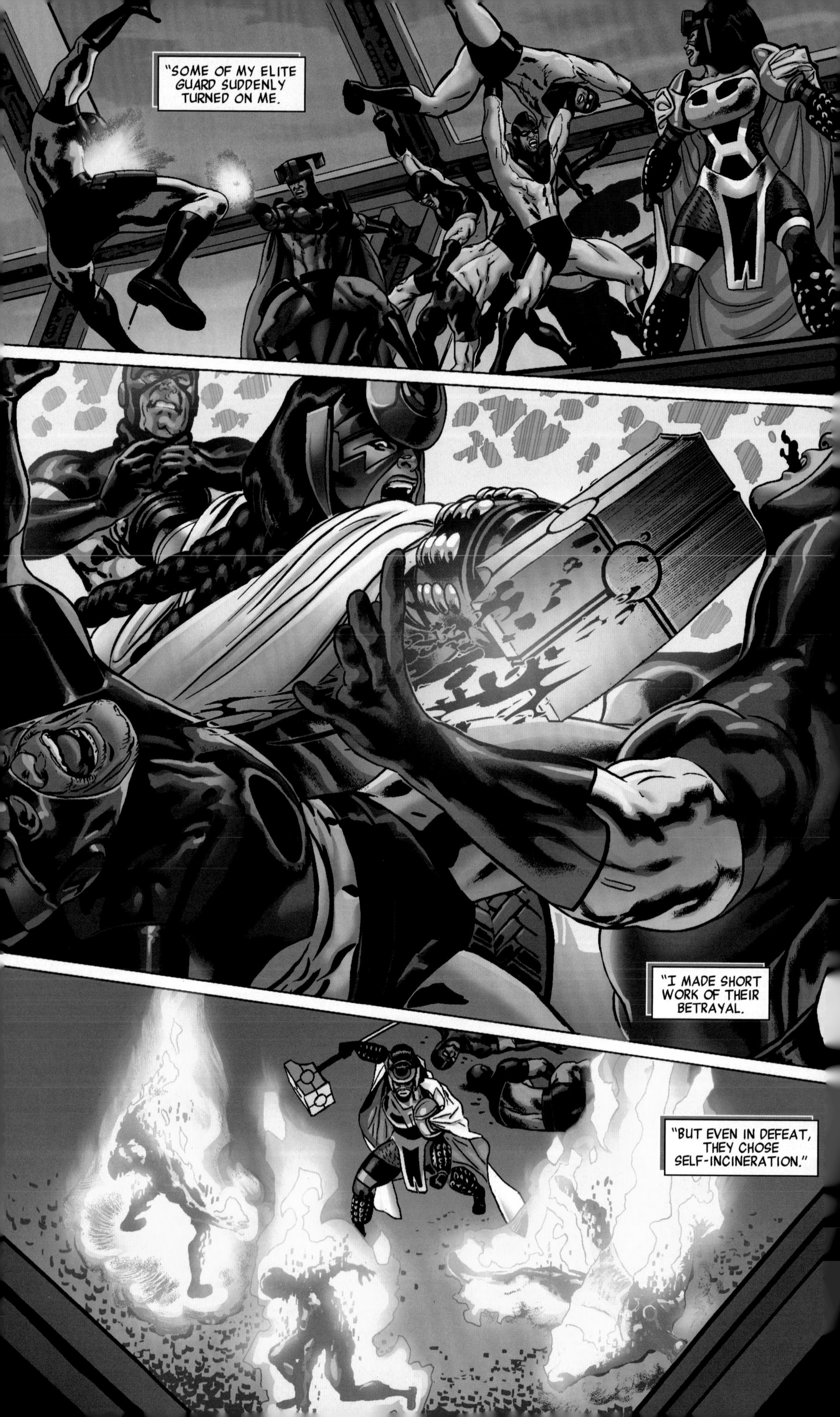
"SOME OF MY ELITE GUARD SUDDENLY TURNED ON ME.
"I MADE SHORT WORK OF THEIR BETRAYAL.
"BUT EVEN IN DEFEAT, THEY CHOSE SELF-INCINERATION."

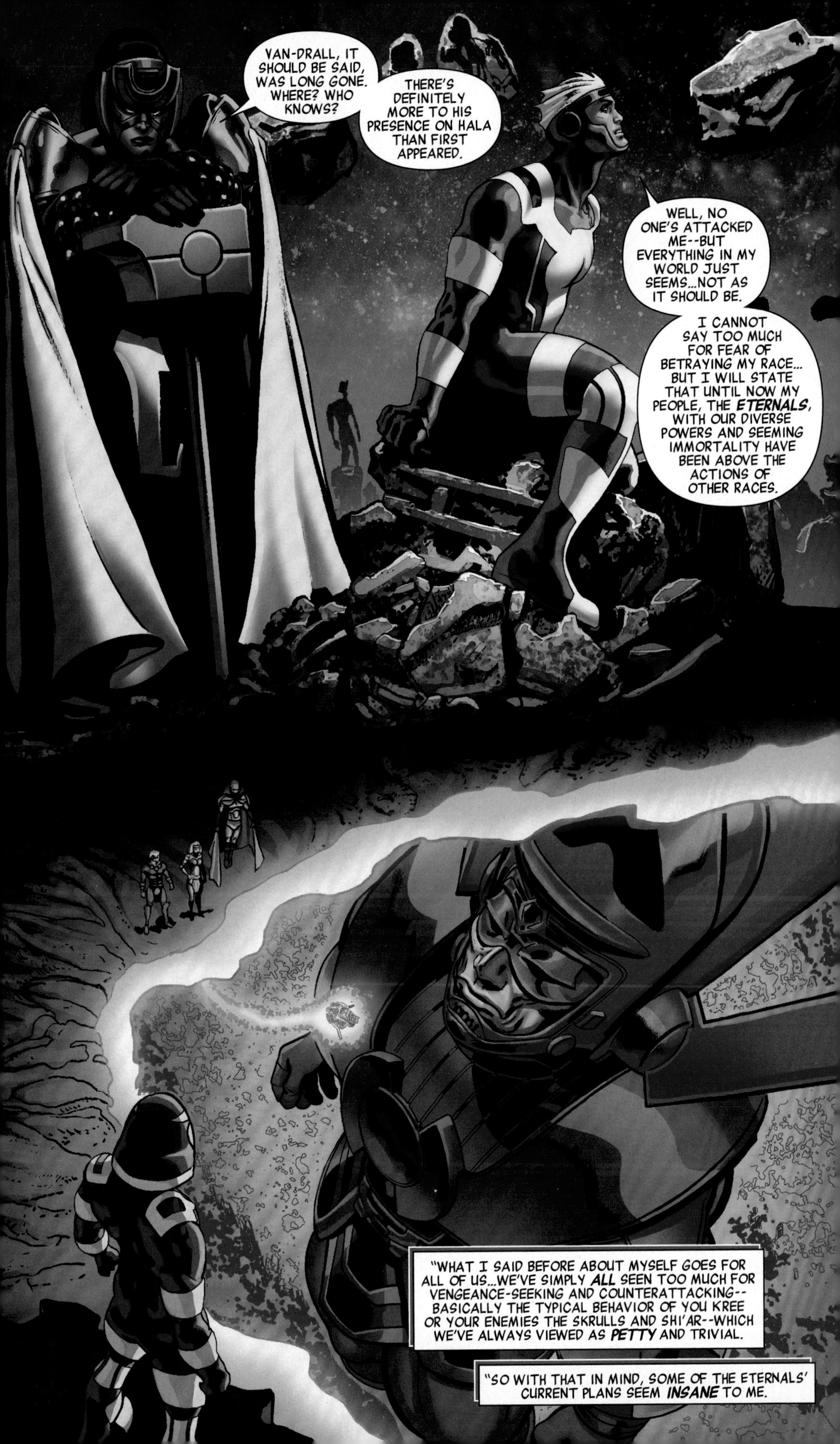
VAN-DRALL, IT SHOULD BE SAID, WAS LONG GONE. WHERE? WHO KNOWS?
THERE'S DEFINITELY MORE TO HIS PRESENCE ON HALA THAN FIRST APPEARED.
WELL, NO ONE'S ATTACKED ME--BUT EVERYTHING IN MY WORLD JUST SEEMS...NOT AS IT SHOULD BE.
I CANNOT SAY TOO MUCH FOR FEAR OF BETRAYING MY RACE... BUT I WILL STATE THAT UNTIL NOW MY PEOPLE, THE ETERNALS, WITH OUR DIVERSE POWERS AND SEEMING IMMORTALITY HAVE BEEN ABOVE THE ACTIONS OF OTHER RACES.
"WHAT I SAID BEFORE ABOUT MYSELF GOES FOR ALL OF US...WE'VE SIMPLY ALL SEEN TOO MUCH FOR VENGEANCE-SEEKING AND COUNTERATTACKING--BASICALLY THE TYPICAL BEHAVIOR OF YOU KREE OR YOUR ENEMIES THE SKRULLS AND SHI'AR--WHICH WE'VE ALWAYS VIEWED AS PETTY AND TRIVIAL.
"SO WITH THAT IN MIND, SOME OF THE ETERNALS' CURRENT PLANS SEEM INSANE TO ME.

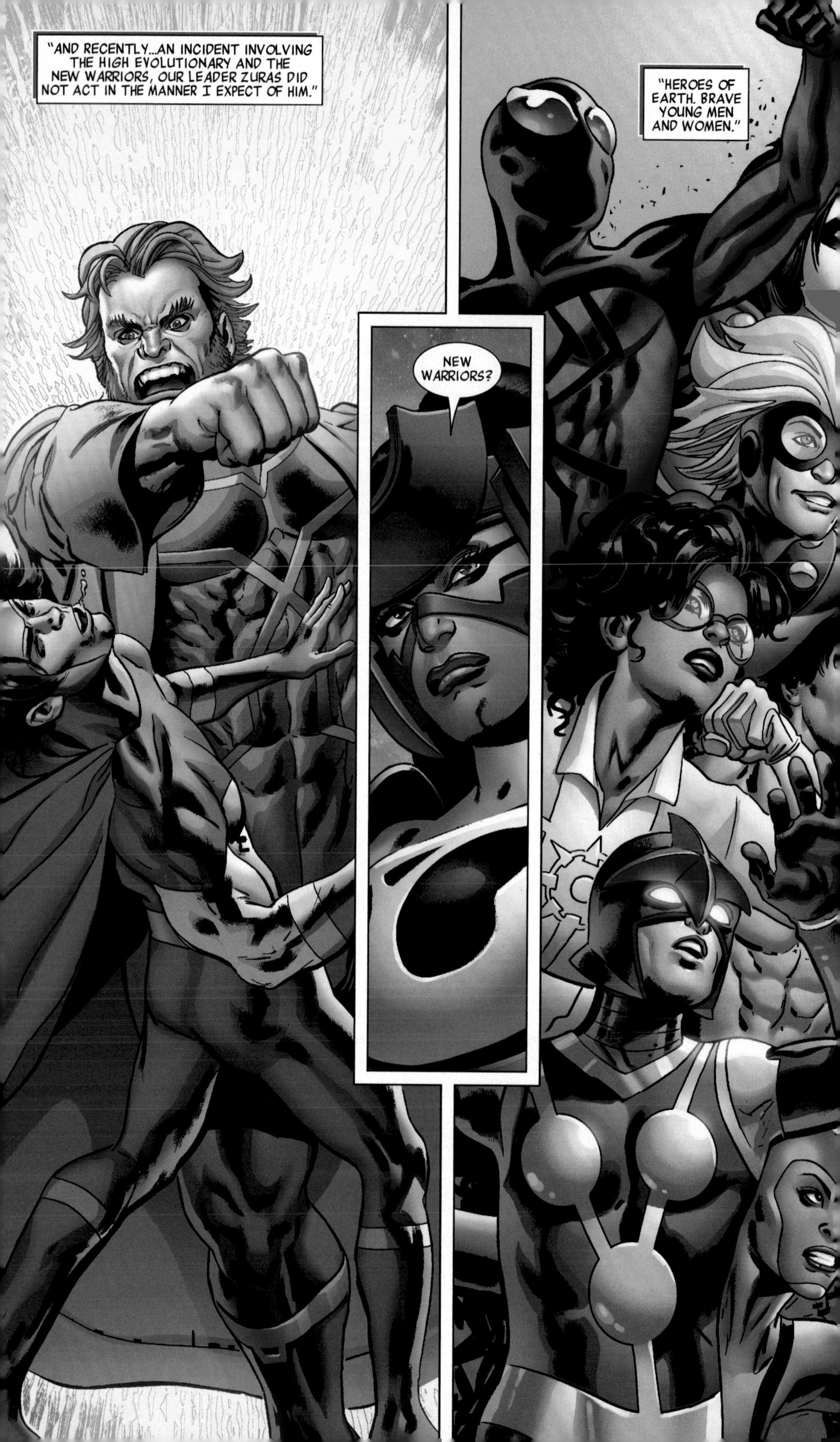

"AND RECENTLY...AN INCIDENT INVOLVING THE HIGH EVOLUTIONARY AND THE NEW WARRIORS, OUR LEADER ZURAS DID NOT ACT IN THE MANNER I EXPECT OF HIM."
"HEROES OF EARTH. BRAVE YOUNG MEN AND WOMEN."
NEW WARRIORS?

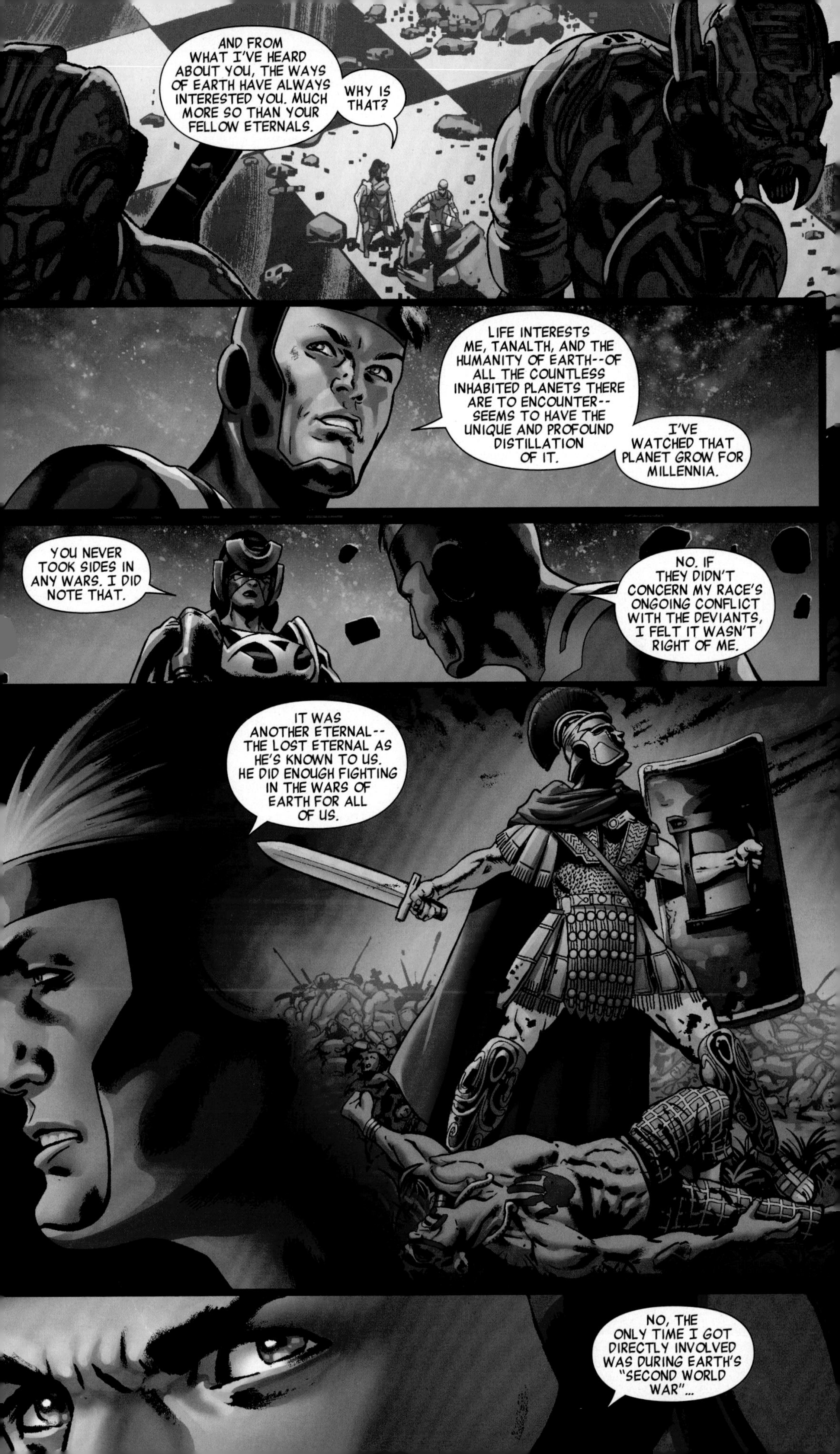
AND FROM WHAT I'VE HEARD ABOUT YOU, THE WAYS OF EARTH HAVE ALWAYS INTERESTED YOU. MUCH MORE SO THAN YOUR FELLOW ETERNALS.
WHY IS THAT?
LIFE INTERESTS ME, TANALTH, AND THE HUMANITY OF EARTH--OF ALL THE COUNTLESS INHABITED PLANETS THERE ARE TO ENCOUNTER--SEEMS TO HAVE THE UNIQUE AND PROFOUND DISTILLATION OF IT.
I'VE WATCHED THAT PLANET GROW FOR MILLENNIA.
YOU NEVER TOOK SIDES IN ANY WARS. I DID NOTE THAT.
NO. IF THEY DIDN'T CONCERN MY RACE'S ONGOING CONFLICT WITH THE DEVIANTS, I FELT IT WASN'T RIGHT OF ME.
IT WAS ANOTHER ETERNAL--THE LOST ETERNAL AS HE'S KNOWN TO US. HE DID ENOUGH FIGHTING IN THE WARS OF EARTH FOR ALL OF US.
NO, THE ONLY TIME I GOT DIRECTLY INVOLVED WAS DURING EARTH'S "SECOND WORLD WAR"...

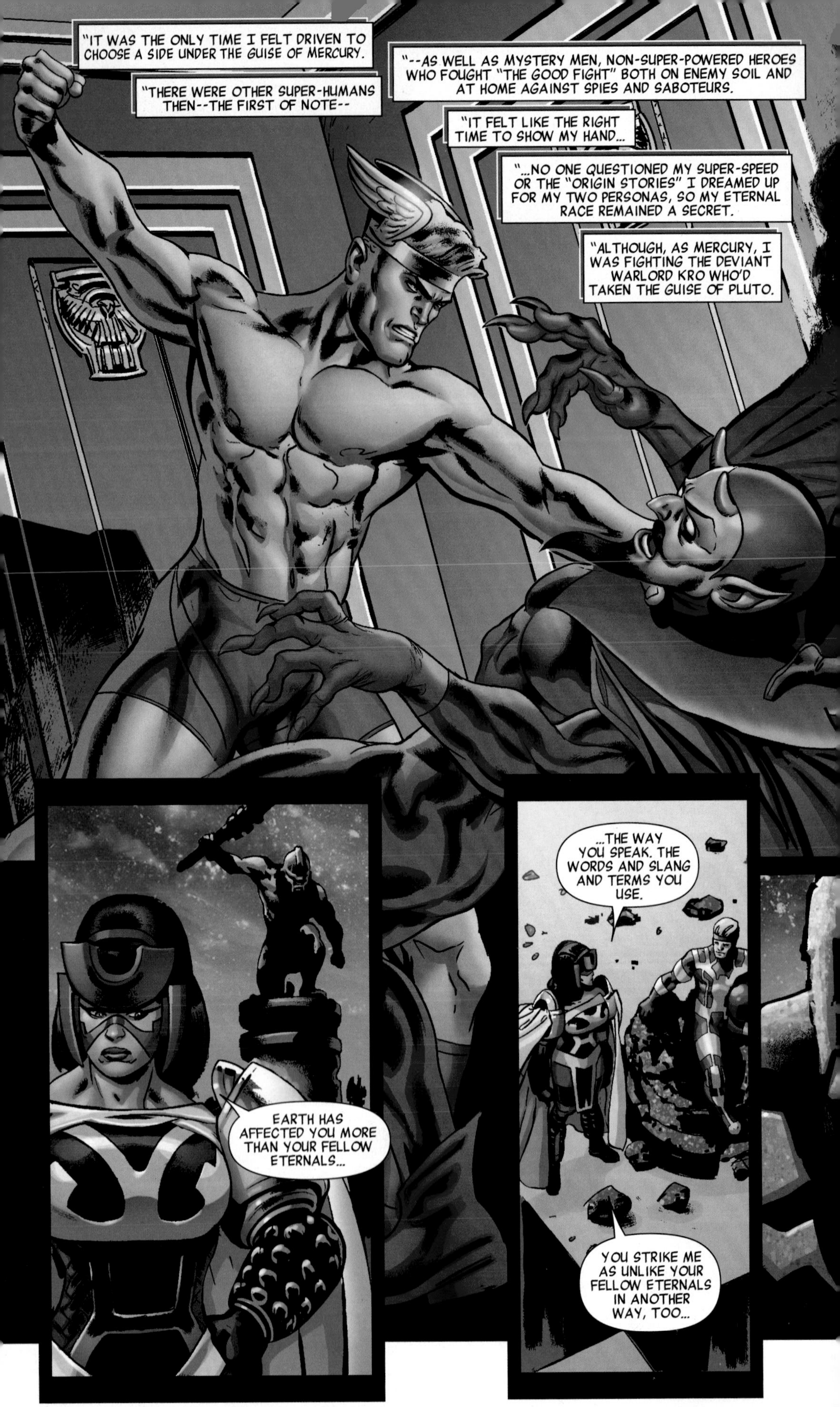
"IT WAS THE ONLY TIME I FELT DRIVEN TO CHOOSE A SIDE UNDER THE GUISE OF MERCURY.
"THERE WERE OTHER SUPER-HUMANS THEN--THE FIRST OF NOTE--
"--AS WELL AS MYSTERY MEN, NON-SUPER-POWERED HEROES WHO FOUGHT "THE GOOD FIGHT" BOTH ON ENEMY SOIL AND AT HOME AGAINST SPIES AND SABOTEURS.
"IT FELT LIKE THE RIGHT TIME TO SHOW MY HAND...
"...NO ONE QUESTIONED MY SUPER-SPEED OR THE "ORIGIN STORIES" I DREAMED UP FOR MY TWO PERSONAS, SO MY ETERNAL RACE REMAINED A SECRET.
"ALTHOUGH, AS MERCURY, I WAS FIGHTING THE DEVIANT WARLORD KRO WHO'D TAKEN THE GUISE OF PLUTO.
EARTH HAS AFFECTED YOU MORE THAN YOUR FELLOW ETERNALS...
...THE WAY YOU SPEAK. THE WORDS AND SLANG AND TERMS YOU USE.
YOU STRIKE ME AS UNLIKE YOUR FELLOW ETERNALS IN ANOTHER WAY, TOO...

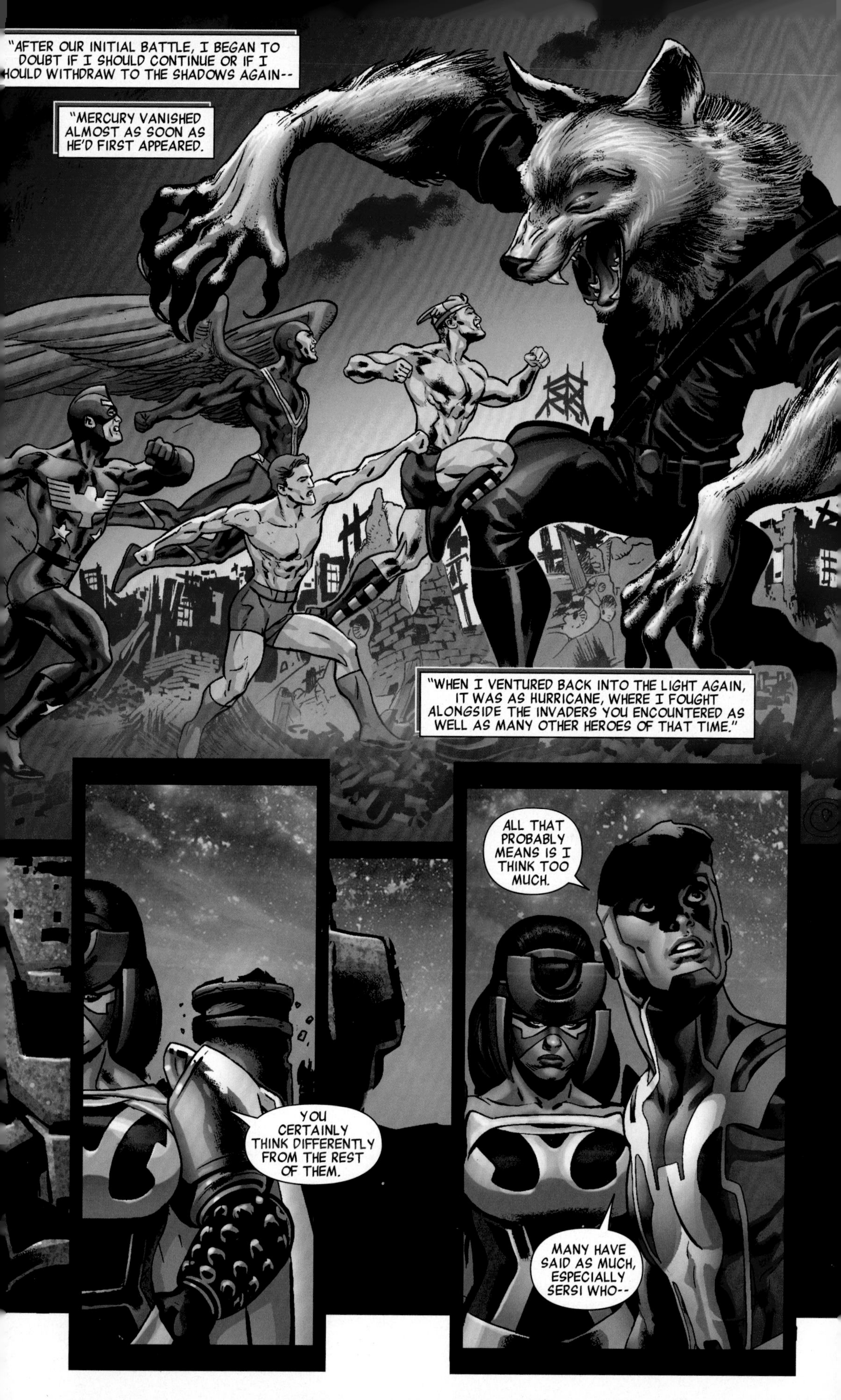
"AFTER OUR INITIAL BATTLE, I BEGAN TO DOUBT IF I SHOULD CONTINUE OR IF I HOULD WITHDRAW TO THE SHADOWS AGAIN--
"MERCURY VANISHED ALMOST AS SOON AS HE'D FIRST APPEARED.
"WHEN I VENTURED BACK INTO THE LIGHT AGAIN, IT WAS AS HURRICANE, WHERE I FOUGHT ALONGSIDE THE INVADERS YOU ENCOUNTERED AS WELL AS MANY OTHER HEROES OF THAT TIME."
YOU CERTAINLY THINK DIFFERENTLY FROM THE REST OF THEM.
ALL THAT PROBABLY MEANS IS I THINK TOO MUCH.
MANY HAVE SAID AS MUCH, ESPECIALLY SERSI WHO--

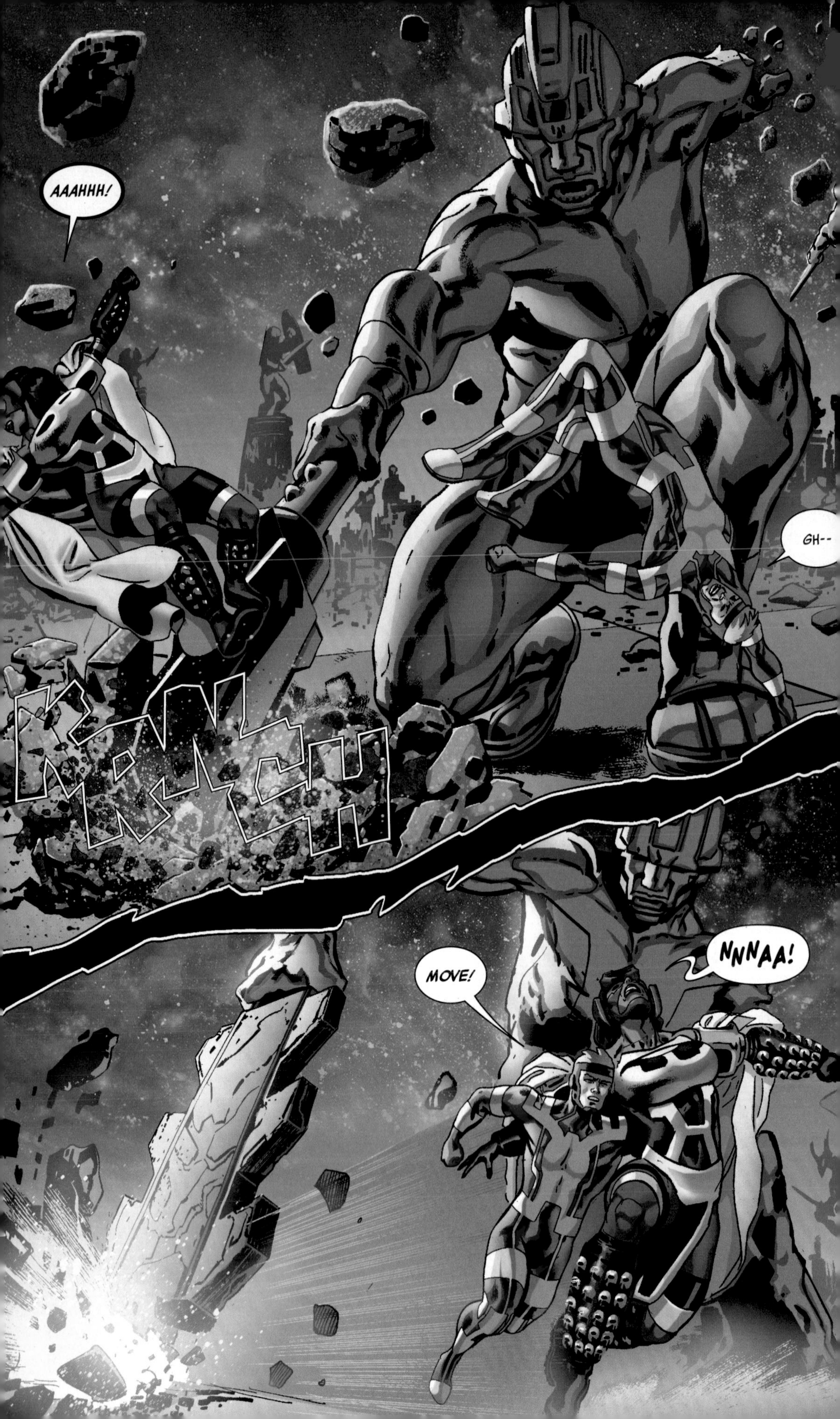
AAAHHH!
GH--
KRUNCH
MOVE!
NNNAA!

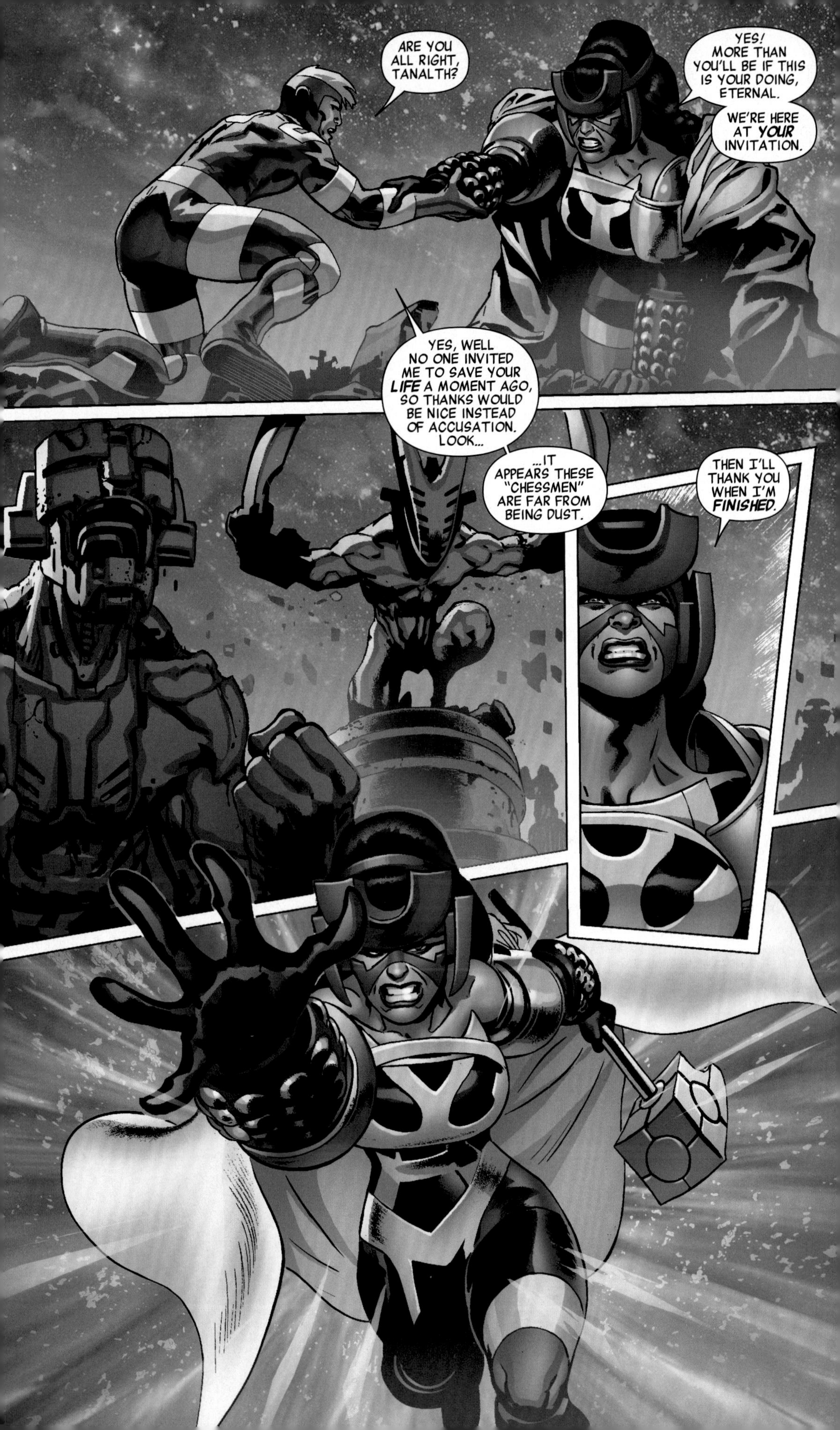

ARE YOU ALL RIGHT, TANALTH?
YES! MORE THAN YOU'LL BE IF THIS IS YOUR DOING, ETERNAL.
WE'RE HERE AT *YOUR* INVITATION.
YES, WELL NO ONE INVITED ME TO SAVE YOUR *LIFE* A MOMENT AGO, SO THANKS WOULD BE NICE INSTEAD OF ACCUSATION. LOOK...
...IT APPEARS THESE "CHESSMEN" ARE FAR FROM BEING DUST.
THEN I'LL THANK YOU WHEN I'M *FINISHED*.

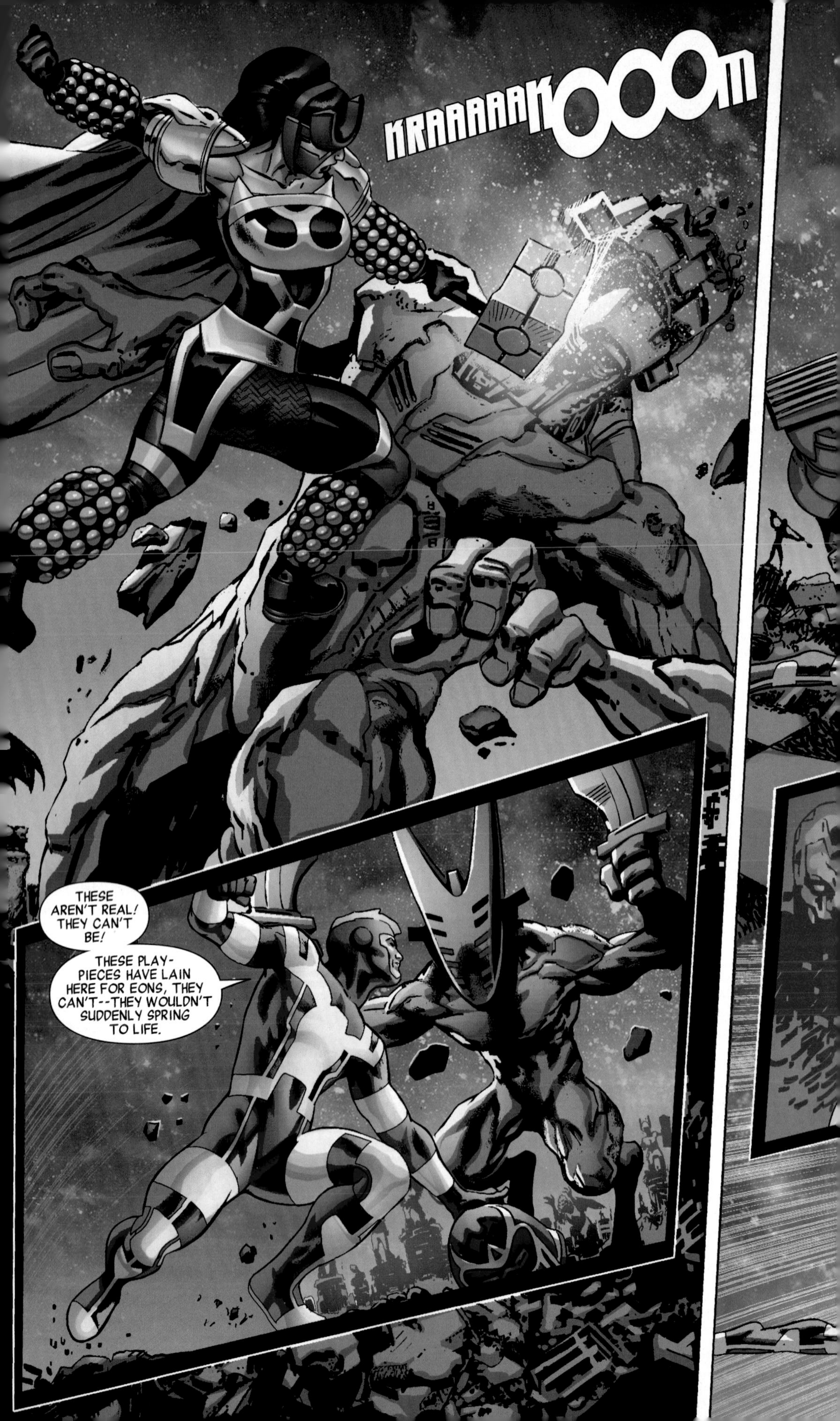
KRAAAAAKOOOM
THESE AREN'T REAL! THEY CAN'T BE!
THESE PLAY-PIECES HAVE LAIN HERE FOR EONS, THEY CAN'T--THEY WOULDN'T SUDDENLY SPRING TO LIFE.

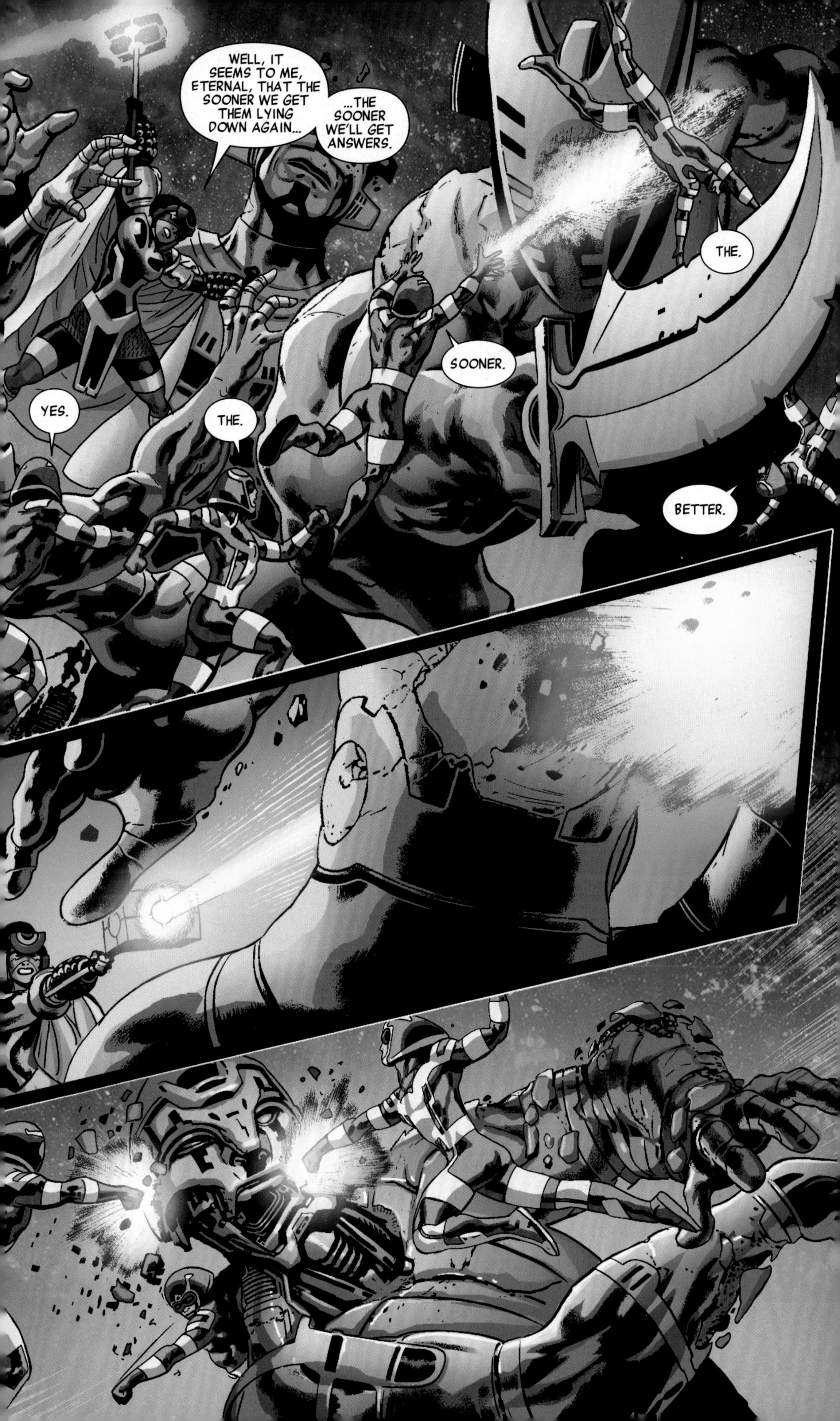
WELL, IT SEEMS TO ME, ETERNAL, THAT THE SOONER WE GET THEM LYING DOWN AGAIN...
...THE SOONER WE'LL GET ANSWERS.
THE.
SOONER.
YES.
THE.
BETTER.

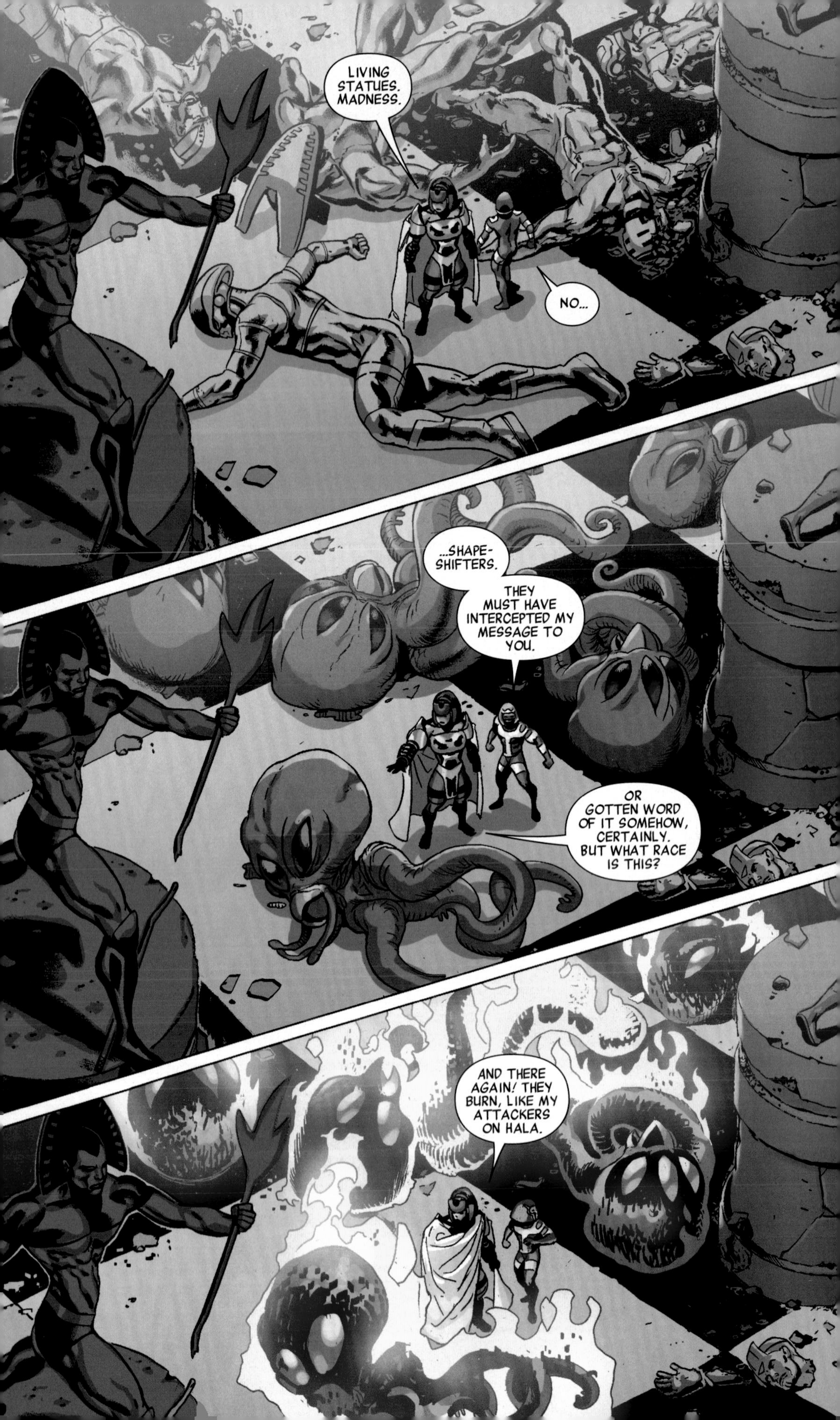
LIVING STATUES. MADNESS.
NO...
...SHAPE-SHIFTERS.
THEY MUST HAVE INTERCEPTED MY MESSAGE TO YOU.
OR GOTTEN WORD OF IT SOMEHOW, CERTAINLY. BUT WHAT RACE IS THIS?
AND THERE AGAIN! THEY BURN, LIKE MY ATTACKERS ON HALA.

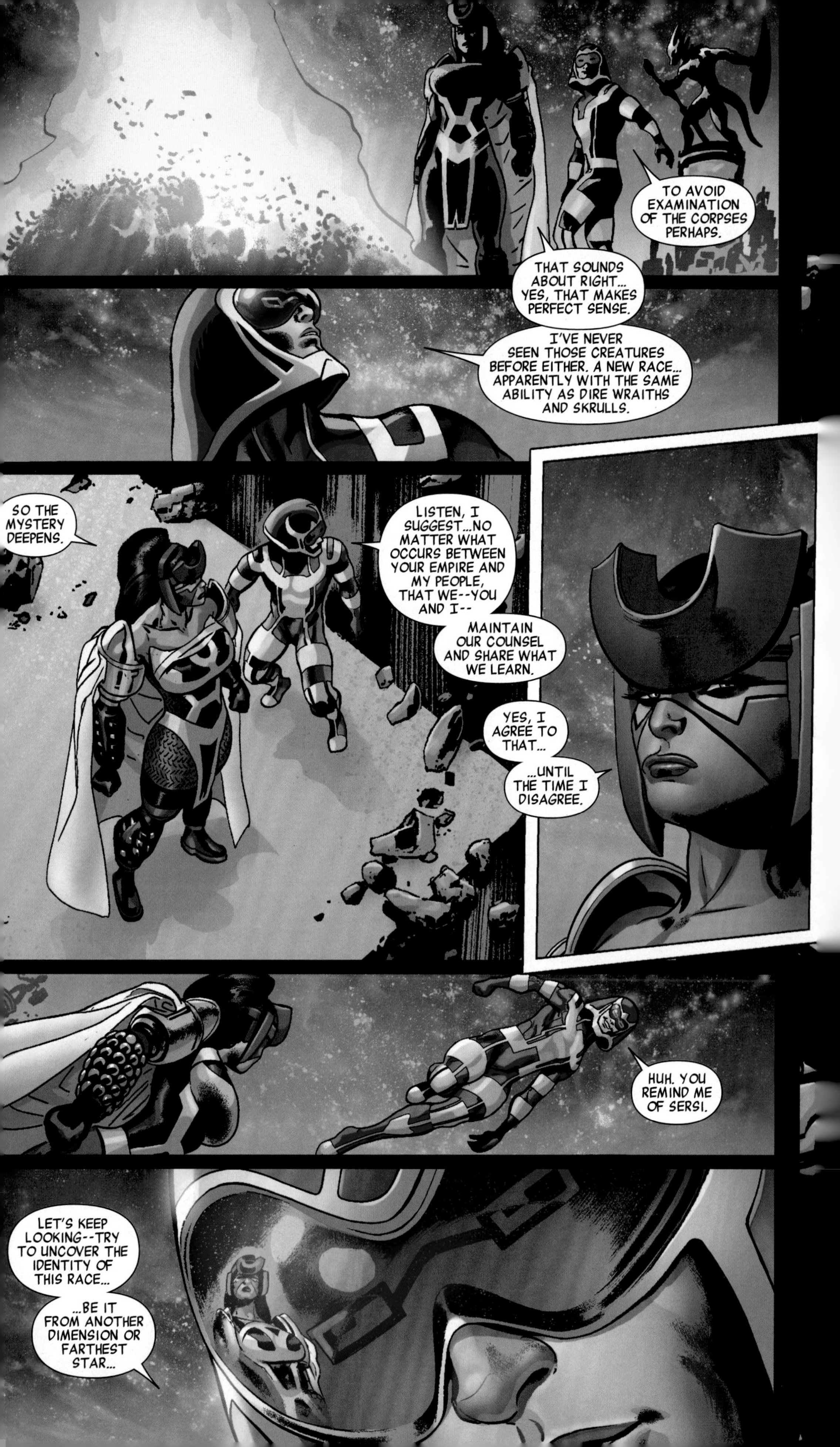
TO AVOID EXAMINATION OF THE CORPSES PERHAPS.
THAT SOUNDS ABOUT RIGHT... YES, THAT MAKES PERFECT SENSE.
I'VE NEVER SEEN THOSE CREATURES BEFORE EITHER. A NEW RACE... APPARENTLY WITH THE SAME ABILITY AS DIRE WRAITHS AND SKRULLS.
SO THE MYSTERY DEEPENS.
LISTEN, I SUGGEST...NO MATTER WHAT OCCURS BETWEEN YOUR EMPIRE AND MY PEOPLE, THAT WE--YOU AND I--
MAINTAIN OUR COUNSEL AND SHARE WHAT WE LEARN.
YES, I AGREE TO THAT...
...UNTIL THE TIME I DISAGREE.
HUH. YOU REMIND ME OF SERSI.
LET'S KEEP LOOKING--TRY TO UNCOVER THE IDENTITY OF THIS RACE...
...BE IT FROM ANOTHER DIMENSION OR FARTHEST STAR...

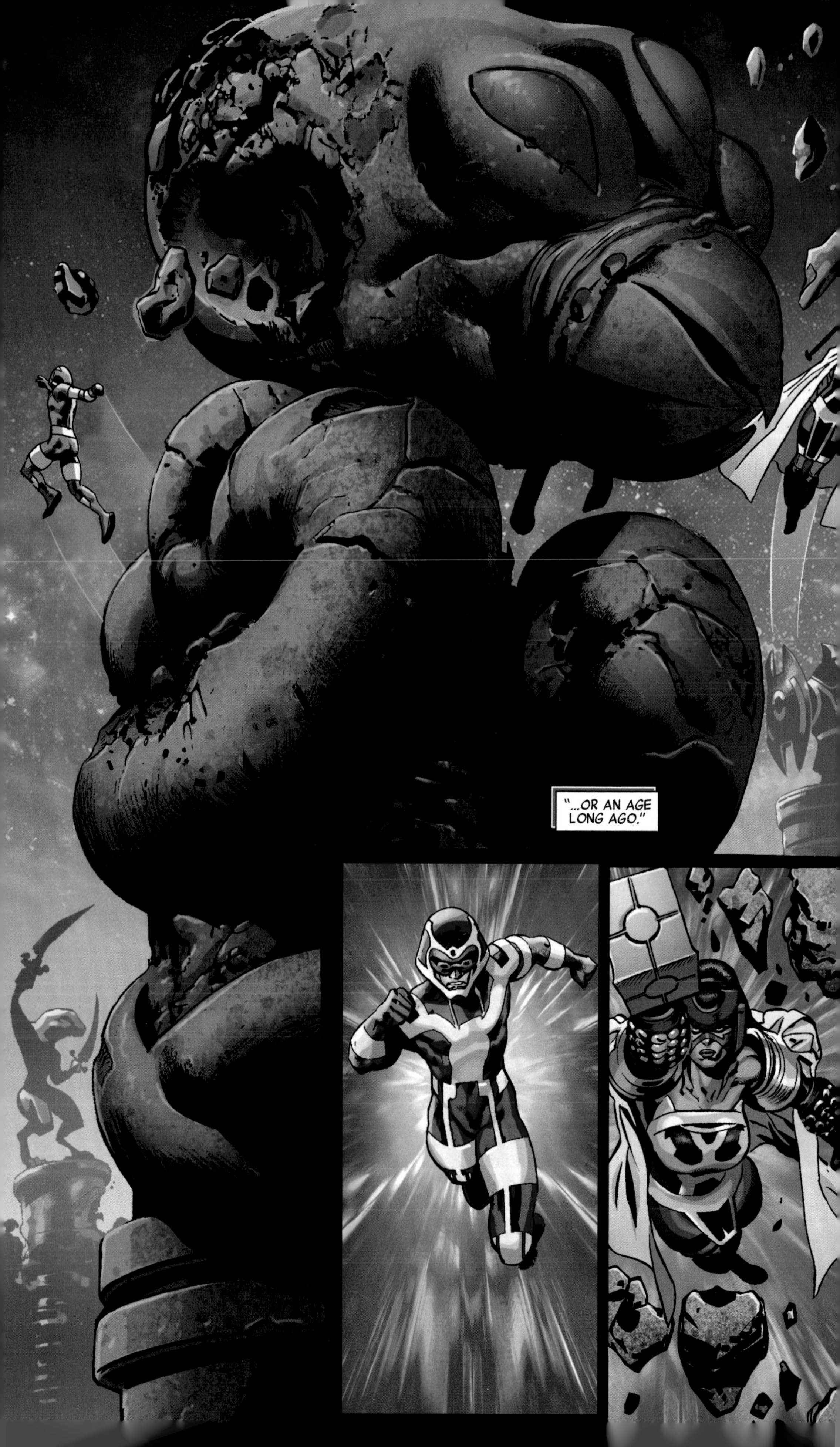
"...OR AN AGE LONG AGO."

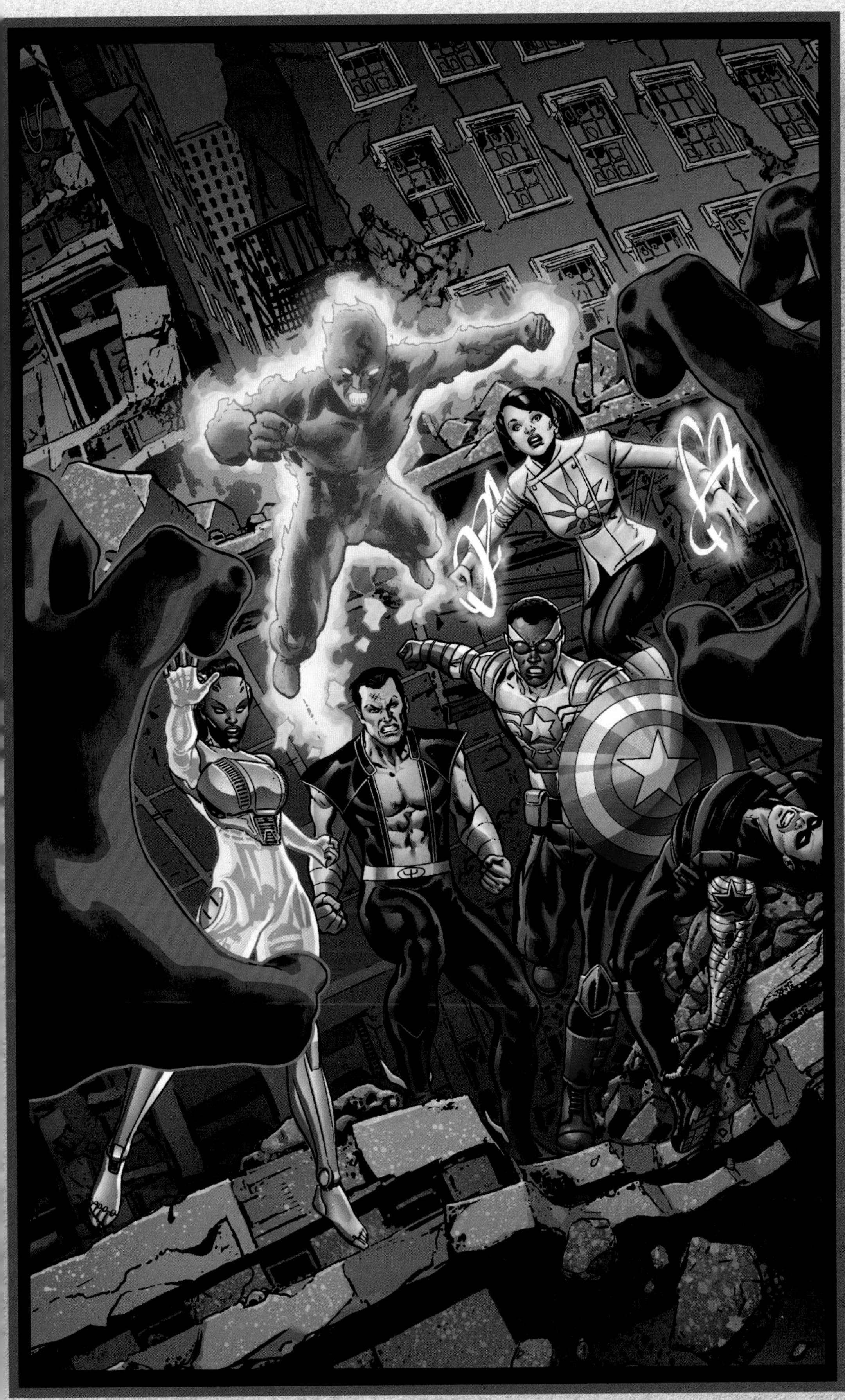

#14

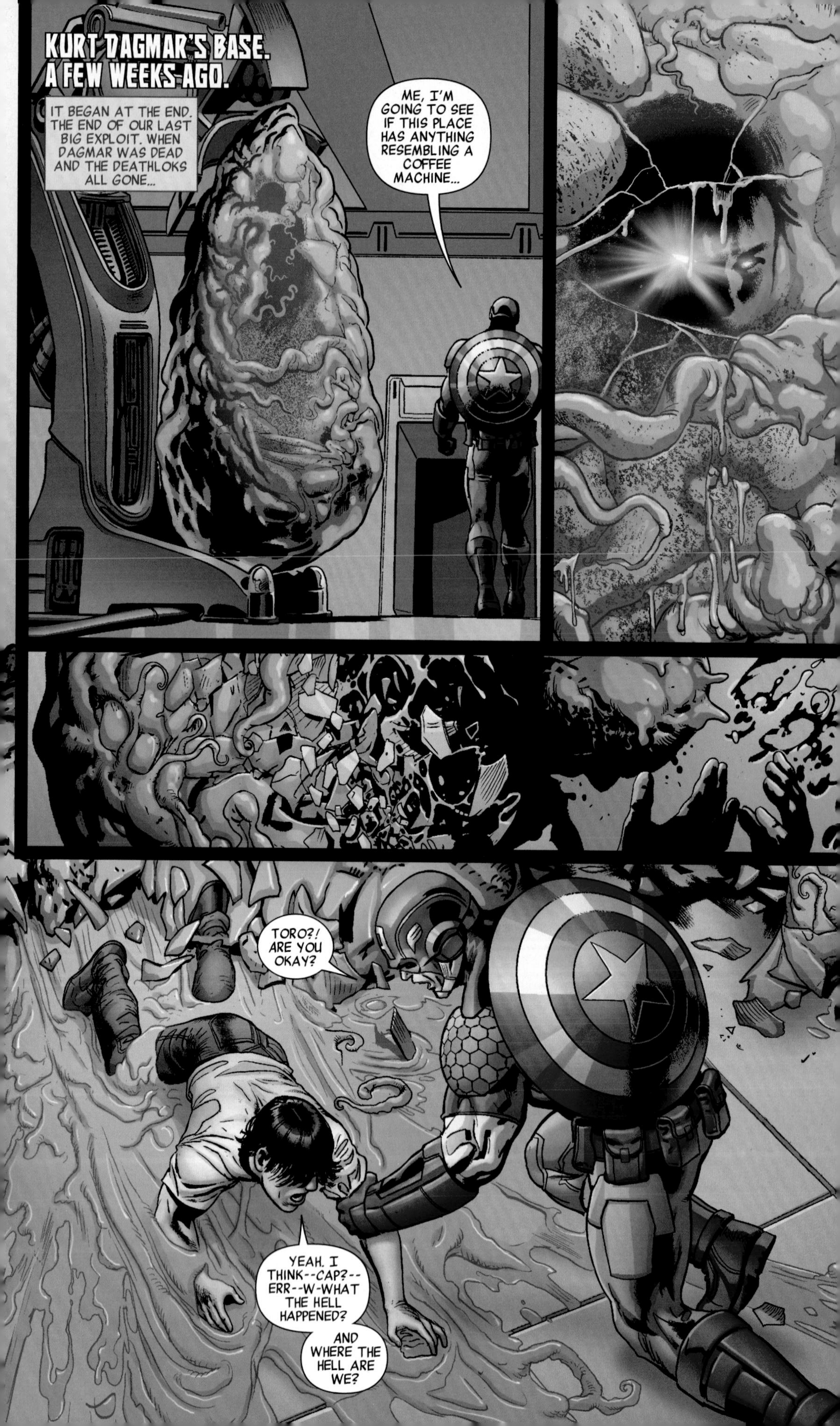
KURT DAGMAR'S BASE. A FEW WEEKS AGO.
IT BEGAN AT THE END. THE END OF OUR LAST BIG EXPLOIT. WHEN DAGMAR WAS DEAD AND THE DEATHLOKS ALL GONE...
ME, I'M GOING TO SEE IF THIS PLACE HAS ANYTHING RESEMBLING A COFFEE MACHINE...
TORO?! ARE YOU OKAY?
YEAH. I THINK--CAP?--ERR--W-WHAT THE HELL HAPPENED?
AND WHERE THE HELL ARE WE?

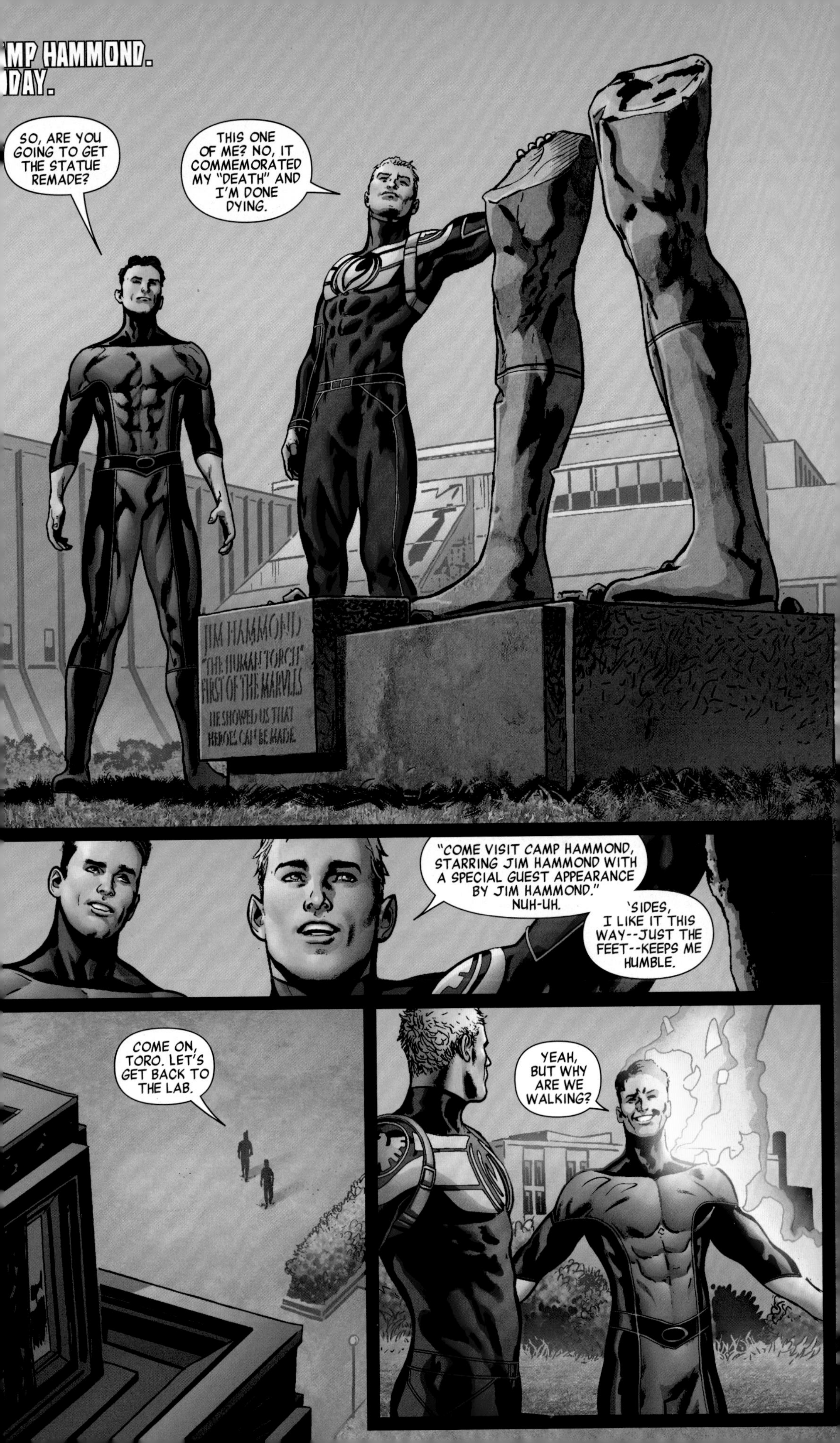
MP HAMMOND.
DAY.
SO, ARE YOU GOING TO GET THE STATUE REMADE?
THIS ONE OF ME? NO, IT COMMEMORATED MY "DEATH" AND I'M DONE DYING.
JIM HAMMOND "THE HUMAN TORCH" FIRST OF THE MARVELS HE SHOWED US THAT HEROES CAN BE MADE.
"COME VISIT CAMP HAMMOND, STARRING JIM HAMMOND WITH A SPECIAL GUEST APPEARANCE BY JIM HAMMOND." NUH-UH.
'SIDES, I LIKE IT THIS WAY--JUST THE FEET--KEEPS ME HUMBLE.
COME ON, TORO. LET'S GET BACK TO THE LAB.
YEAH, BUT WHY ARE WE WALKING?

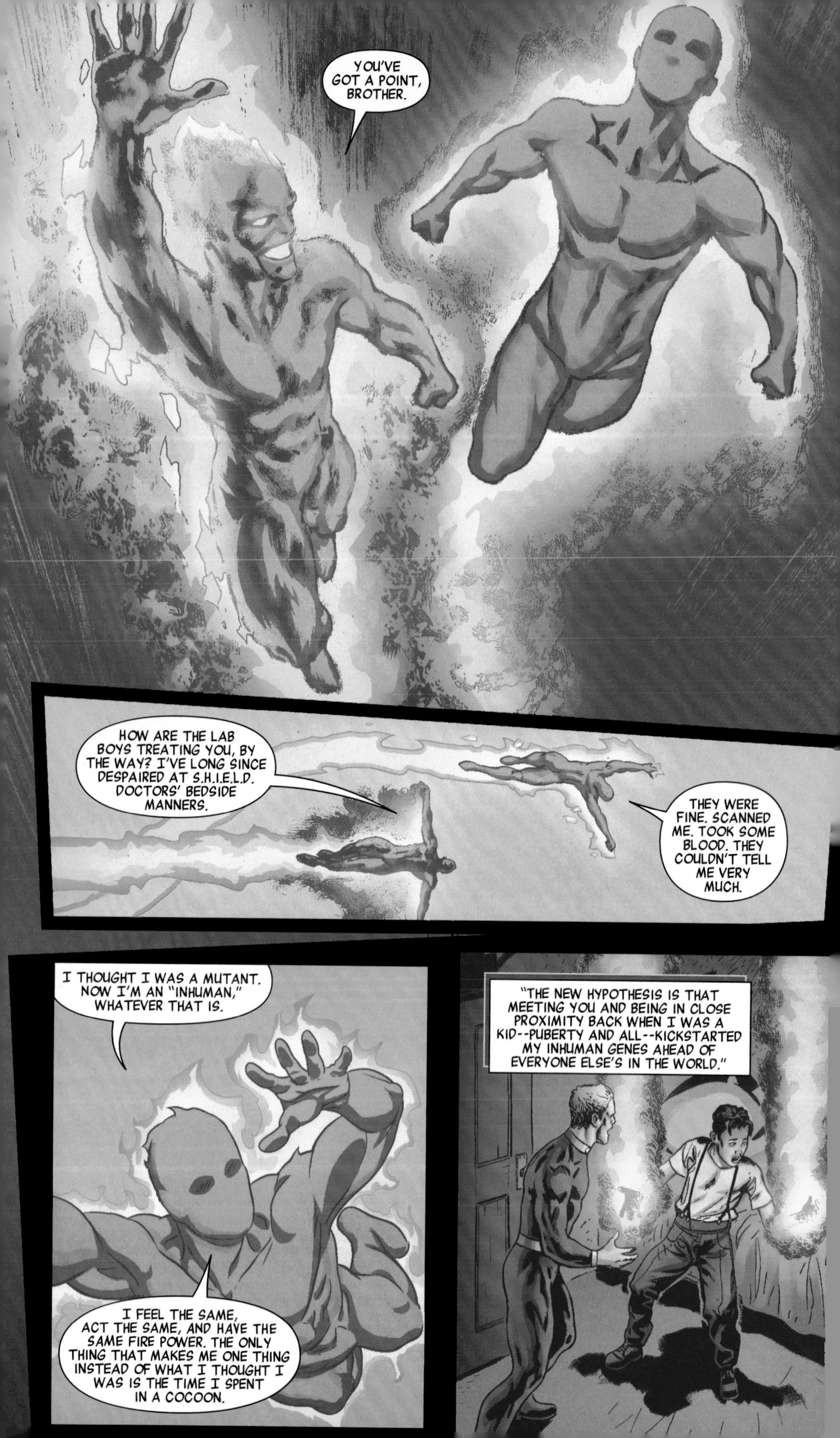
YOU'VE GOT A POINT, BROTHER.
HOW ARE THE LAB BOYS TREATING YOU, BY THE WAY? I'VE LONG SINCE DESPAIRED AT S.H.I.E.L.D. DOCTORS' BEDSIDE MANNERS.
THEY WERE FINE. SCANNED ME. TOOK SOME BLOOD. THEY COULDN'T TELL ME VERY MUCH.
I THOUGHT I WAS A MUTANT. NOW I'M AN "INHUMAN," WHATEVER THAT IS.
I FEEL THE SAME, ACT THE SAME, AND HAVE THE SAME FIRE POWER. THE ONLY THING THAT MAKES ME ONE THING INSTEAD OF WHAT I THOUGHT I WAS IS THE TIME I SPENT IN A COCOON.
"THE NEW HYPOTHESIS IS THAT MEETING YOU AND BEING IN CLOSE PROXIMITY BACK WHEN I WAS A KID--PUBERTY AND ALL--KICKSTARTED MY INHUMAN GENES AHEAD OF EVERYONE ELSE'S IN THE WORLD."

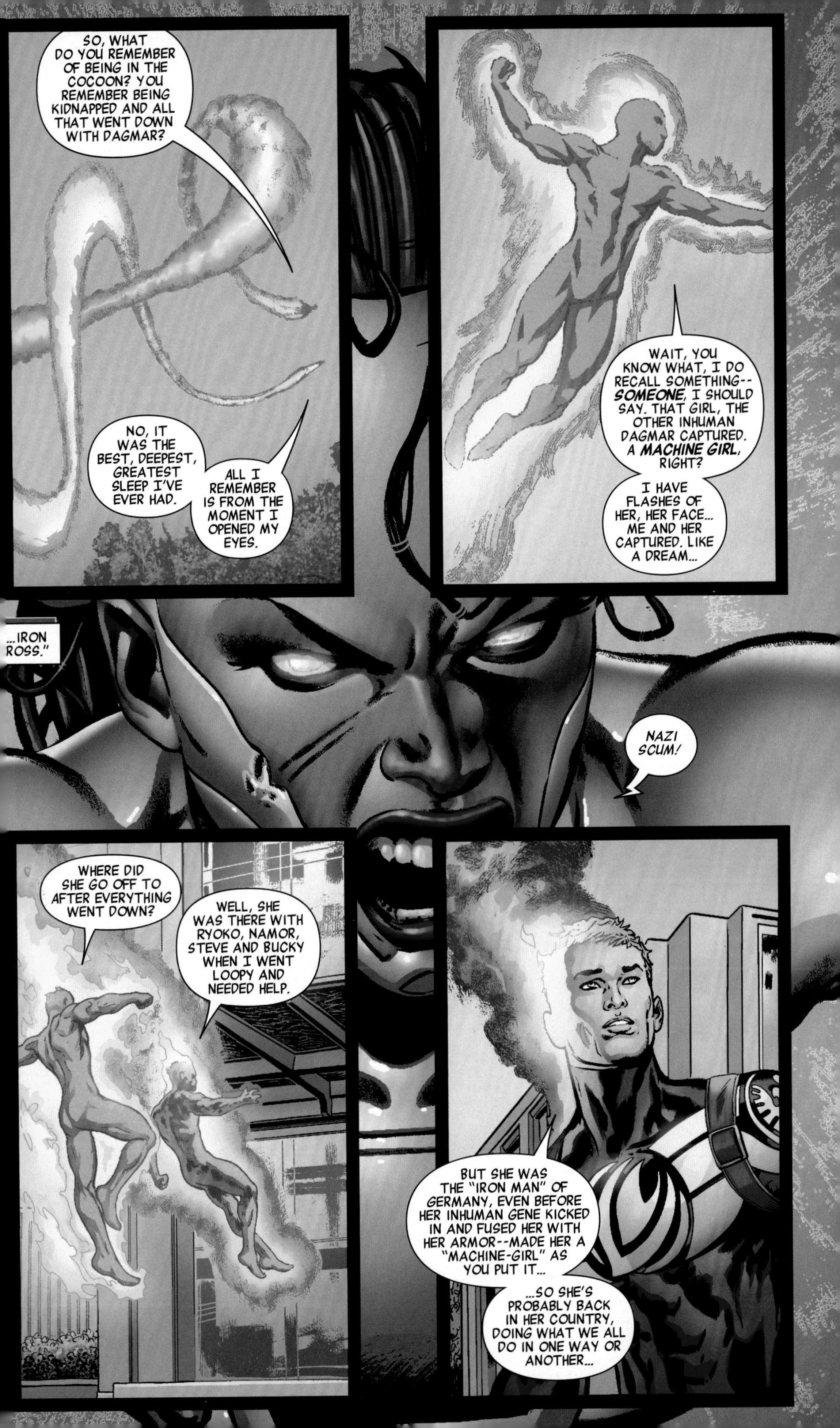
SO, WHAT DO YOU REMEMBER OF BEING IN THE COCOON? YOU REMEMBER BEING KIDNAPPED AND ALL THAT WENT DOWN WITH DAGMAR?
NO, IT WAS THE BEST, DEEPEST, GREATEST SLEEP I'VE EVER HAD.
ALL I REMEMBER IS FROM THE MOMENT I OPENED MY EYES.
WAIT, YOU KNOW WHAT, I DO RECALL SOMETHING-- *SOMEONE*, I SHOULD SAY. THAT GIRL, THE OTHER INHUMAN DAGMAR CAPTURED. A *MACHINE GIRL*, RIGHT?
I HAVE FLASHES OF HER, HER FACE... ME AND HER CAPTURED. LIKE A DREAM...
...IRON ROSS."
NAZI SCUM!
WHERE DID SHE GO OFF TO AFTER EVERYTHING WENT DOWN?
WELL, SHE WAS THERE WITH RYOKO, NAMOR, STEVE AND BUCKY WHEN I WENT LOOPY AND NEEDED HELP.
BUT SHE WAS THE "IRON MAN" OF GERMANY, EVEN BEFORE HER INHUMAN GENE KICKED IN AND FUSED HER WITH HER ARMOR--MADE HER A "MACHINE-GIRL" AS YOU PUT IT...
...SO SHE'S PROBABLY BACK IN HER COUNTRY, DOING WHAT WE ALL DO IN ONE WAY OR ANOTHER...

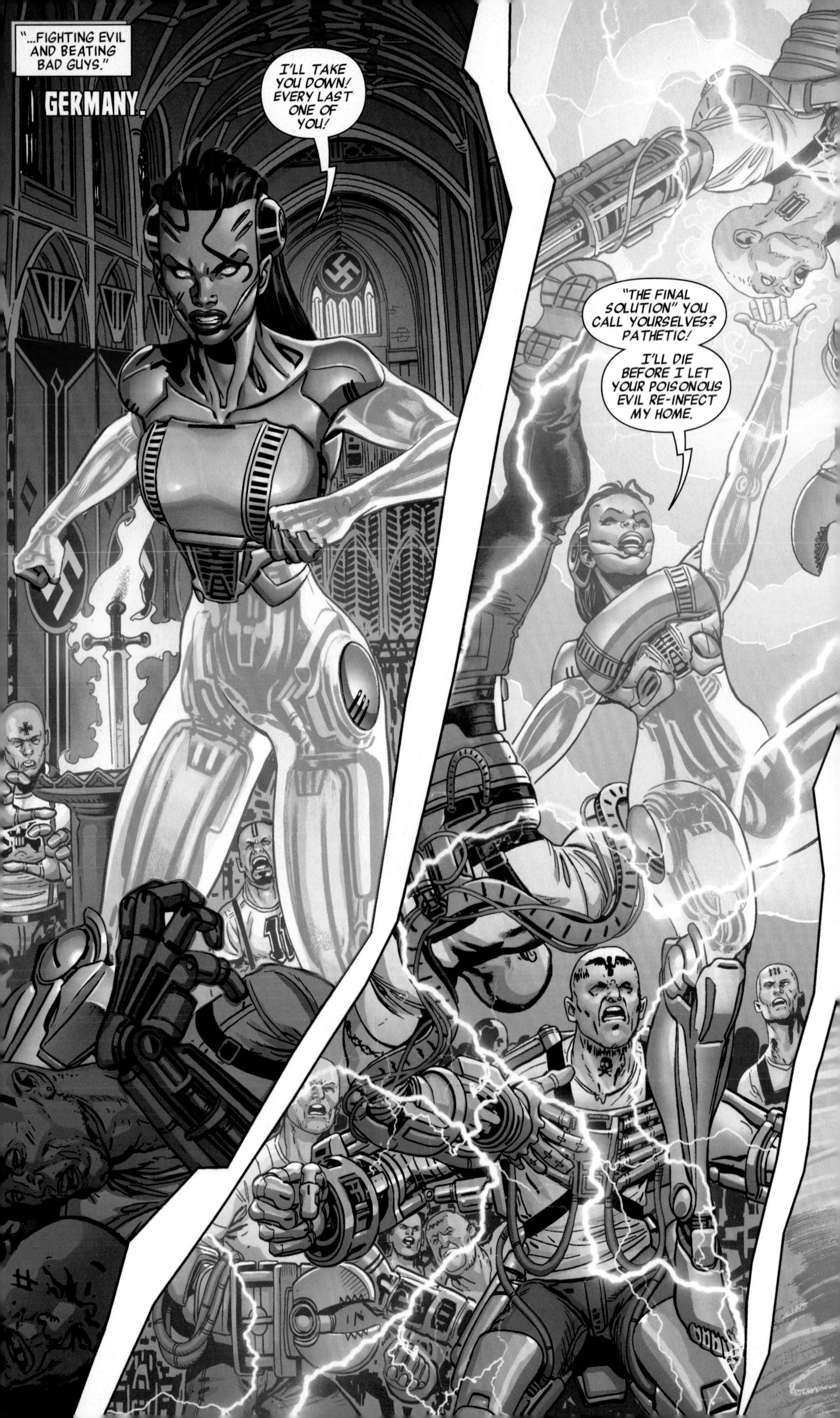

"...FIGHTING EVIL AND BEATING BAD GUYS."
GERMANY.
I'LL TAKE YOU DOWN! EVERY LAST ONE OF YOU!
"THE FINAL SOLUTION" YOU CALL YOURSELVES? PATHETIC!
I'LL DIE BEFORE I LET YOUR POISONOUS EVIL RE-INFECT MY HOME.

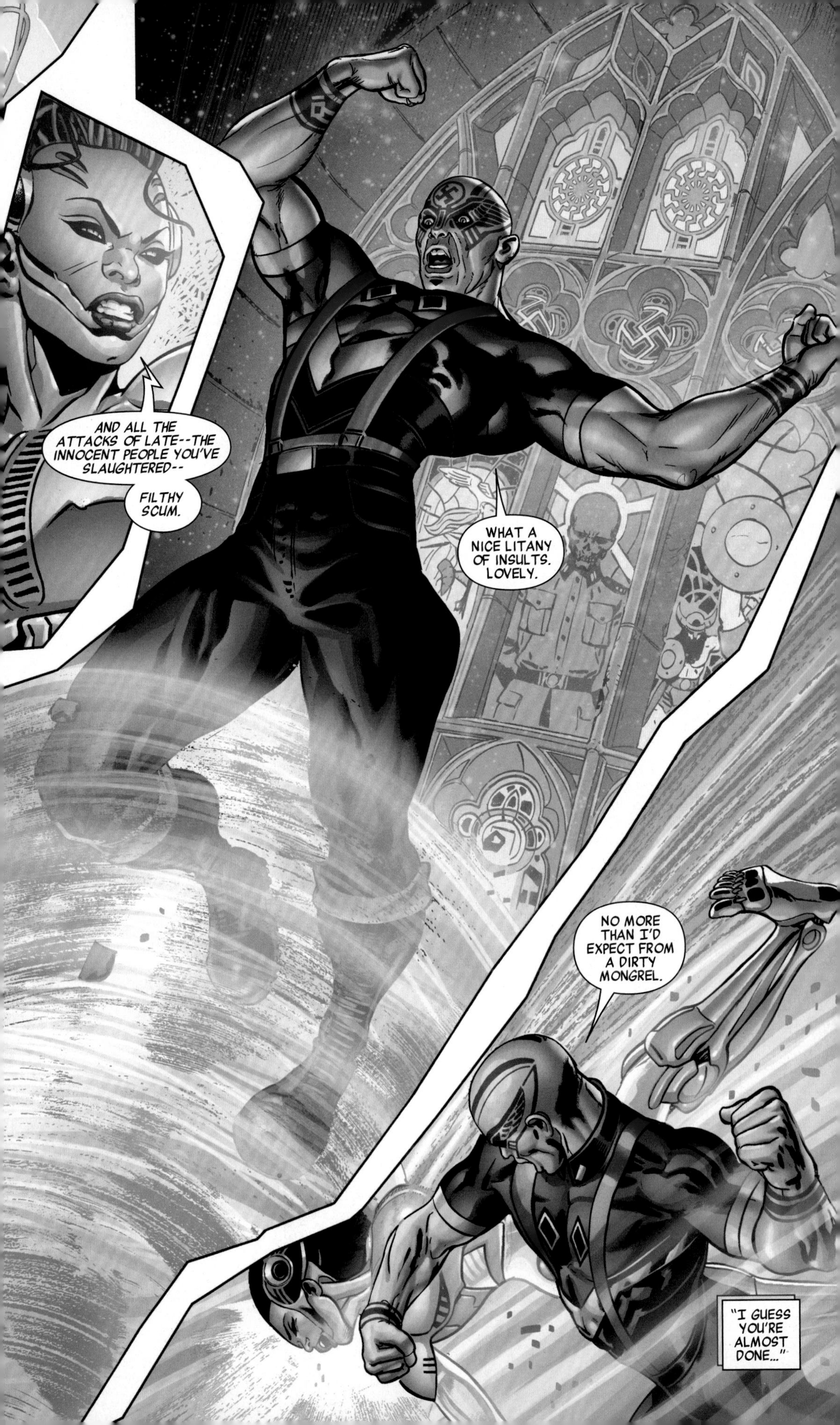
AND ALL THE ATTACKS OF LATE--THE INNOCENT PEOPLE YOU'VE SLAUGHTERED--
FILTHY SCUM.
WHAT A NICE LITANY OF INSULTS. LOVELY.
NO MORE THAN I'D EXPECT FROM A DIRTY MONGREL.
"I GUESS YOU'RE ALMOST DONE..."

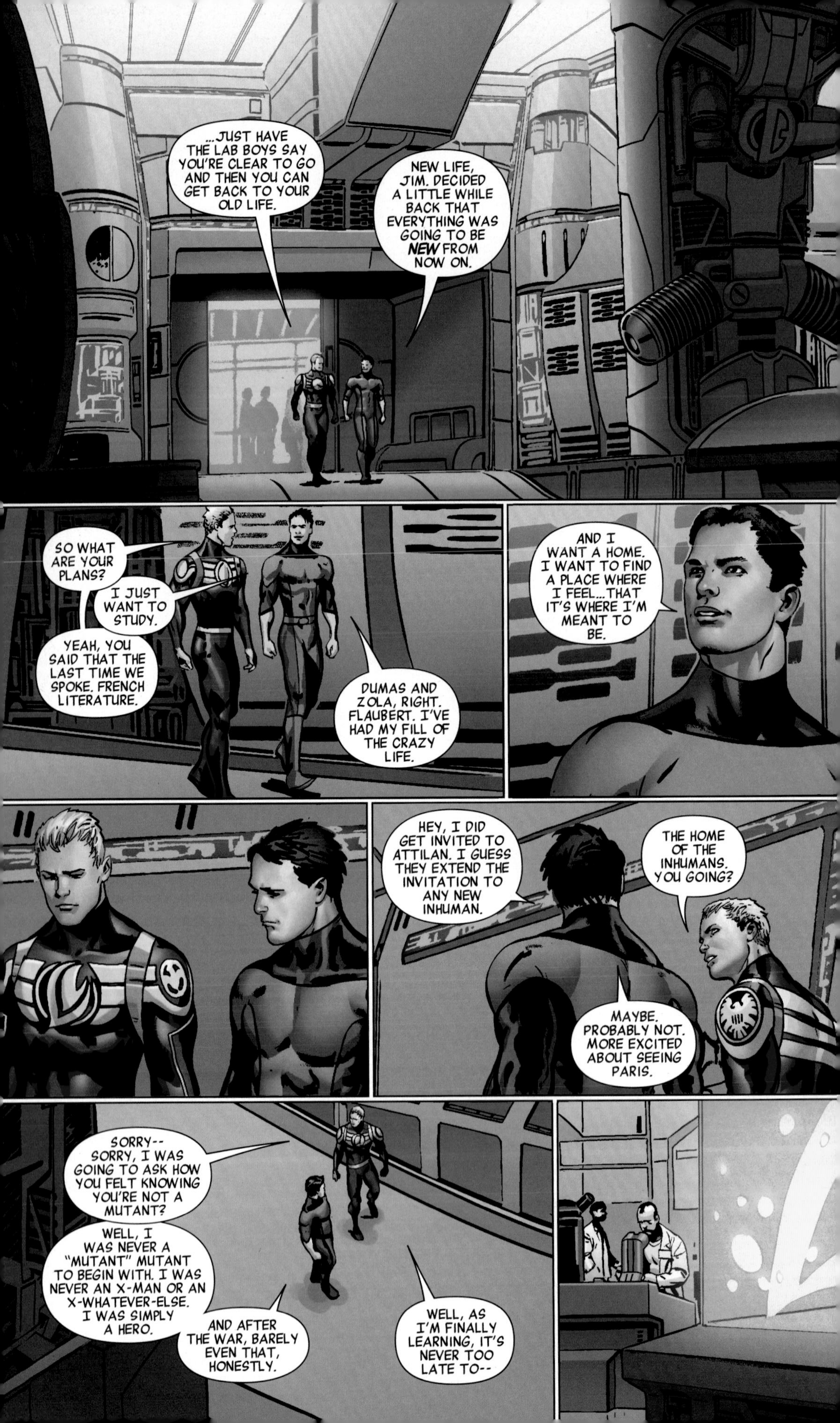
...JUST HAVE THE LAB BOYS SAY YOU'RE CLEAR TO GO AND THEN YOU CAN GET BACK TO YOUR OLD LIFE.
NEW LIFE, JIM. DECIDED A LITTLE WHILE BACK THAT EVERYTHING WAS GOING TO BE *NEW* FROM NOW ON.
SO WHAT ARE YOUR PLANS?
I JUST WANT TO STUDY.
YEAH, YOU SAID THAT THE LAST TIME WE SPOKE. FRENCH LITERATURE.
DUMAS AND ZOLA, RIGHT. FLAUBERT. I'VE HAD MY FILL OF THE CRAZY LIFE.
AND I WANT A HOME. I WANT TO FIND A PLACE WHERE I FEEL...THAT IT'S WHERE I'M MEANT TO BE.
HEY, I DID GET INVITED TO ATTILAN. I GUESS THEY EXTEND THE INVITATION TO ANY NEW INHUMAN.
THE HOME OF THE INHUMANS. YOU GOING?
MAYBE. PROBABLY NOT. MORE EXCITED ABOUT SEEING PARIS.
SORRY-- SORRY, I WAS GOING TO ASK HOW YOU FELT KNOWING YOU'RE NOT A MUTANT?
WELL, I WAS NEVER A "MUTANT" MUTANT TO BEGIN WITH. I WAS NEVER AN X-MAN OR AN X-WHATEVER-ELSE. I WAS SIMPLY A HERO.
AND AFTER THE WAR, BARELY EVEN THAT, HONESTLY.
WELL, AS I'M FINALLY LEARNING, IT'S NEVER TOO LATE TO--

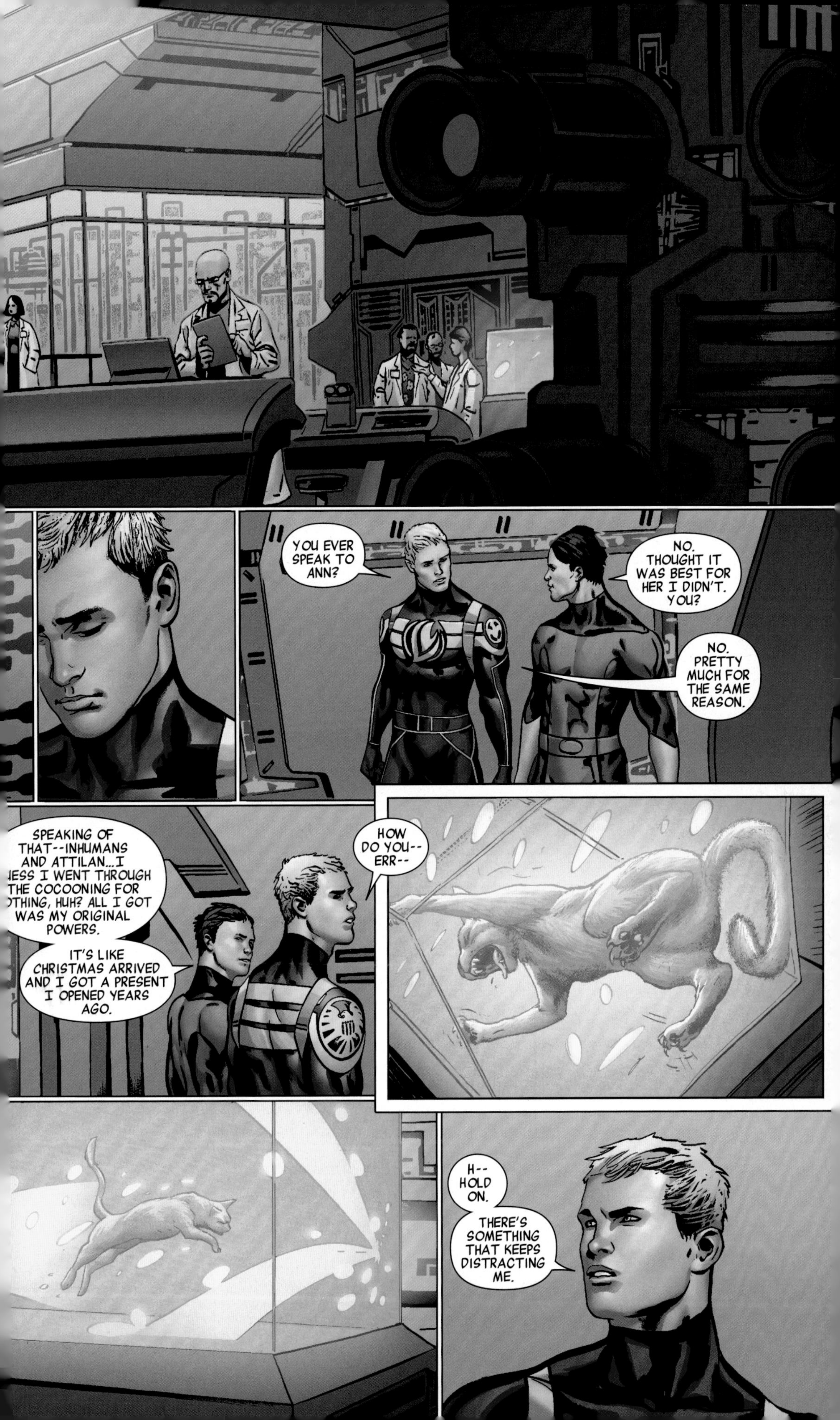
YOU EVER SPEAK TO ANN?
NO. THOUGHT IT WAS BEST FOR HER I DIDN'T. YOU?
NO. PRETTY MUCH FOR THE SAME REASON.
SPEAKING OF THAT--INHUMANS AND ATTILAN...I UESS I WENT THROUGH THE COCOONING FOR OTHING, HUH? ALL I GOT WAS MY ORIGINAL POWERS.
IT'S LIKE CHRISTMAS ARRIVED AND I GOT A PRESENT I OPENED YEARS AGO.
HOW DO YOU-- ERR--
H-- HOLD ON.
THERE'S SOMETHING THAT KEEPS DISTRACTING ME.

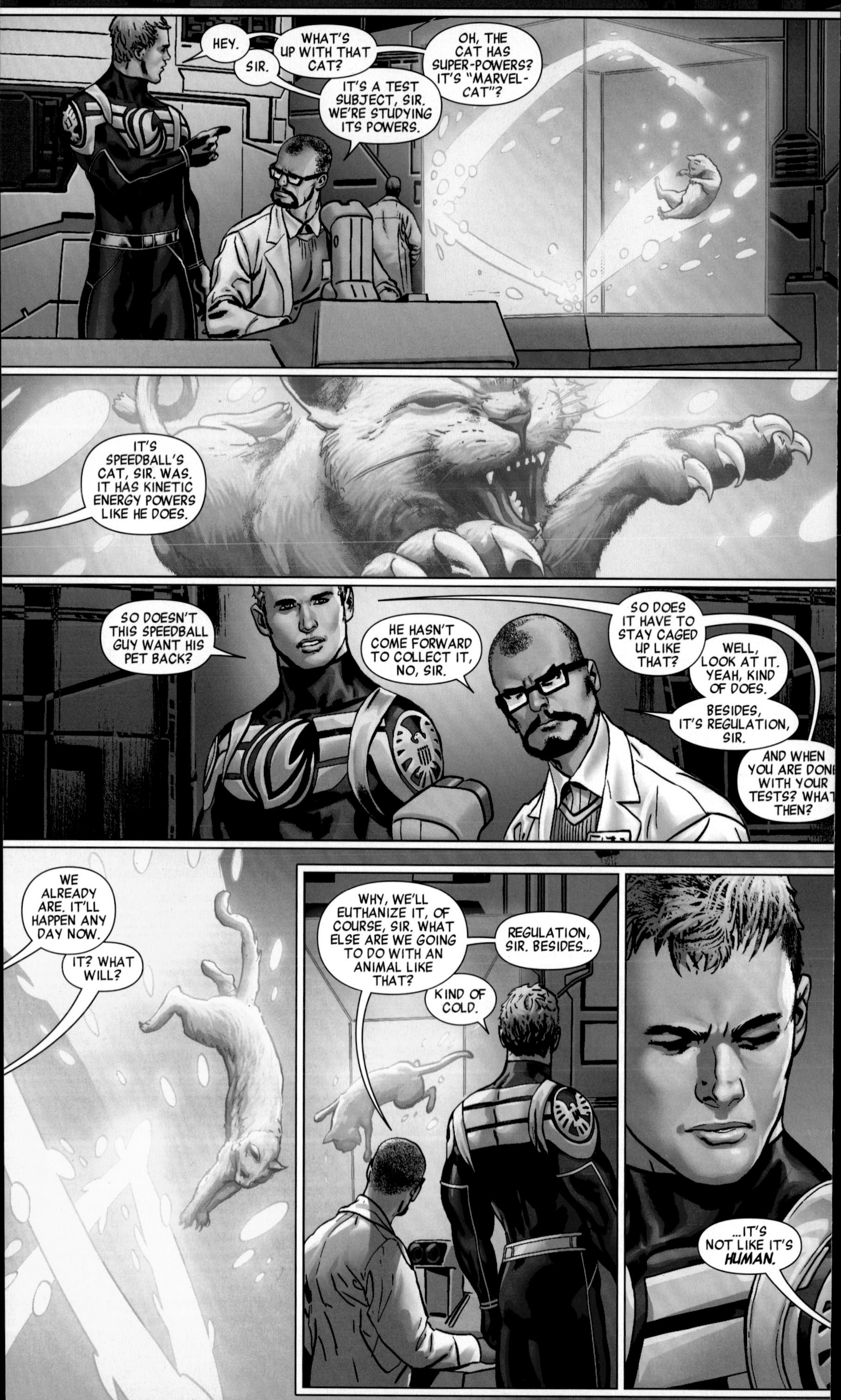
HEY.
SIR.
WHAT'S UP WITH THAT CAT?
IT'S A TEST SUBJECT, SIR. WE'RE STUDYING ITS POWERS.
OH, THE CAT HAS SUPER-POWERS? IT'S "MARVEL-CAT"?
IT'S SPEEDBALL'S CAT, SIR. WAS. IT HAS KINETIC ENERGY POWERS LIKE HE DOES.
SO DOESN'T THIS SPEEDBALL GUY WANT HIS PET BACK?
HE HASN'T COME FORWARD TO COLLECT IT, NO, SIR.
SO DOES IT HAVE TO STAY CAGED UP LIKE THAT?
WELL, LOOK AT IT. YEAH, KIND OF DOES.
BESIDES, IT'S REGULATION, SIR.
AND WHEN YOU ARE DONE WITH YOUR TESTS? WHAT THEN?
WE ALREADY ARE. IT'LL HAPPEN ANY DAY NOW.
IT? WHAT WILL?
WHY, WE'LL EUTHANIZE IT, OF COURSE, SIR. WHAT ELSE ARE WE GOING TO DO WITH AN ANIMAL LIKE THAT?
KIND OF COLD.
REGULATION, SIR. BESIDES...
...IT'S NOT LIKE IT'S *HUMAN.*

SORRY, THAT WAS BOTHERING ME.

NO PROBLEM, JIM. HOW ARE YOU DOING, ANYWAY? YOU HAVEN'T REALLY SAID.

YOU'RE A S.H.I.E.L.D. AGENT NOW...AND MORE IN THE SPOTLIGHT THAN YOU'VE BEEN IN QUITE A WHILE.

GREAT. I GUESS. I MEAN--YOU KNOW WHAT? HOW I'M DOING ISN'T IMPORTANT--

TORO... TOM...I HAVE TO SAY THIS. I'M SORRY I'VE BEEN A BAD FRIEND. RUNNING OFF, HIDING, NOT STANDING UP AND BEING A MAN.

I SHOULD HAVE BEEN AROUND MORE... DEFINITELY SHOULD HAVE WHEN YOU WERE IN YOUR COCOON. S.H.I.E.L.D. IS THE START OF ME CHANGING THAT.

SIR.

SON. WHAT'S UP?

DIRECTOR HILL JUST RADIOED INTEL SHE THOUGHT YOU'D WANT TO HANDLE YOURSELF.

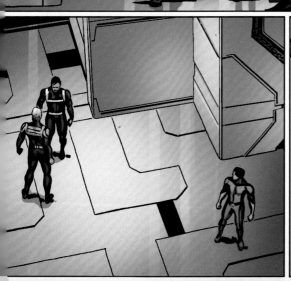

TROUBLE?

YEAH...

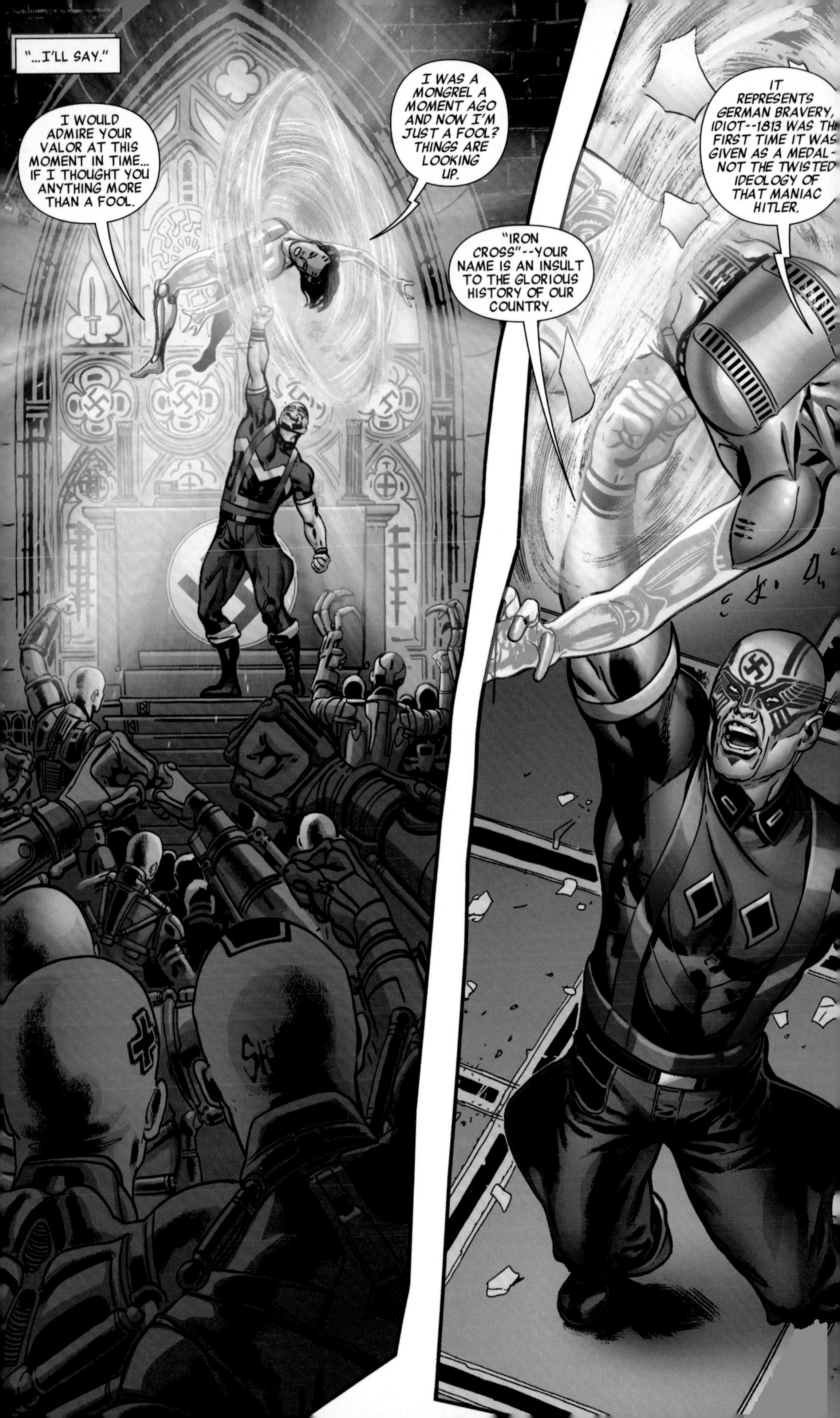
"...I'LL SAY."
I WOULD ADMIRE YOUR VALOR AT THIS MOMENT IN TIME... IF I THOUGHT YOU ANYTHING MORE THAN A FOOL.
I WAS A MONGREL A MOMENT AGO AND NOW I'M JUST A FOOL? THINGS ARE LOOKING UP.
"IRON CROSS"--YOUR NAME IS AN INSULT TO THE GLORIOUS HISTORY OF OUR COUNTRY.
IT REPRESENTS GERMAN BRAVERY, IDIOT--1813 WAS THE FIRST TIME IT WAS GIVEN AS A MEDAL-NOT THE TWISTED IDEOLOGY OF THAT MANIAC HITLER.

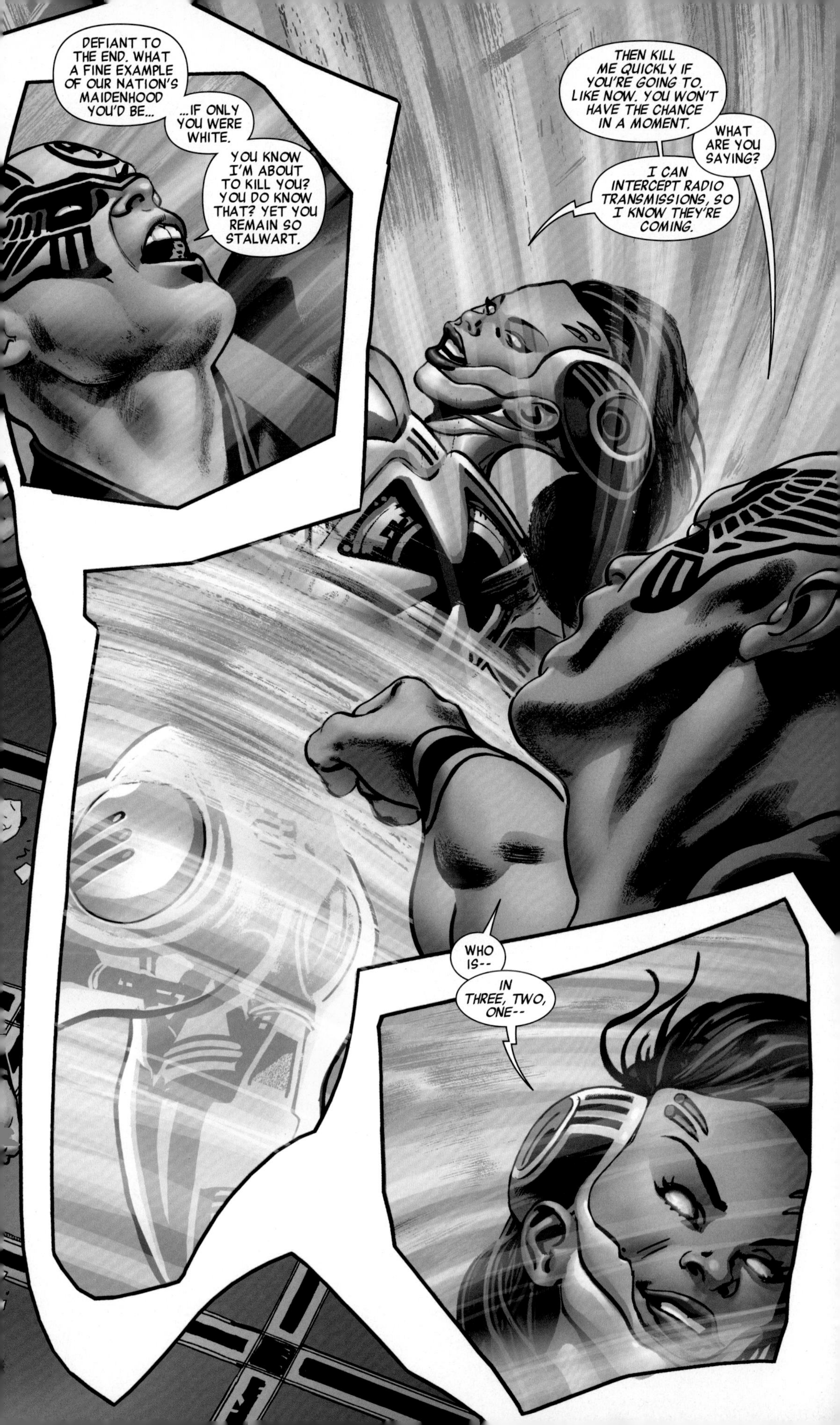
DEFIANT TO THE END. WHAT A FINE EXAMPLE OF OUR NATION'S MAIDENHOOD YOU'D BE...
...IF ONLY YOU WERE WHITE.
YOU KNOW I'M ABOUT TO KILL YOU? YOU DO KNOW THAT? YET YOU REMAIN SO STALWART.
THEN KILL ME QUICKLY IF YOU'RE GOING TO. LIKE NOW. YOU WON'T HAVE THE CHANCE IN A MOMENT.
WHAT ARE YOU SAYING?
I CAN INTERCEPT RADIO TRANSMISSIONS, SO I KNOW THEY'RE COMING.
WHO IS--
IN THREE, TWO, ONE--

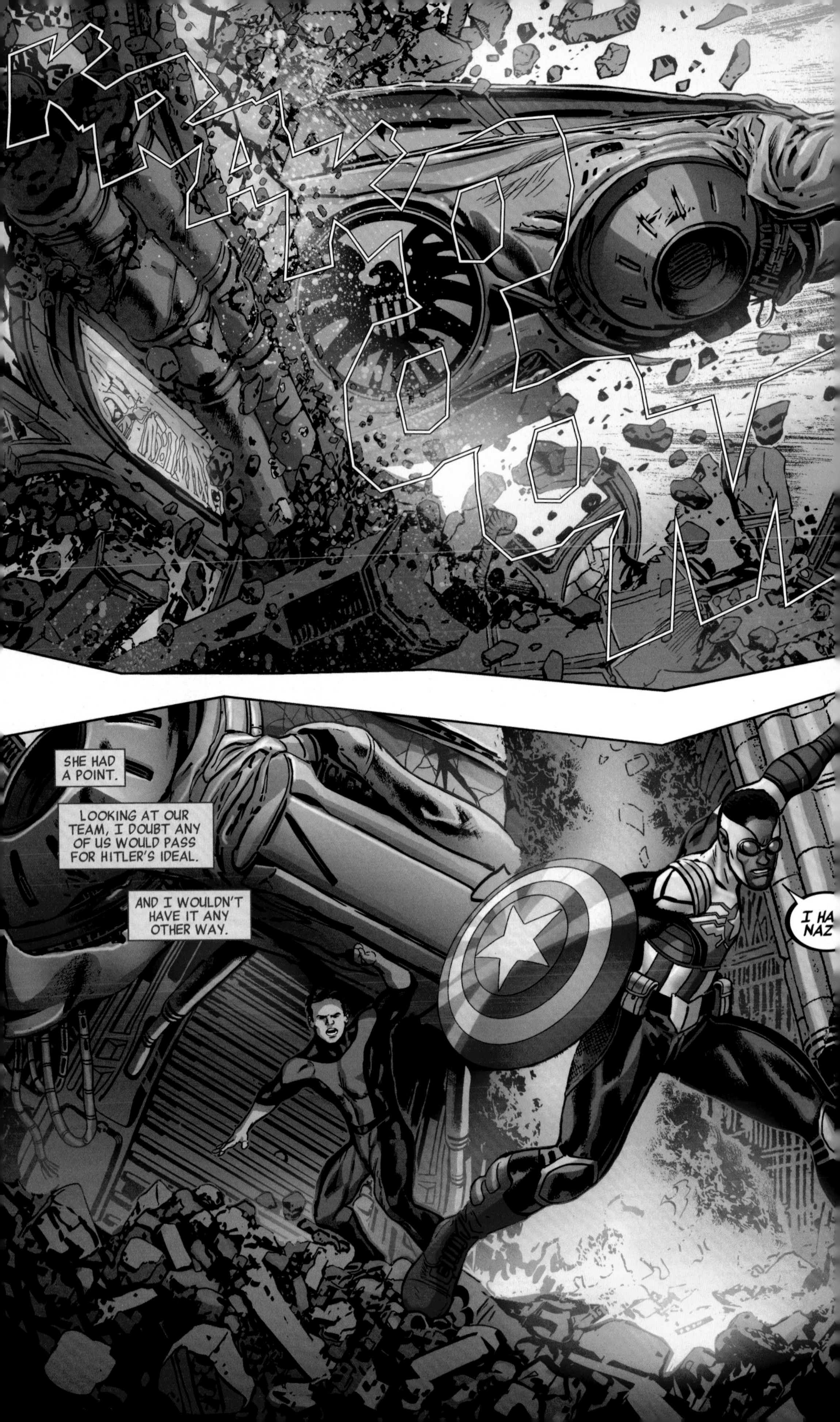
SHE HAD A POINT.
LOOKING AT OUR TEAM, I DOUBT ANY OF US WOULD PASS FOR HITLER'S IDEAL.
AND I WOULDN'T HAVE IT ANY OTHER WAY.
I HA NAZ

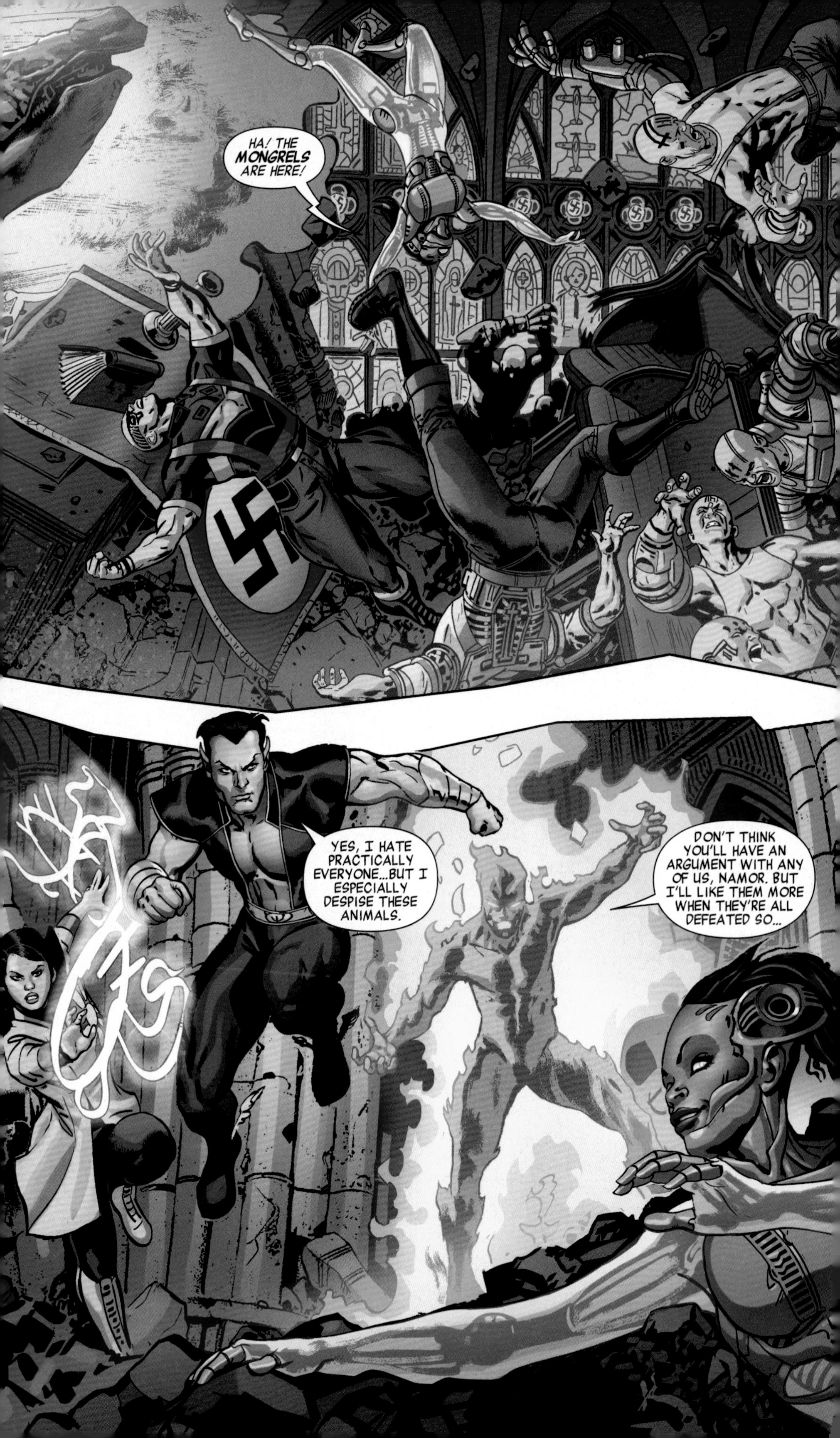
HA! THE MONGRELS ARE HERE!
YES, I HATE PRACTICALLY EVERYONE...BUT I ESPECIALLY DESPISE THESE ANIMALS.
DON'T THINK YOU'LL HAVE AN ARGUMENT WITH ANY OF US, NAMOR. BUT I'LL LIKE THEM MORE WHEN THEY'RE ALL DEFEATED SO...

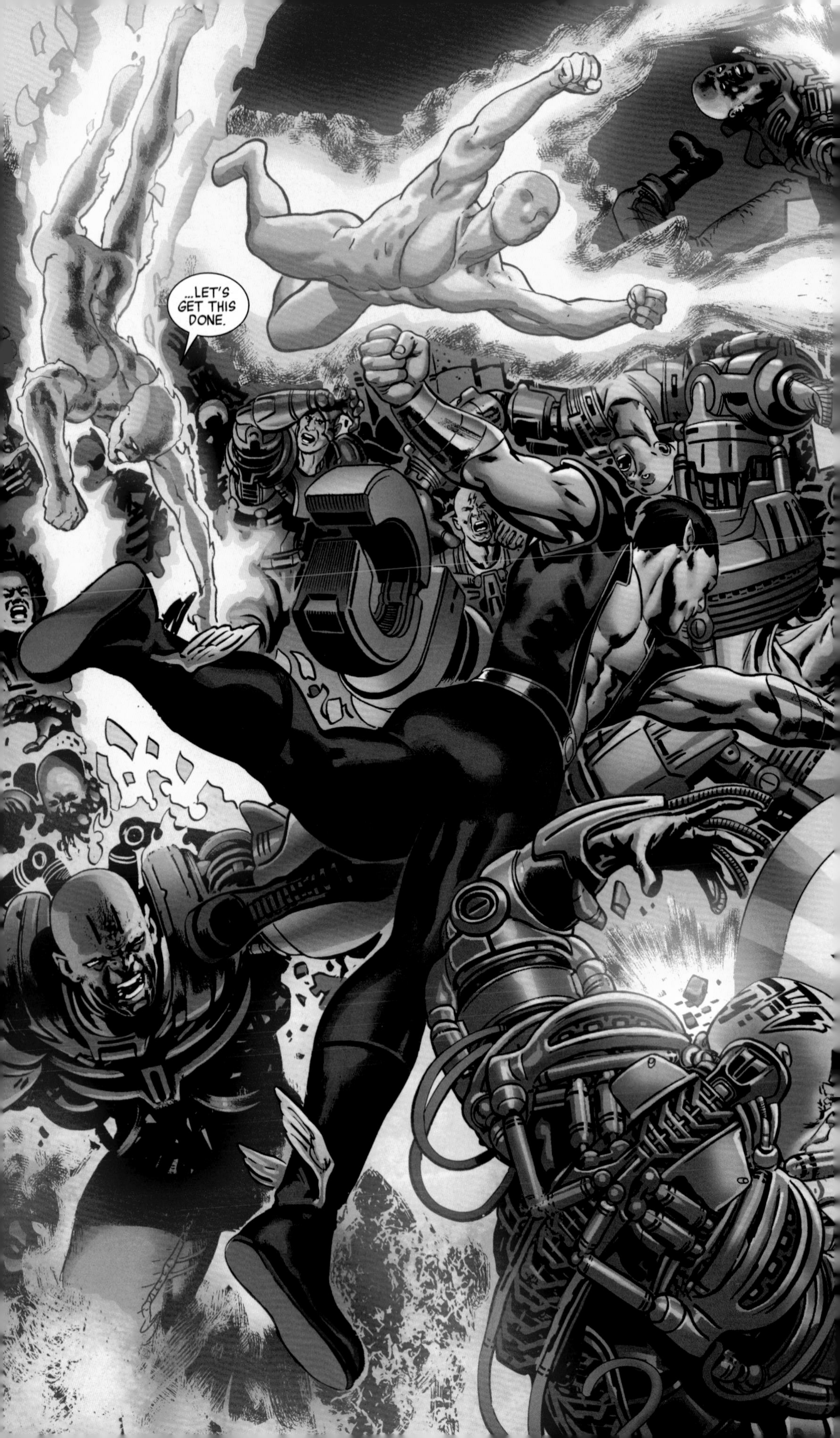
...LET'S GET THIS DONE.

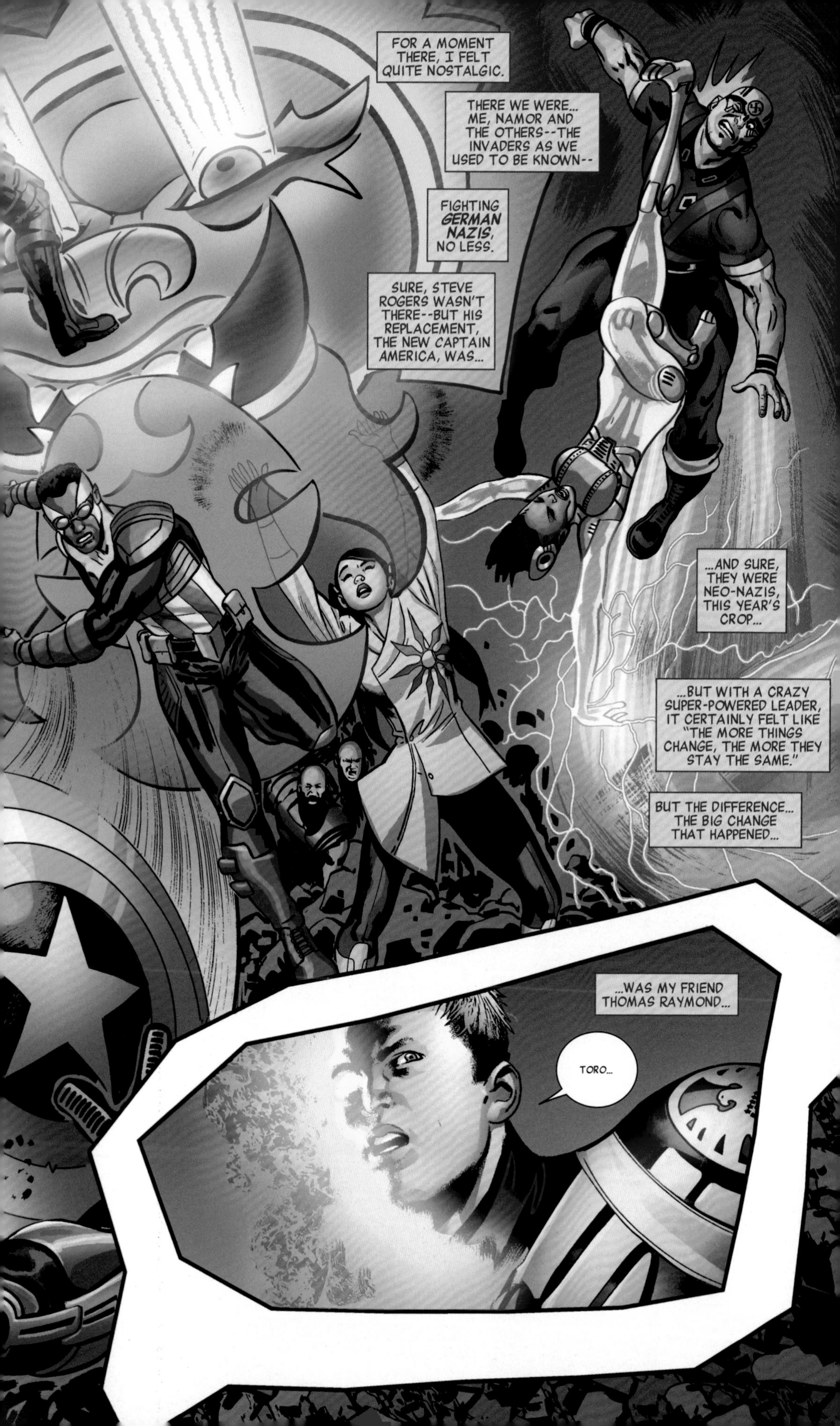
FOR A MOMENT THERE, I FELT QUITE NOSTALGIC.
THERE WE WERE... ME, NAMOR AND THE OTHERS--THE INVADERS AS WE USED TO BE KNOWN--
FIGHTING *GERMAN NAZIS*, NO LESS.
SURE, STEVE ROGERS WASN'T THERE--BUT HIS REPLACEMENT, THE NEW CAPTAIN AMERICA, WAS...
...AND SURE, THEY WERE NEO-NAZIS, THIS YEAR'S CROP...
...BUT WITH A CRAZY SUPER-POWERED LEADER, IT CERTAINLY FELT LIKE "THE MORE THINGS CHANGE, THE MORE THEY STAY THE SAME."
BUT THE DIFFERENCE... THE BIG CHANGE THAT HAPPENED...
...WAS MY FRIEND THOMAS RAYMOND...
TORO...

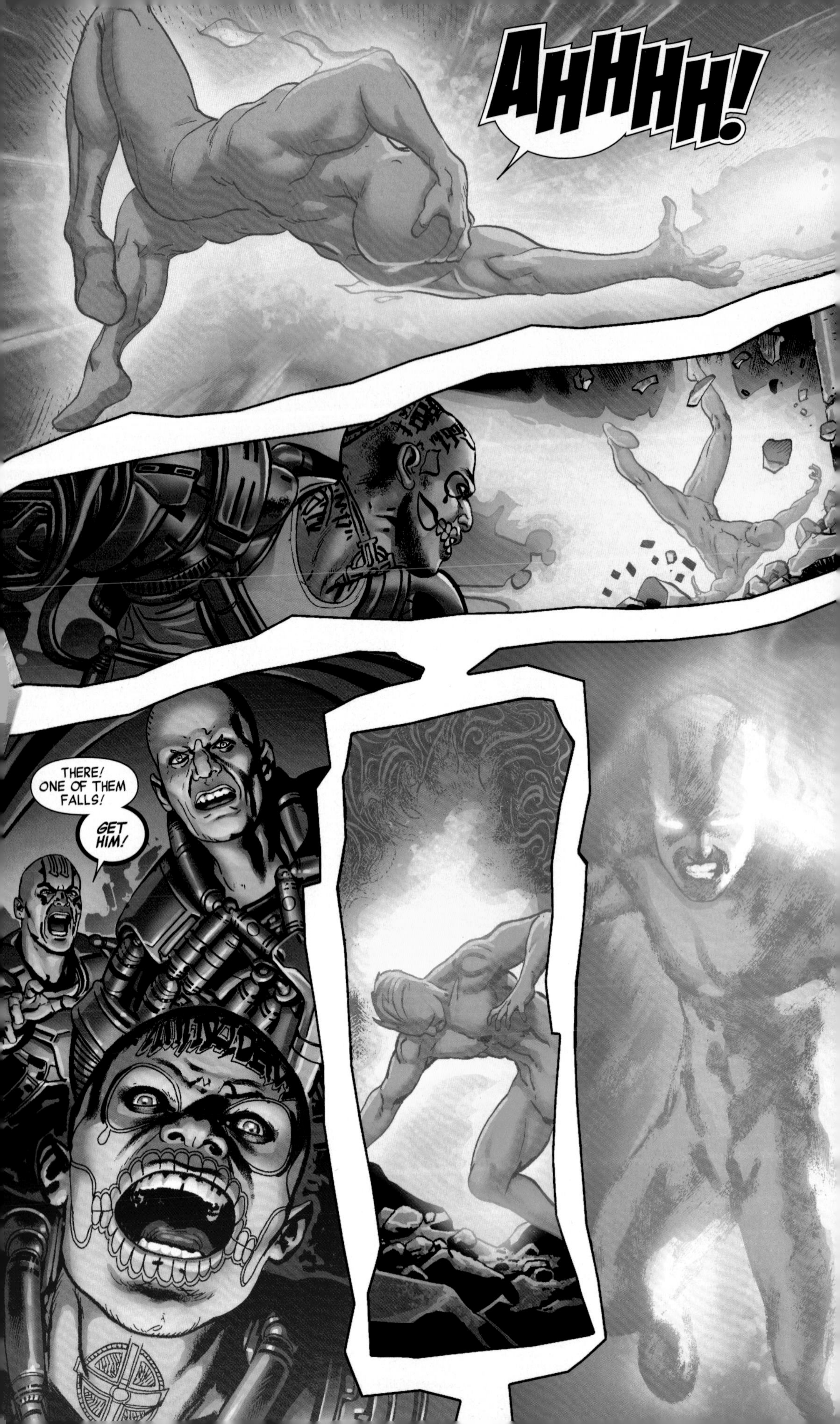
AHHHH!
THERE! ONE OF THEM FALLS!
GET HIM!

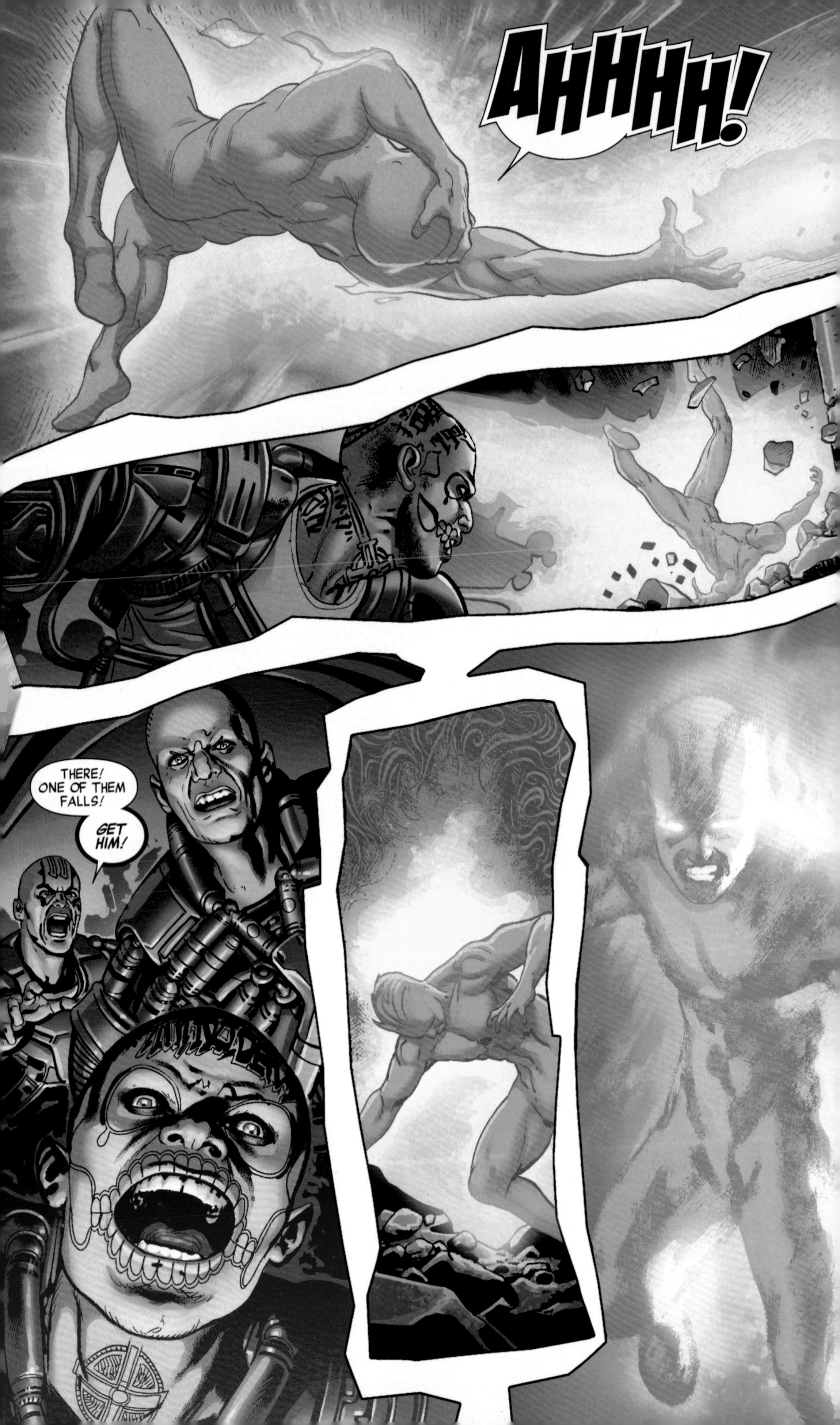
AHHHH!
THERE! ONE OF THEM FALLS!
GET HIM!

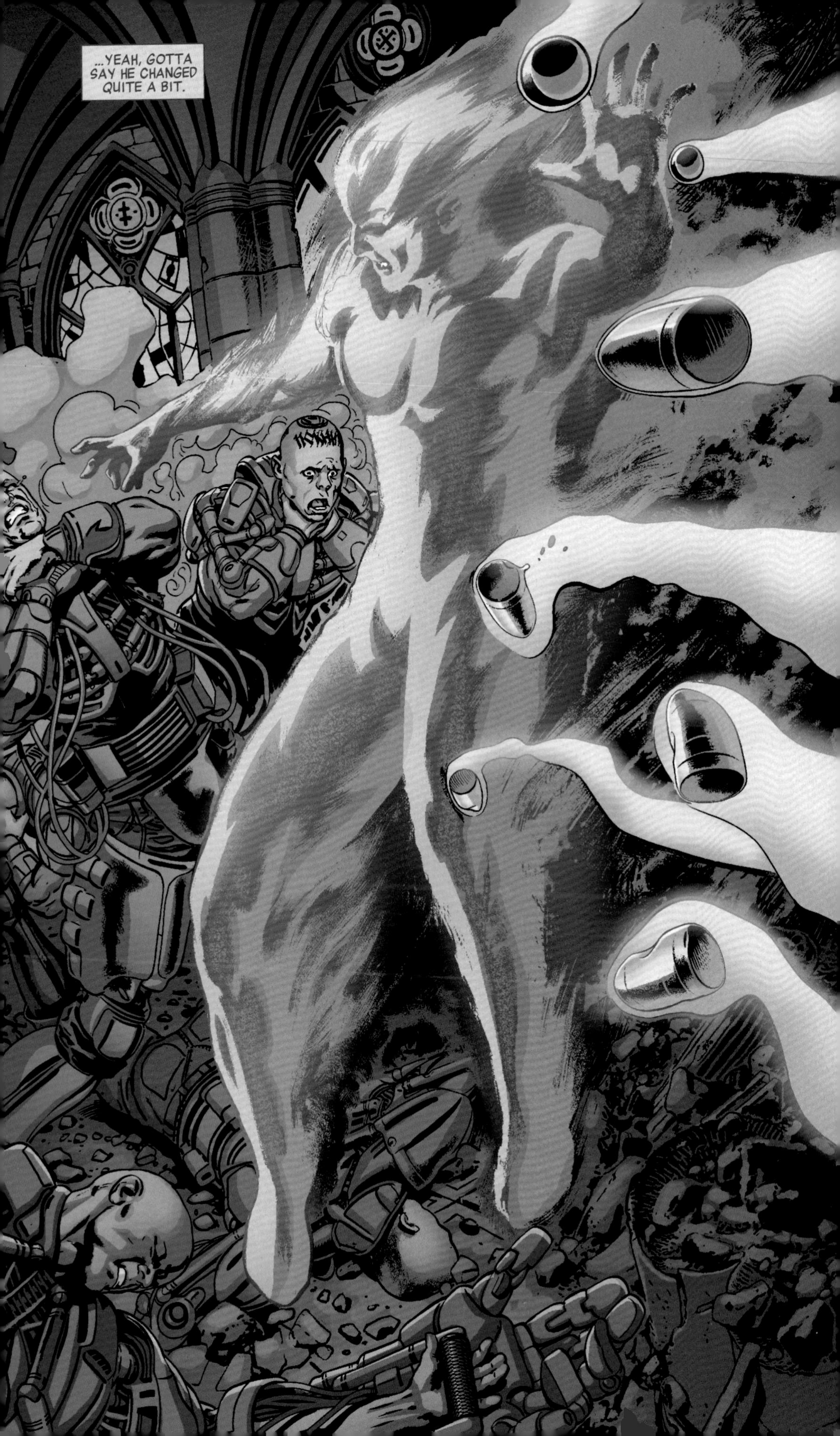
...YEAH, GOTTA SAY HE CHANGED QUITE A BIT.

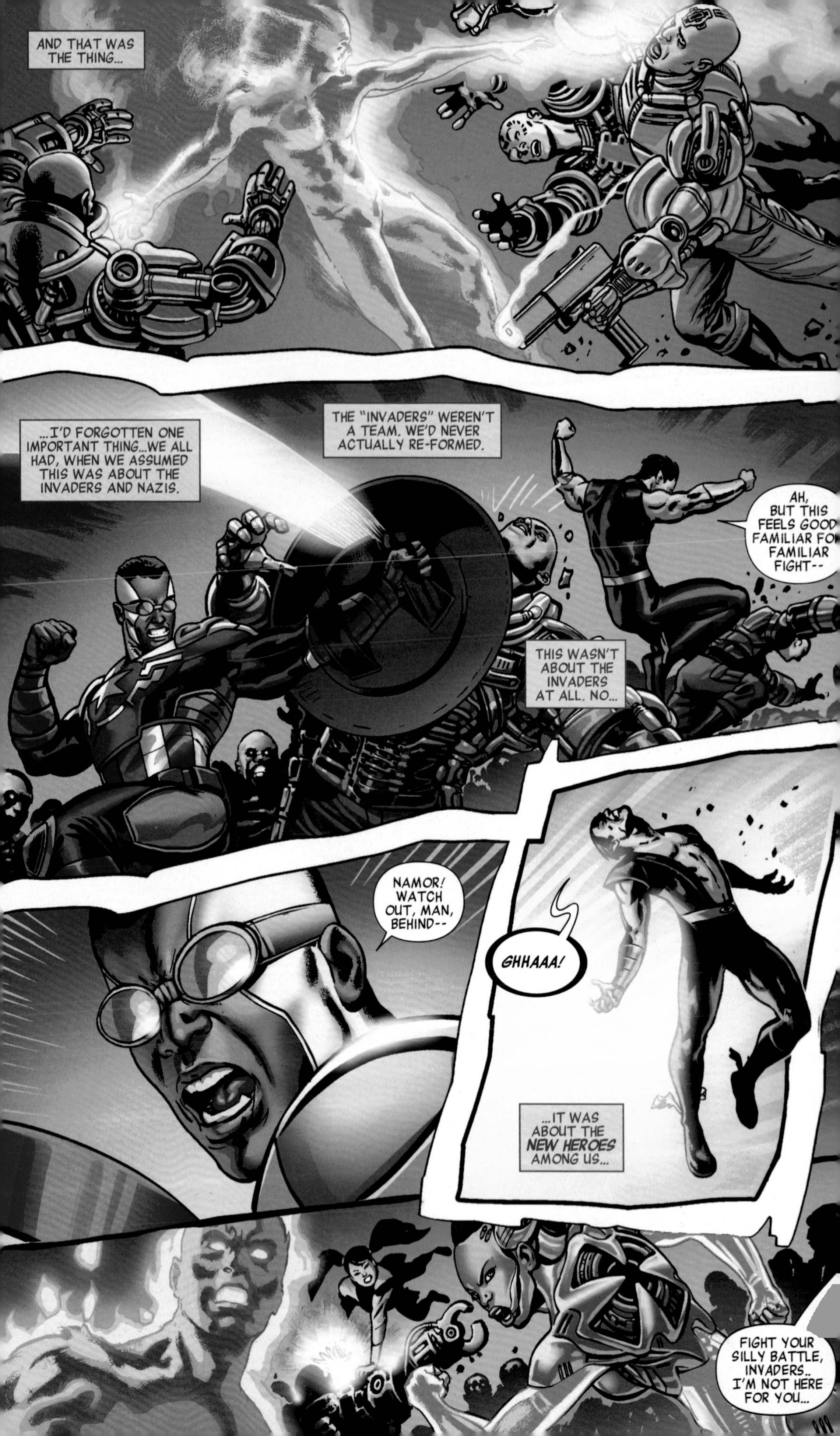
AND THAT WAS THE THING...
...I'D FORGOTTEN ONE IMPORTANT THING...WE ALL HAD, WHEN WE ASSUMED THIS WAS ABOUT THE INVADERS AND NAZIS.
THE "INVADERS" WEREN'T A TEAM. WE'D NEVER ACTUALLY RE-FORMED.
AH, BUT THIS FEELS GOOD FAMILIAR FO FAMILIAR FIGHT--
THIS WASN'T ABOUT THE INVADERS AT ALL. NO...
NAMOR! WATCH OUT, MAN, BEHIND--
GHHAAA!
...IT WAS ABOUT THE NEW HEROES AMONG US...
FIGHT YOUR SILLY BATTLE, INVADERS.. I'M NOT HERE FOR YOU...

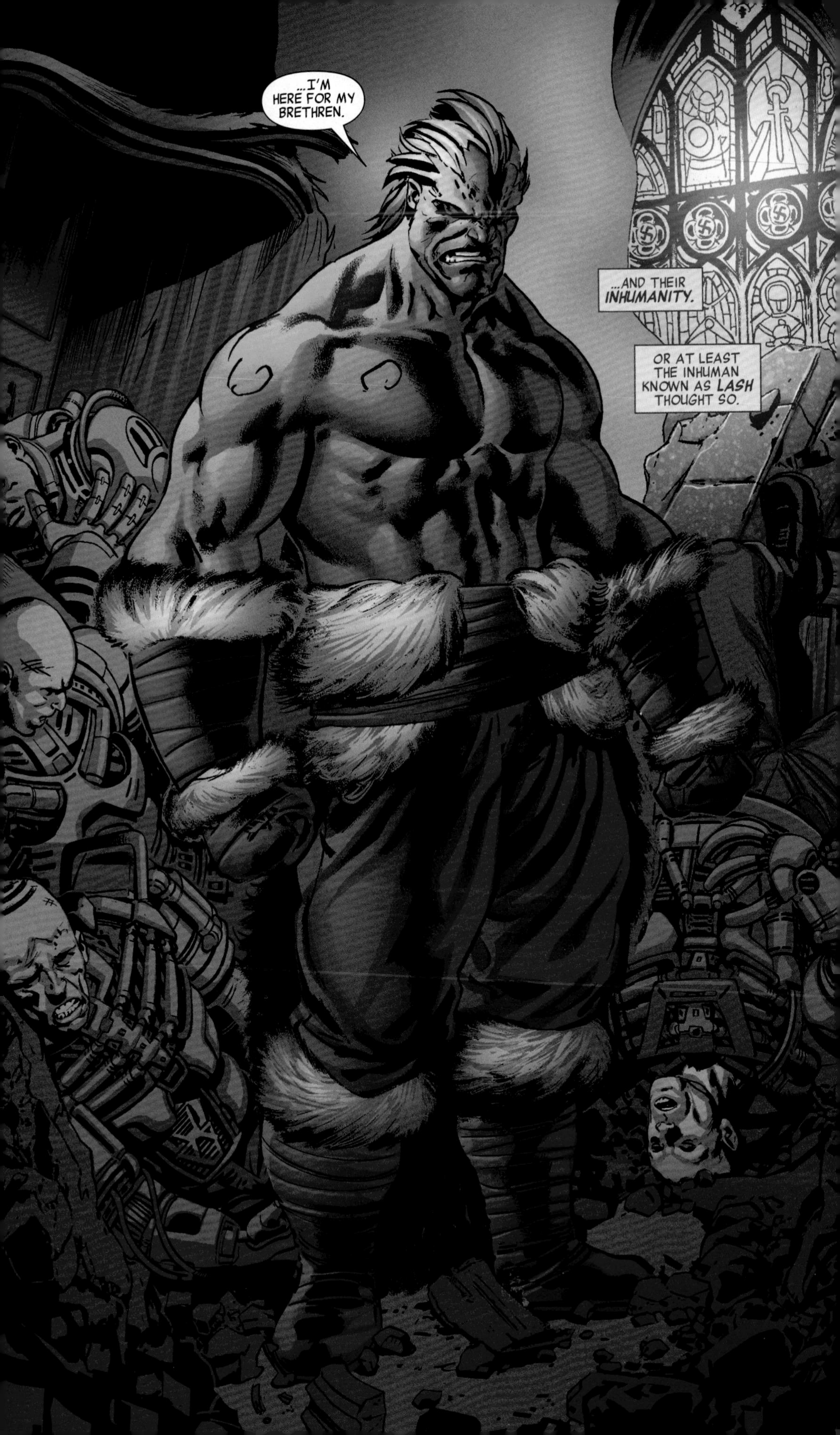
...I'M HERE FOR MY BRETHREN.
...AND THEIR INHUMANITY.
OR AT LEAST THE INHUMAN KNOWN AS LASH THOUGHT SO.

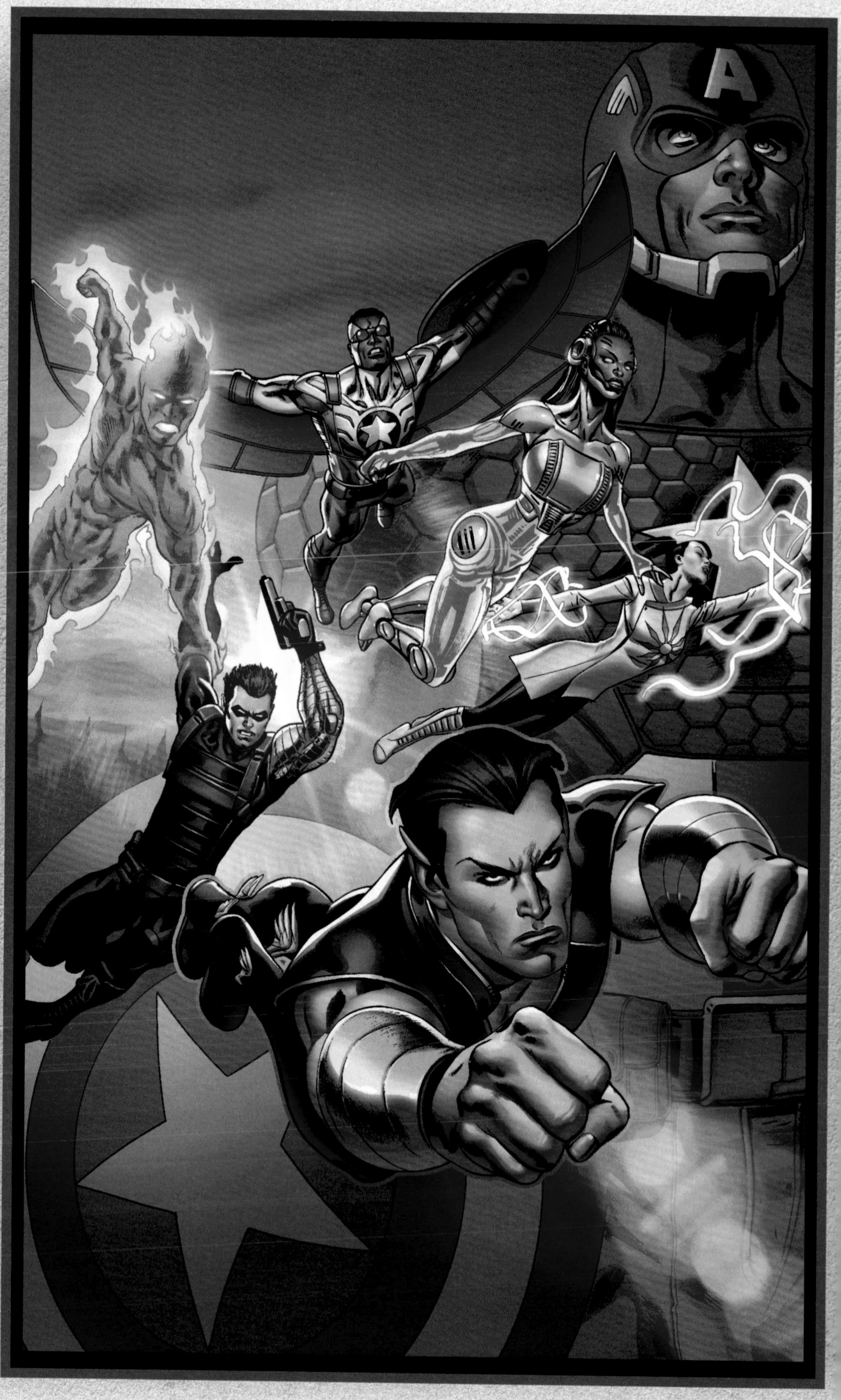
A

#15

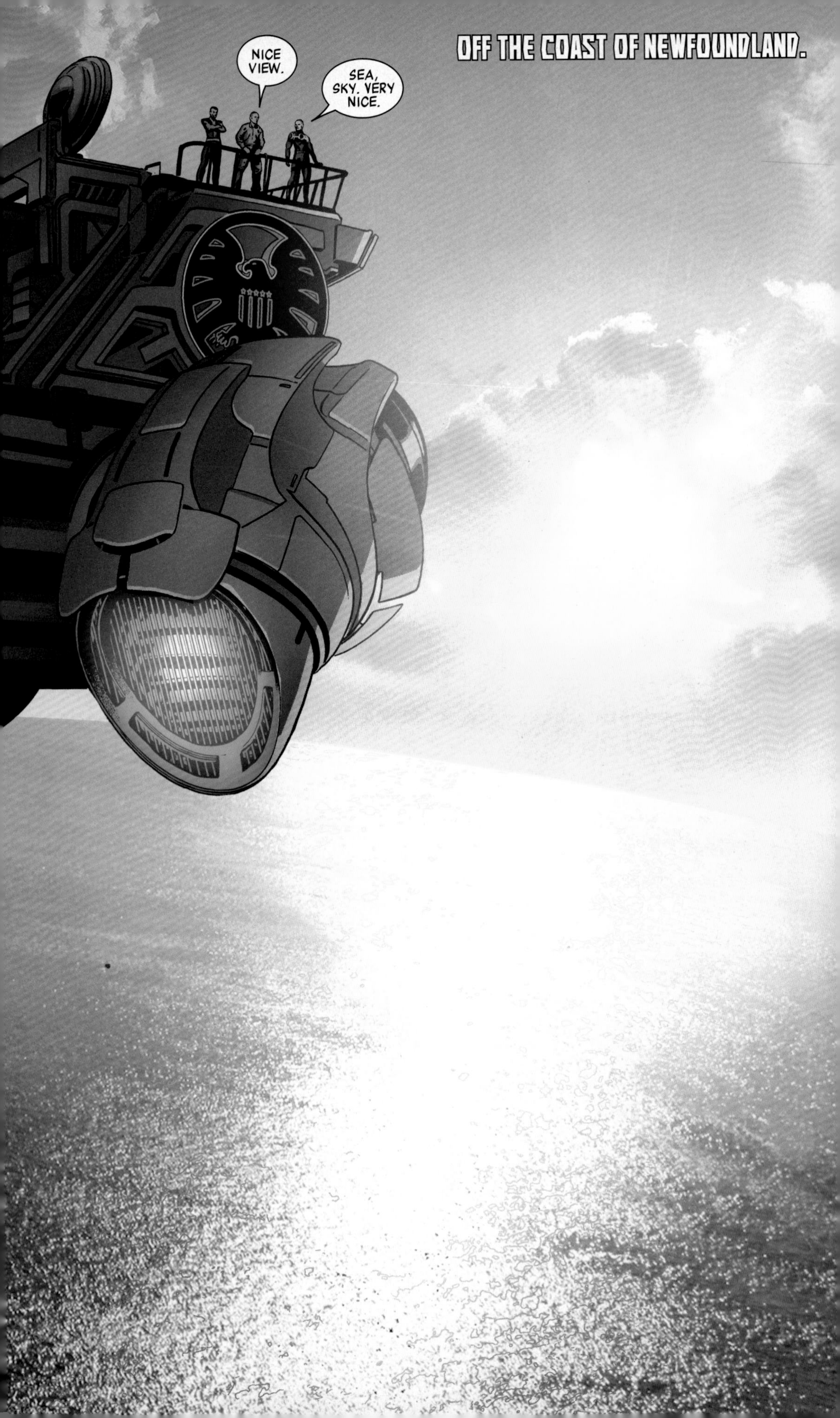
OFF THE COAST OF NEWFOUNDLAND.
NICE VIEW.
SEA, SKY. VERY NICE.

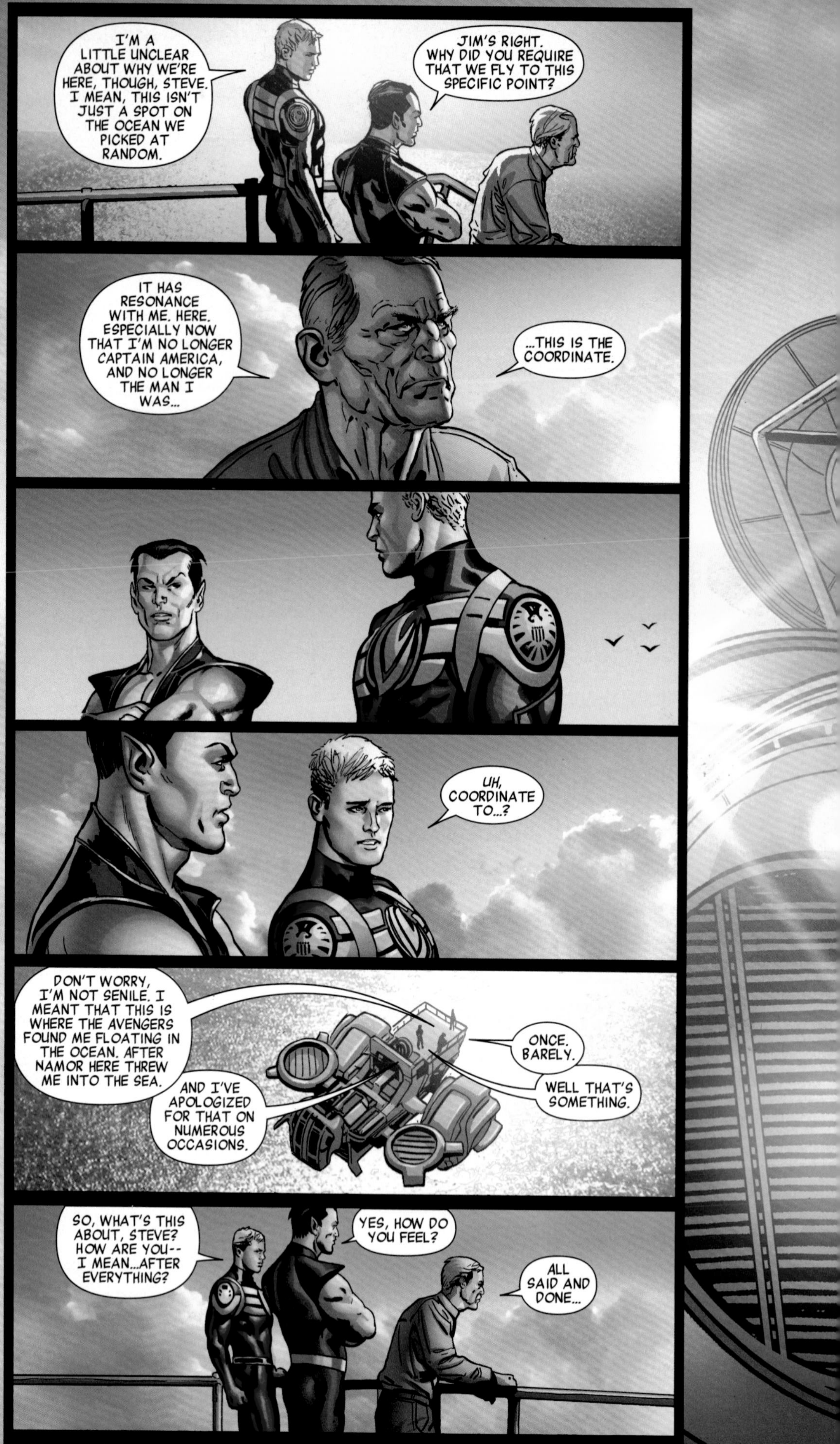
I'M A LITTLE UNCLEAR ABOUT WHY WE'RE HERE, THOUGH, STEVE. I MEAN, THIS ISN'T JUST A SPOT ON THE OCEAN WE PICKED AT RANDOM.
JIM'S RIGHT. WHY DID YOU REQUIRE THAT WE FLY TO THIS SPECIFIC POINT?
IT HAS RESONANCE WITH ME. HERE. ESPECIALLY NOW THAT I'M NO LONGER CAPTAIN AMERICA, AND NO LONGER THE MAN I WAS...
...THIS IS THE COORDINATE.
UH, COORDINATE TO...?
DON'T WORRY, I'M NOT SENILE. I MEANT THAT THIS IS WHERE THE AVENGERS FOUND ME FLOATING IN THE OCEAN. AFTER NAMOR HERE THREW ME INTO THE SEA.
AND I'VE APOLOGIZED FOR THAT ON NUMEROUS OCCASIONS.
ONCE. BARELY.
WELL THAT'S SOMETHING.
SO, WHAT'S THIS ABOUT, STEVE? HOW ARE YOU-- I MEAN...AFTER EVERYTHING?
YES, HOW DO YOU FEEL?
ALL SAID AND DONE...

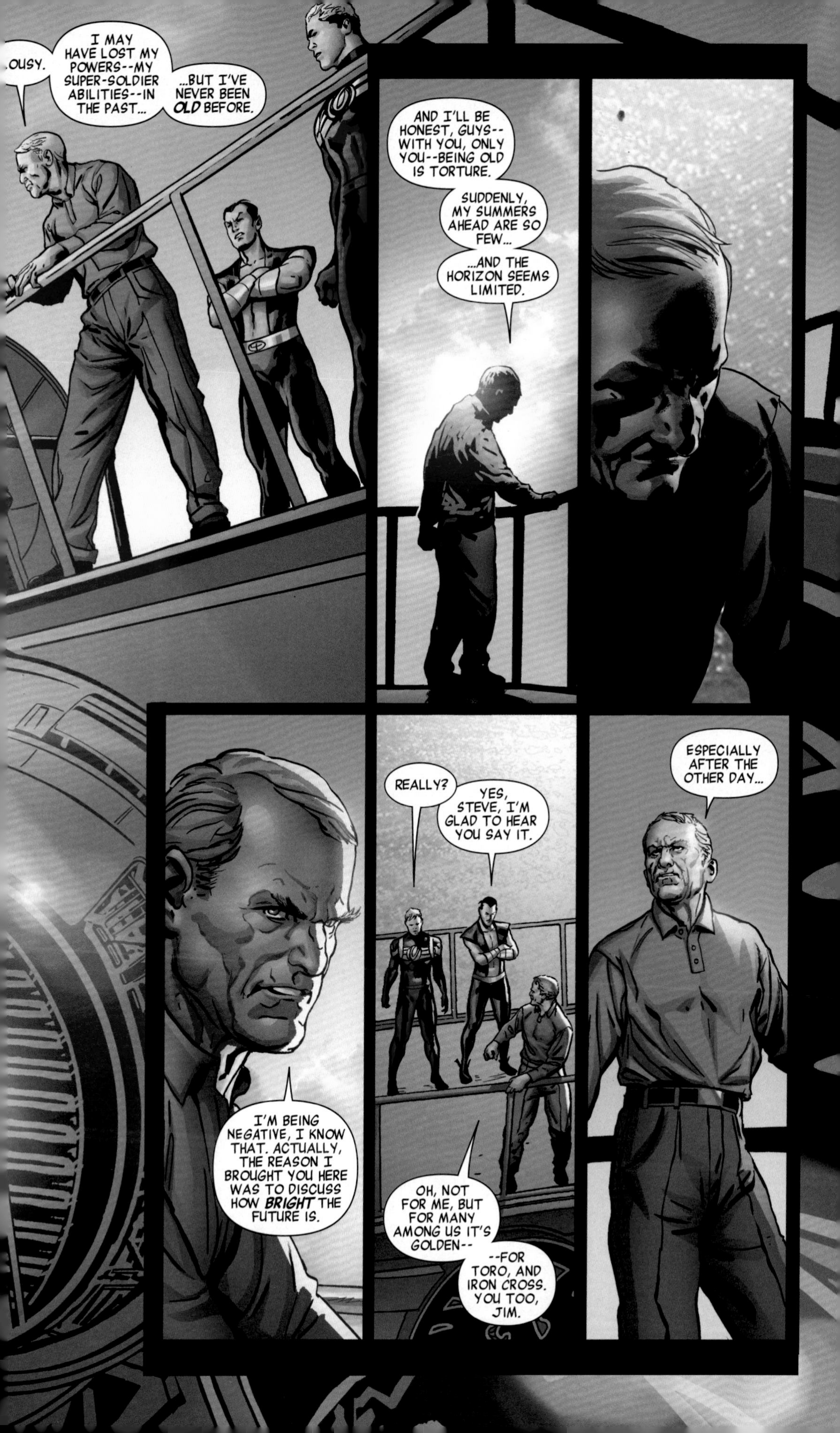
LOUSY.
I MAY HAVE LOST MY POWERS--MY SUPER-SOLDIER ABILITIES--IN THE PAST...
...BUT I'VE NEVER BEEN OLD BEFORE.
AND I'LL BE HONEST, GUYS--WITH YOU, ONLY YOU--BEING OLD IS TORTURE.
SUDDENLY, MY SUMMERS AHEAD ARE SO FEW...
...AND THE HORIZON SEEMS LIMITED.
I'M BEING NEGATIVE, I KNOW THAT. ACTUALLY, THE REASON I BROUGHT YOU HERE WAS TO DISCUSS HOW BRIGHT THE FUTURE IS.
REALLY?
YES, STEVE, I'M GLAD TO HEAR YOU SAY IT.
OH, NOT FOR ME, BUT FOR MANY AMONG US IT'S GOLDEN--
--FOR TORO, AND IRON CROSS. YOU TOO, JIM.
ESPECIALLY AFTER THE OTHER DAY...

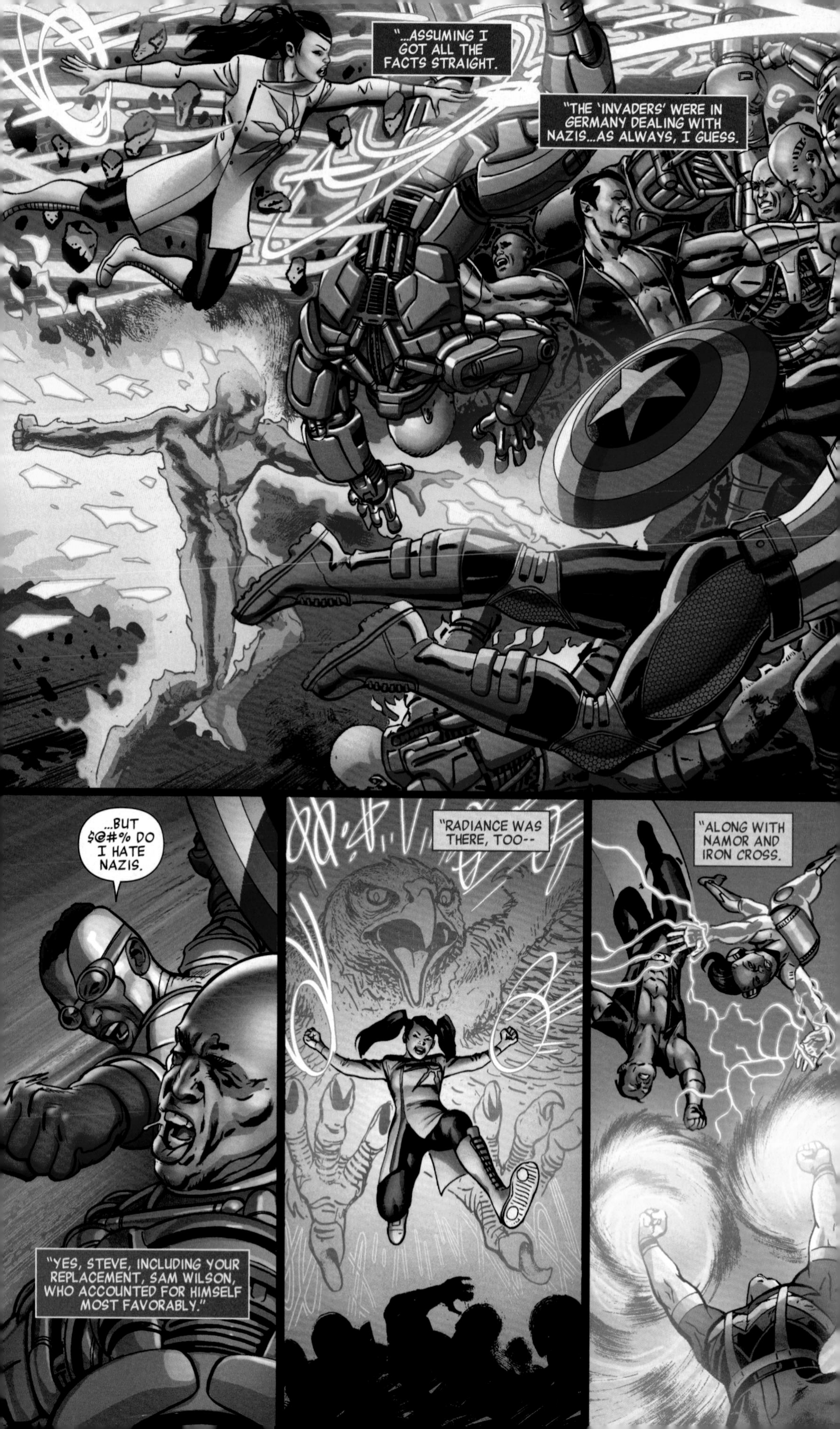
"...ASSUMING I GOT ALL THE FACTS STRAIGHT.
"THE 'INVADERS' WERE IN GERMANY DEALING WITH NAZIS...AS ALWAYS, I GUESS.
...BUT $@#% DO I HATE NAZIS.
"YES, STEVE, INCLUDING YOUR REPLACEMENT, SAM WILSON, WHO ACCOUNTED FOR HIMSELF MOST FAVORABLY."
"RADIANCE WAS THERE, TOO--
"ALONG WITH NAMOR AND IRON CROSS.

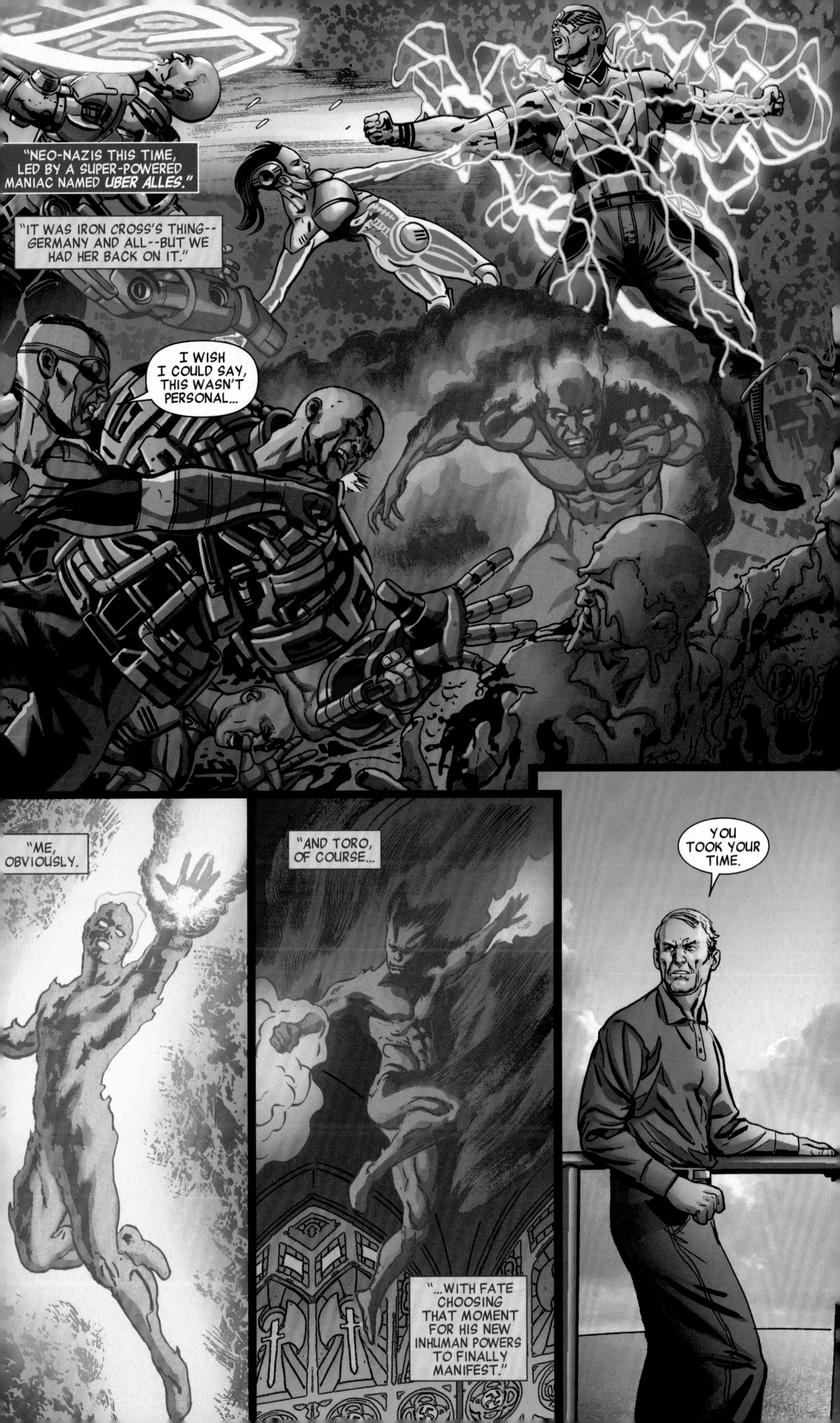
"NEO-NAZIS THIS TIME, LED BY A SUPER-POWERED MANIAC NAMED UBER ALLES."
"IT WAS IRON CROSS'S THING--GERMANY AND ALL--BUT WE HAD HER BACK ON IT."
I WISH I COULD SAY, THIS WASN'T PERSONAL...
"ME, OBVIOUSLY.
"AND TORO, OF COURSE...
"...WITH FATE CHOOSING THAT MOMENT FOR HIS NEW INHUMAN POWERS TO FINALLY MANIFEST."
YOU TOOK YOUR TIME.

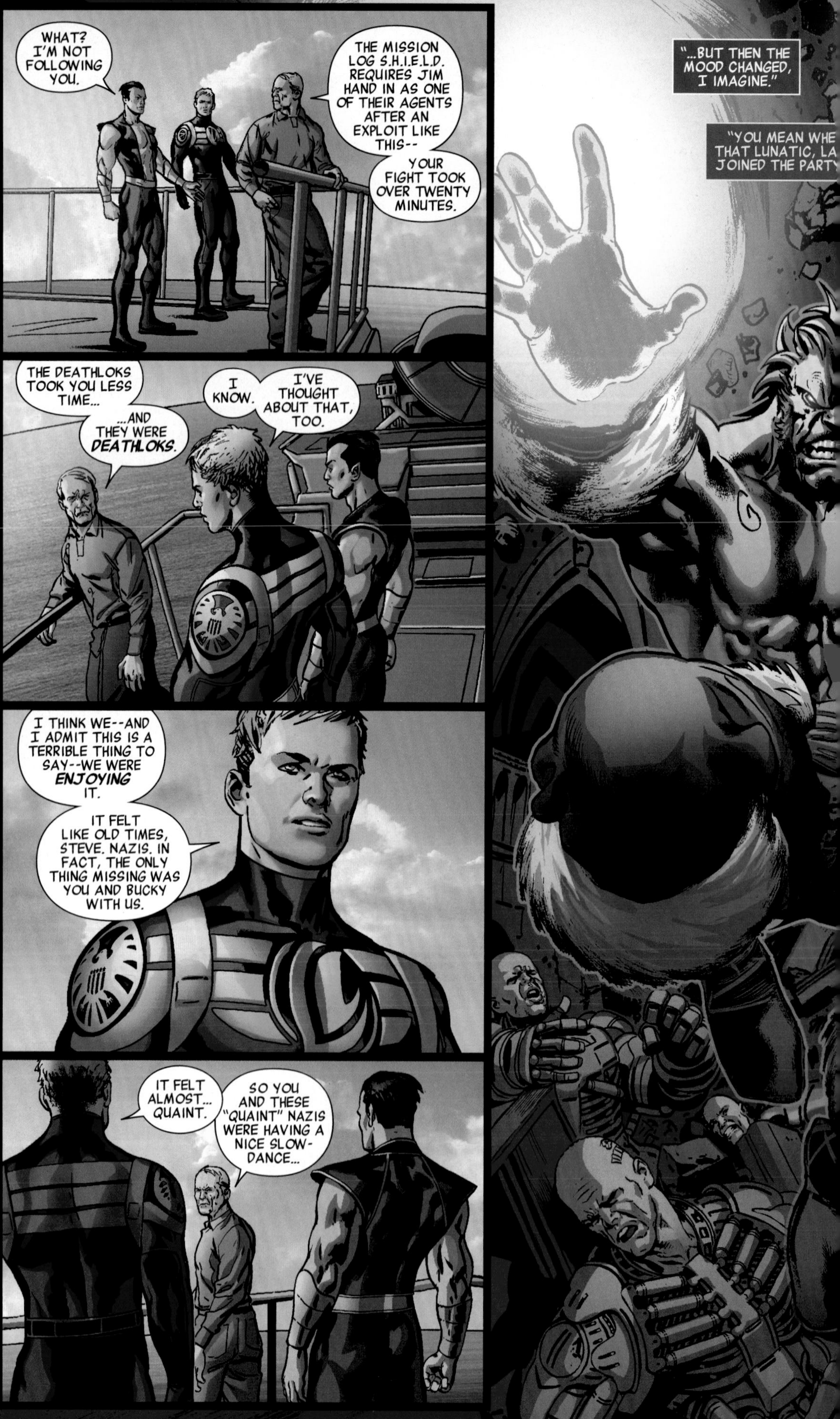
WHAT? I'M NOT FOLLOWING YOU.
THE MISSION LOG S.H.I.E.L.D. REQUIRES JIM HAND IN AS ONE OF THEIR AGENTS AFTER AN EXPLOIT LIKE THIS--
YOUR FIGHT TOOK OVER TWENTY MINUTES.
THE DEATHLOKS TOOK YOU LESS TIME...
...AND THEY WERE *DEATHLOKS*.
I KNOW.
I'VE THOUGHT ABOUT THAT, TOO.
I THINK WE--AND I ADMIT THIS IS A TERRIBLE THING TO SAY--WE WERE *ENJOYING* IT.
IT FELT LIKE OLD TIMES, STEVE. NAZIS. IN FACT, THE ONLY THING MISSING WAS YOU AND BUCKY WITH US.
IT FELT ALMOST... QUAINT.
SO YOU AND THESE "QUAINT" NAZIS WERE HAVING A NICE SLOW-DANCE...
"...BUT THEN THE MOOD CHANGED, I IMAGINE."
"YOU MEAN WHE THAT LUNATIC, LA JOINED THE PARTY

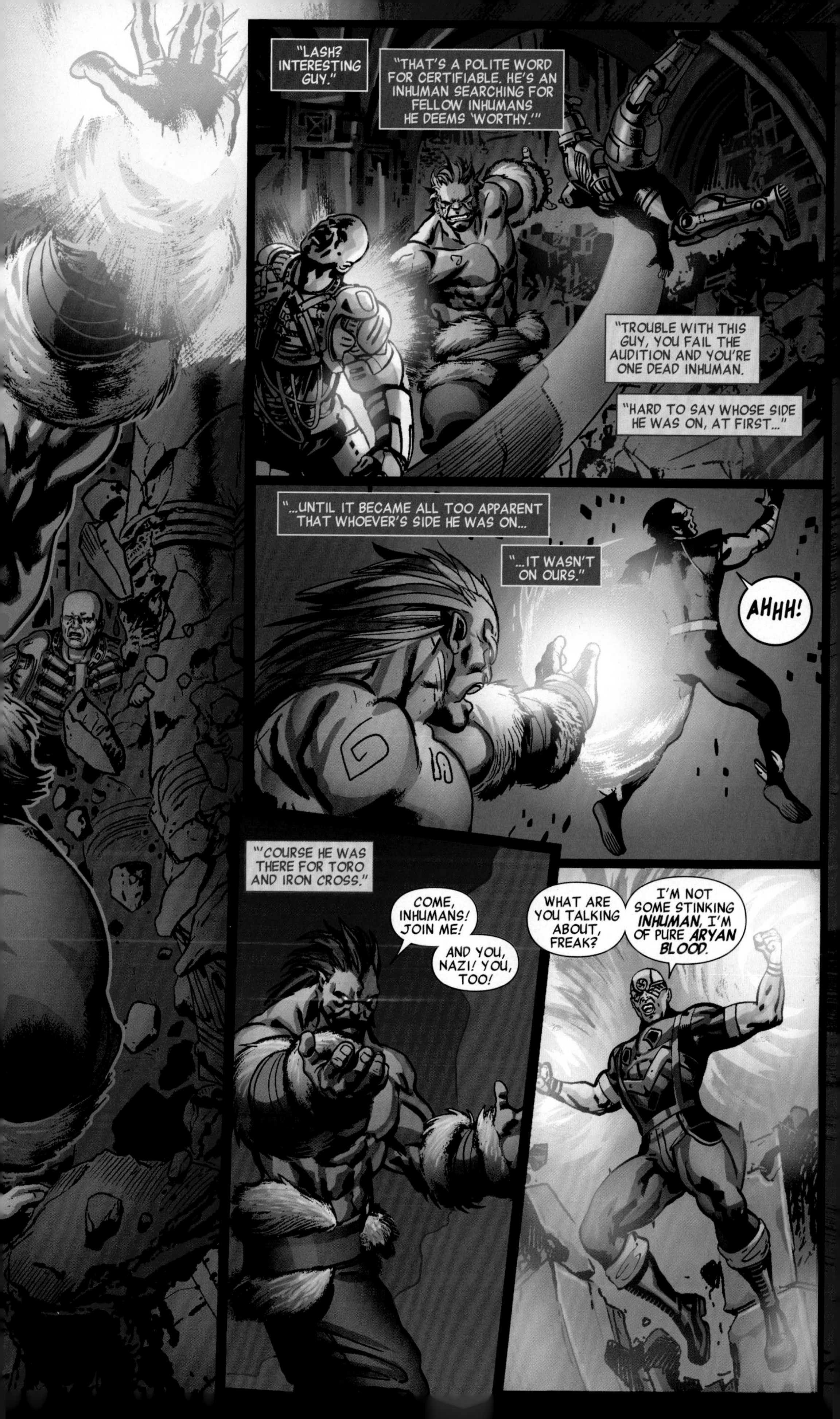
"LASH? INTERESTING GUY."
"THAT'S A POLITE WORD FOR CERTIFIABLE. HE'S AN INHUMAN SEARCHING FOR FELLOW INHUMANS HE DEEMS 'WORTHY.'"
"TROUBLE WITH THIS GUY, YOU FAIL THE AUDITION AND YOU'RE ONE DEAD INHUMAN.
"HARD TO SAY WHOSE SIDE HE WAS ON, AT FIRST..."
"...UNTIL IT BECAME ALL TOO APPARENT THAT WHOEVER'S SIDE HE WAS ON...
"...IT WASN'T ON OURS."
AHHH!
"'COURSE HE WAS THERE FOR TORO AND IRON CROSS."
COME, INHUMANS! JOIN ME!
AND YOU, NAZI! YOU, TOO!
WHAT ARE YOU TALKING ABOUT, FREAK?
I'M NOT SOME STINKING INHUMAN, I'M OF PURE ARYAN BLOOD.

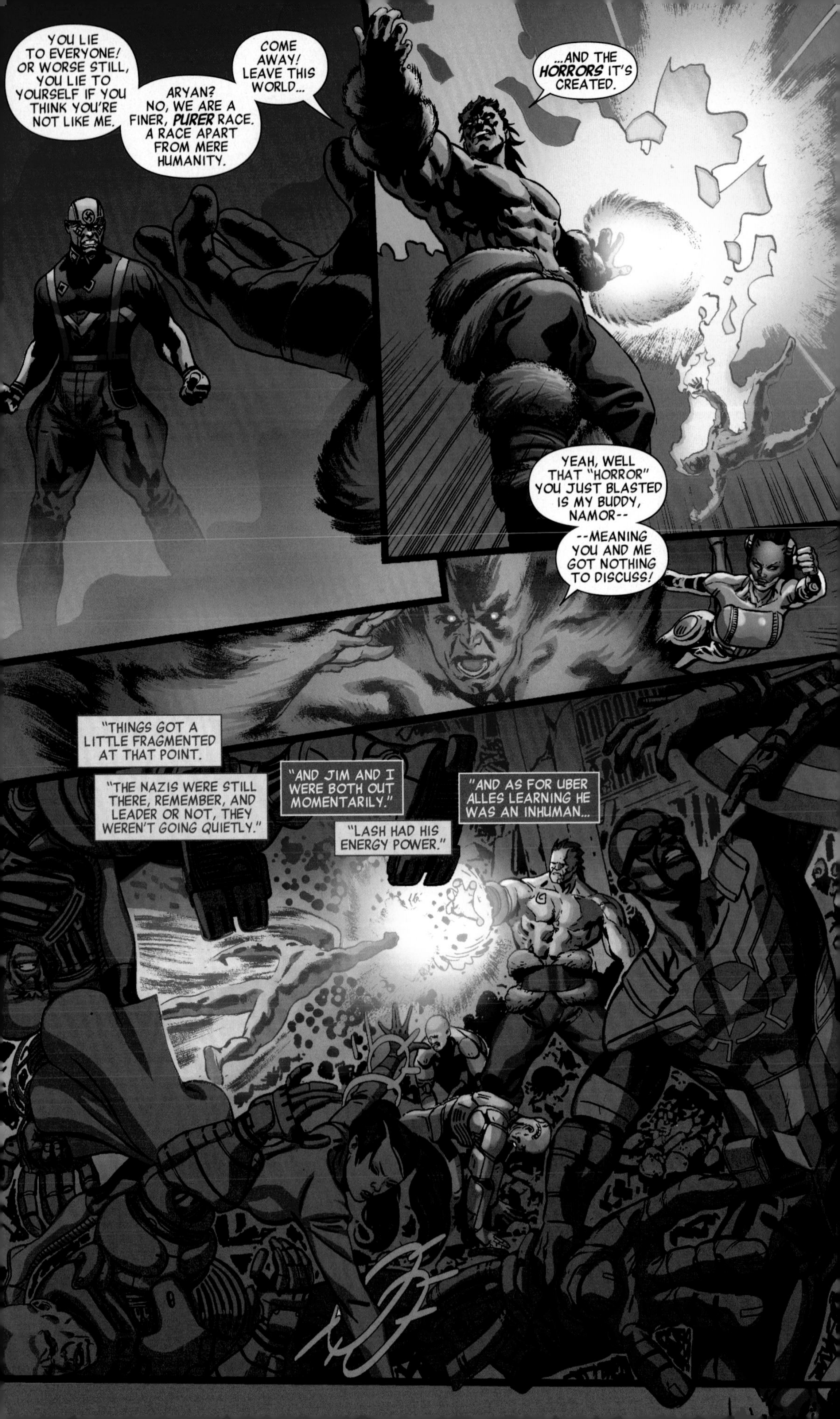
YOU LIE TO EVERYONE! OR WORSE STILL, YOU LIE TO YOURSELF IF YOU THINK YOU'RE NOT LIKE ME.
ARYAN? NO, WE ARE A FINER, PURER RACE. A RACE APART FROM MERE HUMANITY.
COME AWAY! LEAVE THIS WORLD...
...AND THE HORRORS IT'S CREATED.
YEAH, WELL THAT "HORROR" YOU JUST BLASTED IS MY BUDDY, NAMOR--
--MEANING YOU AND ME GOT NOTHING TO DISCUSS!
"THINGS GOT A LITTLE FRAGMENTED AT THAT POINT.
"THE NAZIS WERE STILL THERE, REMEMBER, AND LEADER OR NOT, THEY WEREN'T GOING QUIETLY."
"AND JIM AND I WERE BOTH OUT MOMENTARILY."
"LASH HAD HIS ENERGY POWER."
"AND AS FOR UBER ALLES LEARNING HE WAS AN INHUMAN...

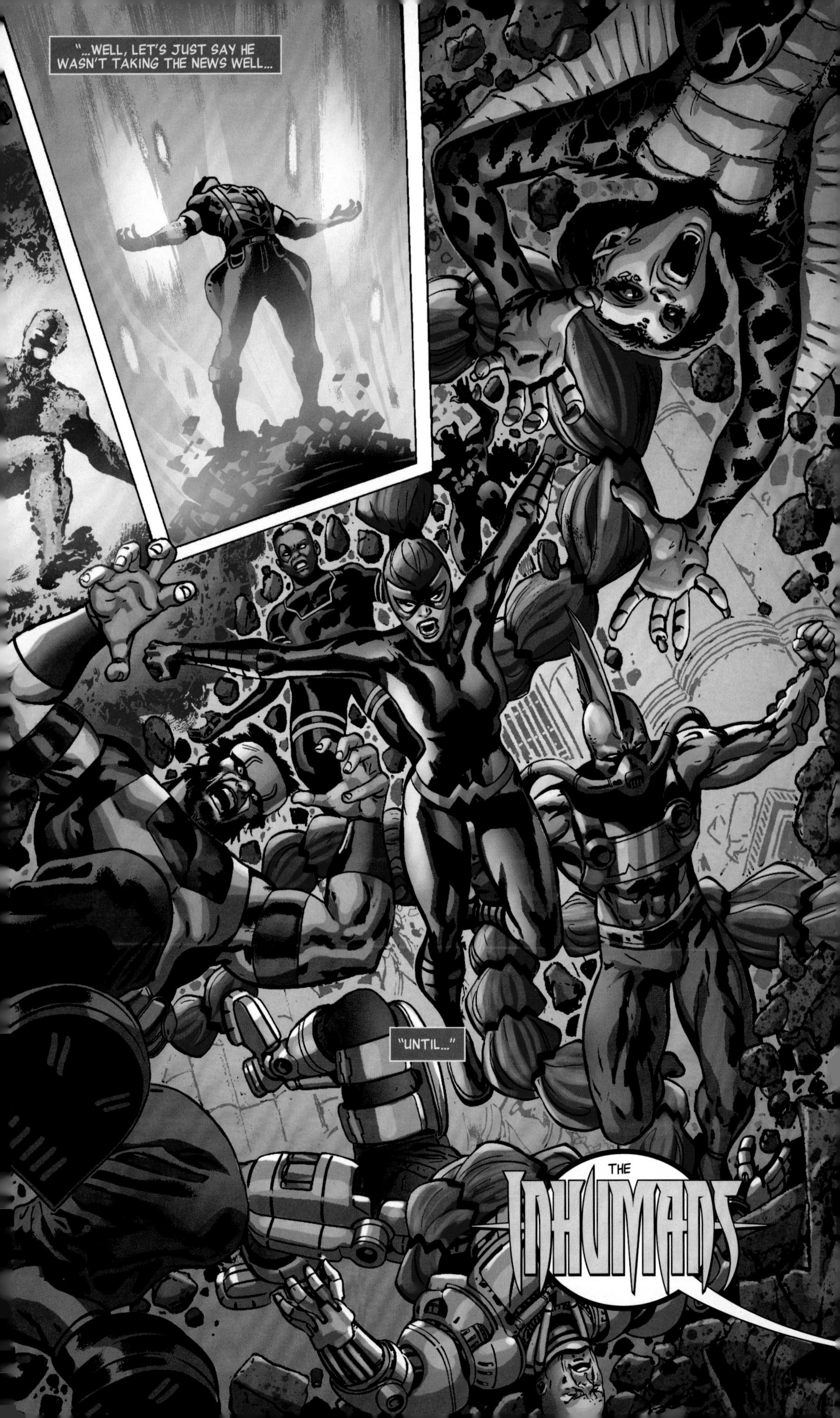
"...WELL, LET'S JUST SAY HE WASN'T TAKING THE NEWS WELL...
"UNTIL..."
THE INHUMANS

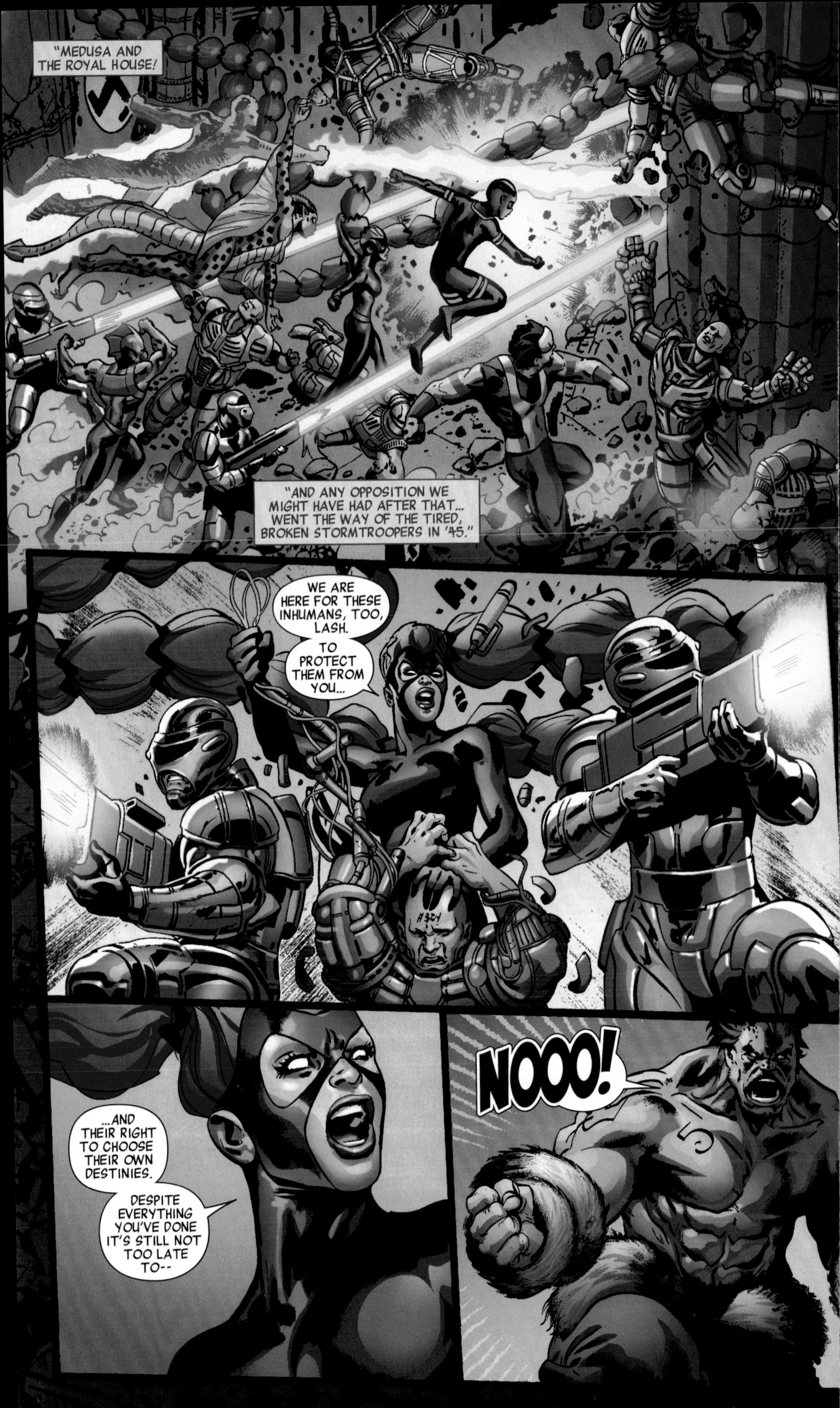
"MEDUSA AND THE ROYAL HOUSE!
"AND ANY OPPOSITION WE MIGHT HAVE HAD AFTER THAT... WENT THE WAY OF THE TIRED, BROKEN STORMTROOPERS IN '45."
WE ARE HERE FOR THESE INHUMANS, TOO, LASH.
TO PROTECT THEM FROM YOU...
...AND THEIR RIGHT TO CHOOSE THEIR OWN DESTINIES.
DESPITE EVERYTHING YOU'VE DONE IT'S STILL NOT TOO LATE TO--
NOOO!

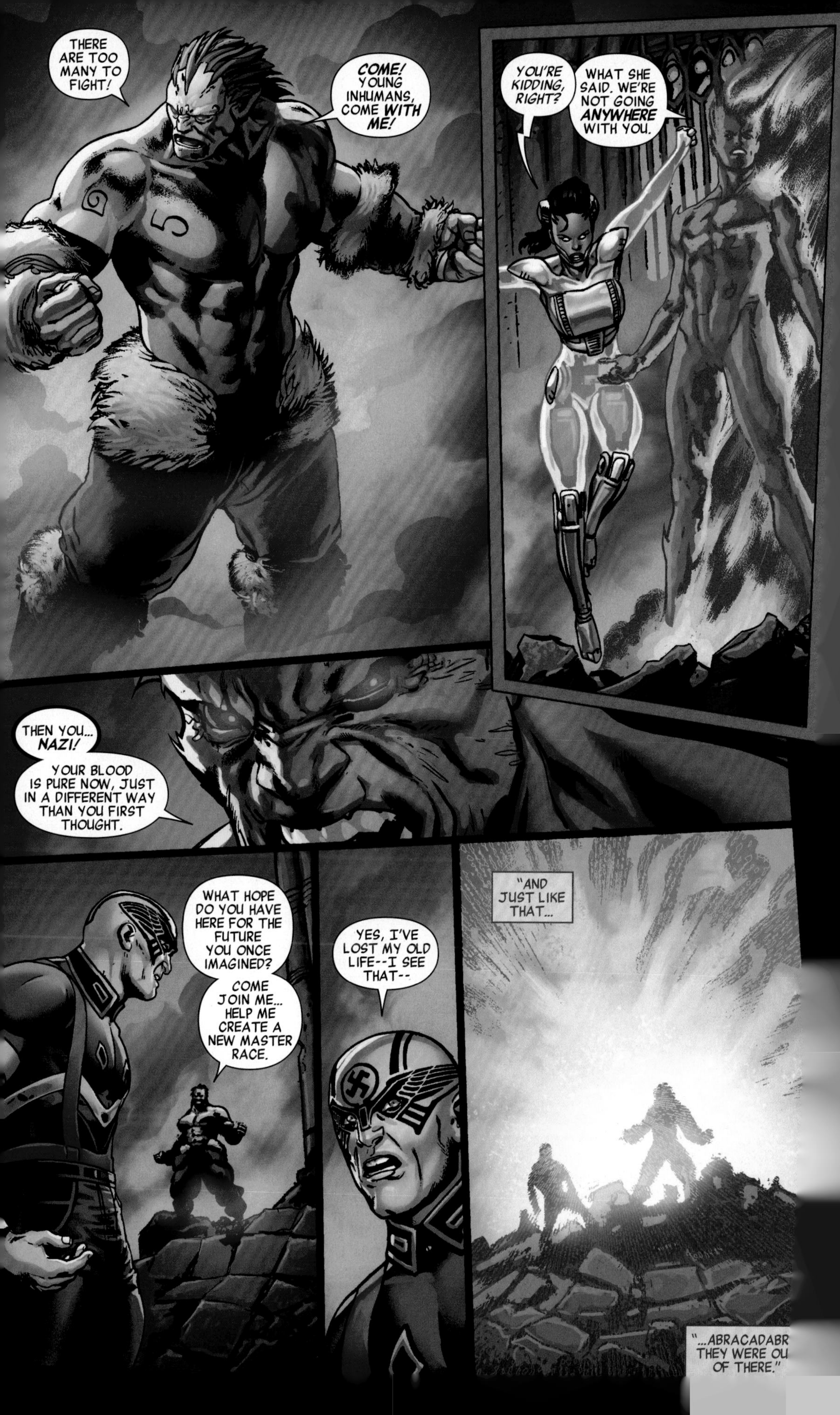
THERE ARE TOO MANY TO FIGHT!
COME! YOUNG INHUMANS, COME WITH ME!
YOU'RE KIDDING, RIGHT?
WHAT SHE SAID. WE'RE NOT GOING ANYWHERE WITH YOU.
THEN YOU... NAZI!
YOUR BLOOD IS PURE NOW, JUST IN A DIFFERENT WAY THAN YOU FIRST THOUGHT.
WHAT HOPE DO YOU HAVE HERE FOR THE FUTURE YOU ONCE IMAGINED?
COME JOIN ME... HELP ME CREATE A NEW MASTER RACE.
YES, I'VE LOST MY OLD LIFE--I SEE THAT--.
"AND JUST LIKE THAT...
"...ABRACADABR THEY WERE OU OF THERE."

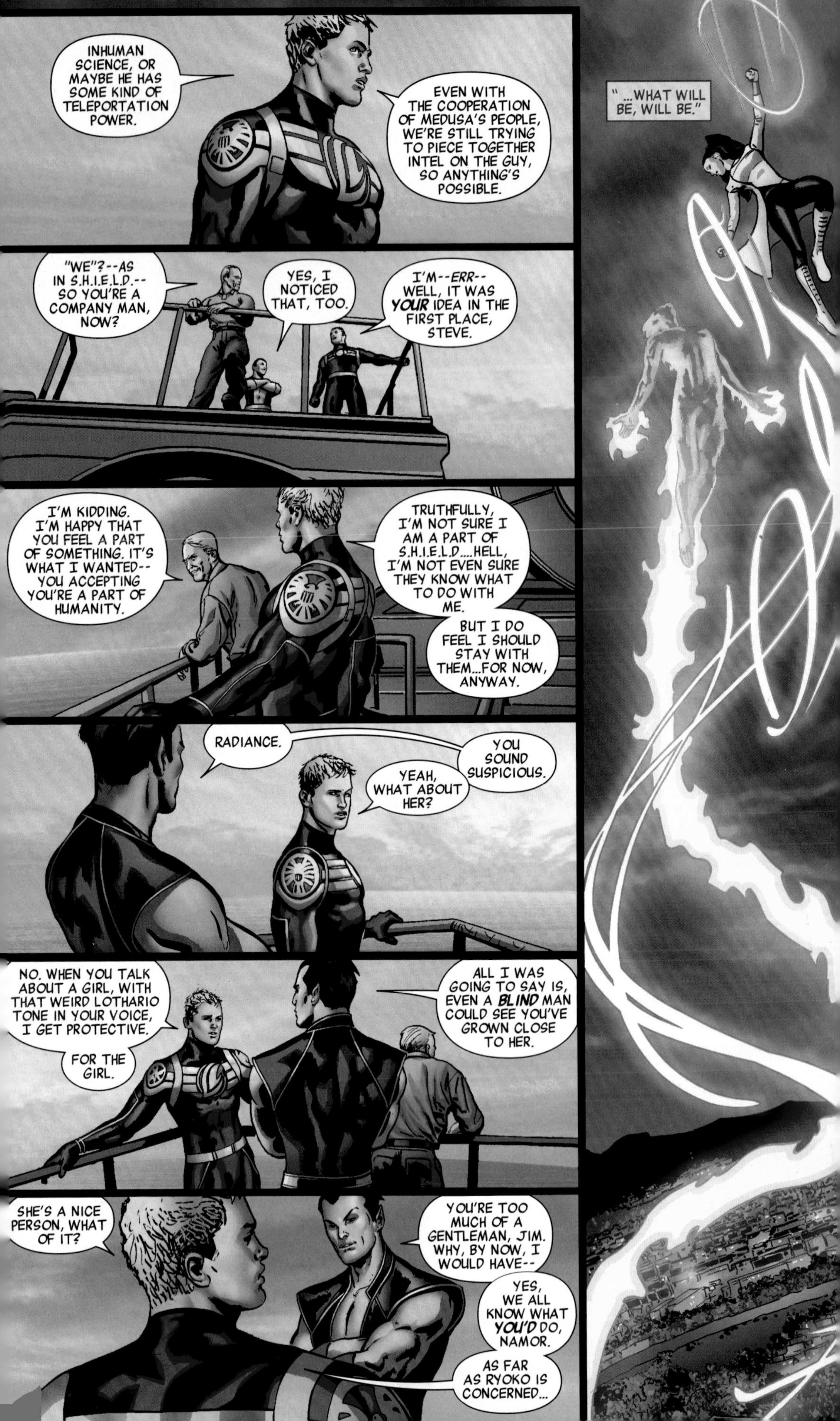
INHUMAN SCIENCE, OR MAYBE HE HAS SOME KIND OF TELEPORTATION POWER.
EVEN WITH THE COOPERATION OF MEDUSA'S PEOPLE, WE'RE STILL TRYING TO PIECE TOGETHER INTEL ON THE GUY, SO ANYTHING'S POSSIBLE.
"WE"?--AS IN S.H.I.E.L.D.--SO YOU'RE A COMPANY MAN, NOW?
YES, I NOTICED THAT, TOO.
I'M--ERR--WELL, IT WAS YOUR IDEA IN THE FIRST PLACE, STEVE.
I'M KIDDING. I'M HAPPY THAT YOU FEEL A PART OF SOMETHING. IT'S WHAT I WANTED--YOU ACCEPTING YOU'RE A PART OF HUMANITY.
TRUTHFULLY, I'M NOT SURE I AM A PART OF S.H.I.E.L.D....HELL, I'M NOT EVEN SURE THEY KNOW WHAT TO DO WITH ME.
BUT I DO FEEL I SHOULD STAY WITH THEM...FOR NOW, ANYWAY.
RADIANCE.
YOU SOUND SUSPICIOUS.
YEAH, WHAT ABOUT HER?
NO. WHEN YOU TALK ABOUT A GIRL, WITH THAT WEIRD LOTHARIO TONE IN YOUR VOICE, I GET PROTECTIVE.
FOR THE GIRL.
ALL I WAS GOING TO SAY IS, EVEN A BLIND MAN COULD SEE YOU'VE GROWN CLOSE TO HER.
SHE'S A NICE PERSON, WHAT OF IT?
YOU'RE TOO MUCH OF A GENTLEMAN, JIM. WHY, BY NOW, I WOULD HAVE--
YES, WE ALL KNOW WHAT YOU'D DO, NAMOR.
AS FAR AS RYOKO IS CONCERNED...
"...WHAT WILL BE, WILL BE."

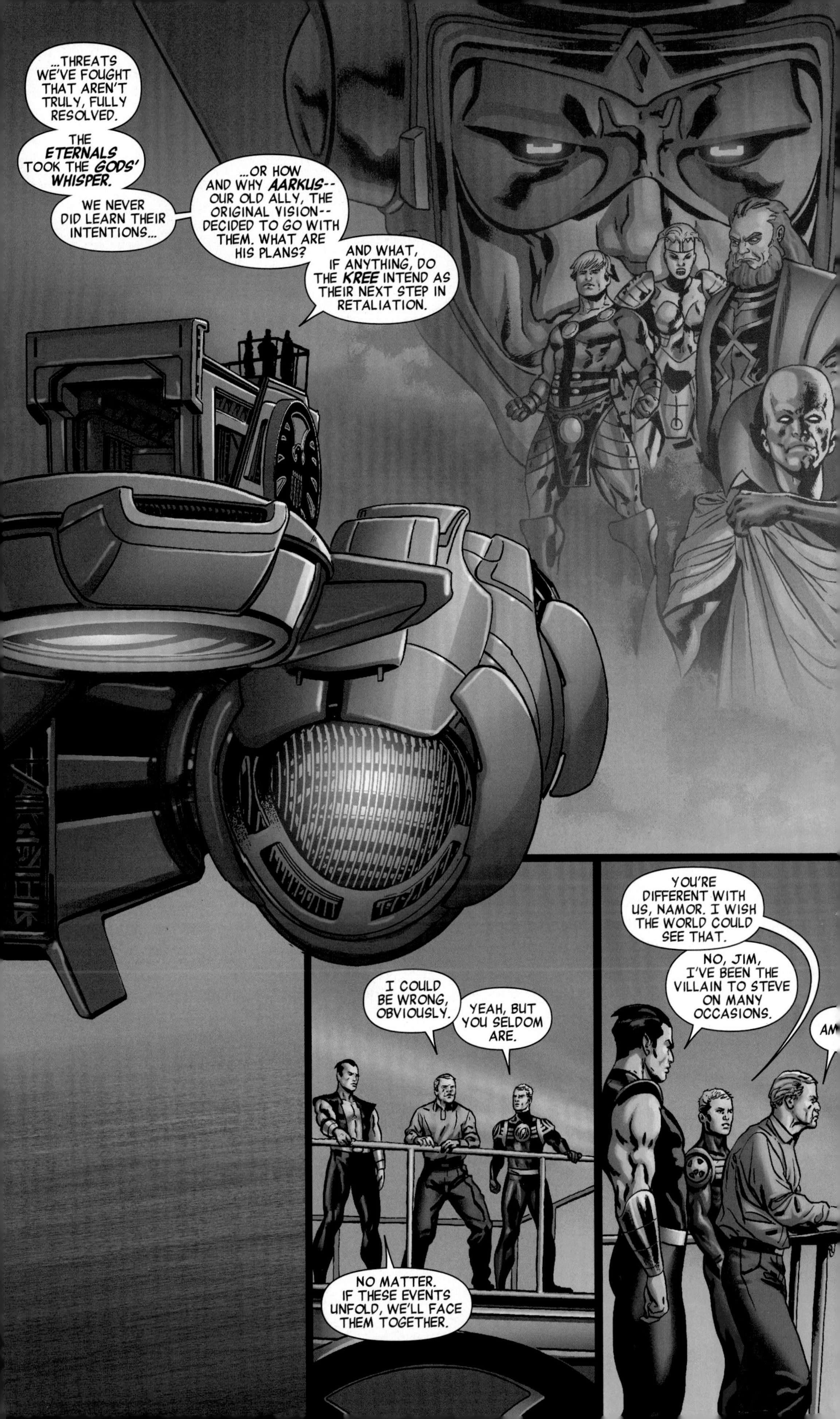
...THREATS WE'VE FOUGHT THAT AREN'T TRULY, FULLY RESOLVED.
THE ETERNALS TOOK THE GODS' WHISPER.
WE NEVER DID LEARN THEIR INTENTIONS...
...OR HOW AND WHY AARKUS-- OUR OLD ALLY, THE ORIGINAL VISION-- DECIDED TO GO WITH THEM. WHAT ARE HIS PLANS?
AND WHAT, IF ANYTHING, DO THE KREE INTEND AS THEIR NEXT STEP IN RETALIATION.
I COULD BE WRONG, OBVIOUSLY.
YEAH, BUT YOU SELDOM ARE.
NO MATTER. IF THESE EVENTS UNFOLD, WE'LL FACE THEM TOGETHER.
YOU'RE DIFFERENT WITH US, NAMOR. I WISH THE WORLD COULD SEE THAT.
NO, JIM, I'VE BEEN THE VILLAIN TO STEVE ON MANY OCCASIONS.

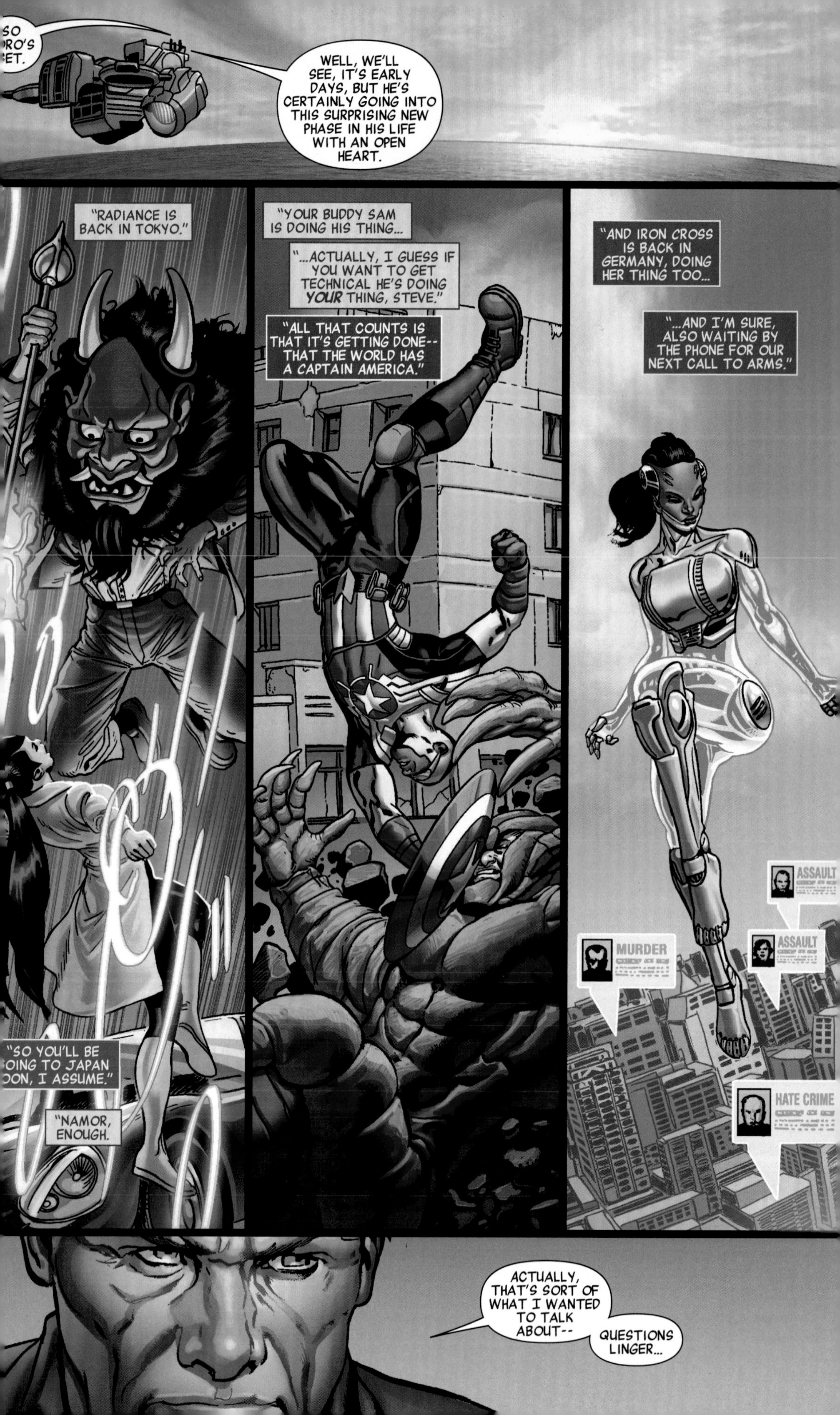
SO RO'S ET.
WELL, WE'LL SEE, IT'S EARLY DAYS, BUT HE'S CERTAINLY GOING INTO THIS SURPRISING NEW PHASE IN HIS LIFE WITH AN OPEN HEART.
"RADIANCE IS BACK IN TOKYO."
"SO YOU'LL BE OING TO JAPAN OON, I ASSUME."
"NAMOR, ENOUGH.
"YOUR BUDDY SAM IS DOING HIS THING...
"...ACTUALLY, I GUESS IF YOU WANT TO GET TECHNICAL HE'S DOING YOUR THING, STEVE."
"ALL THAT COUNTS IS THAT IT'S GETTING DONE-- THAT THE WORLD HAS A CAPTAIN AMERICA."
"AND IRON CROSS IS BACK IN GERMANY, DOING HER THING TOO...
"...AND I'M SURE, ALSO WAITING BY THE PHONE FOR OUR NEXT CALL TO ARMS."
ASSAULT
MURDER
ASSAULT
HATE CRIME
ACTUALLY, THAT'S SORT OF WHAT I WANTED TO TALK ABOUT--
QUESTIONS LINGER...

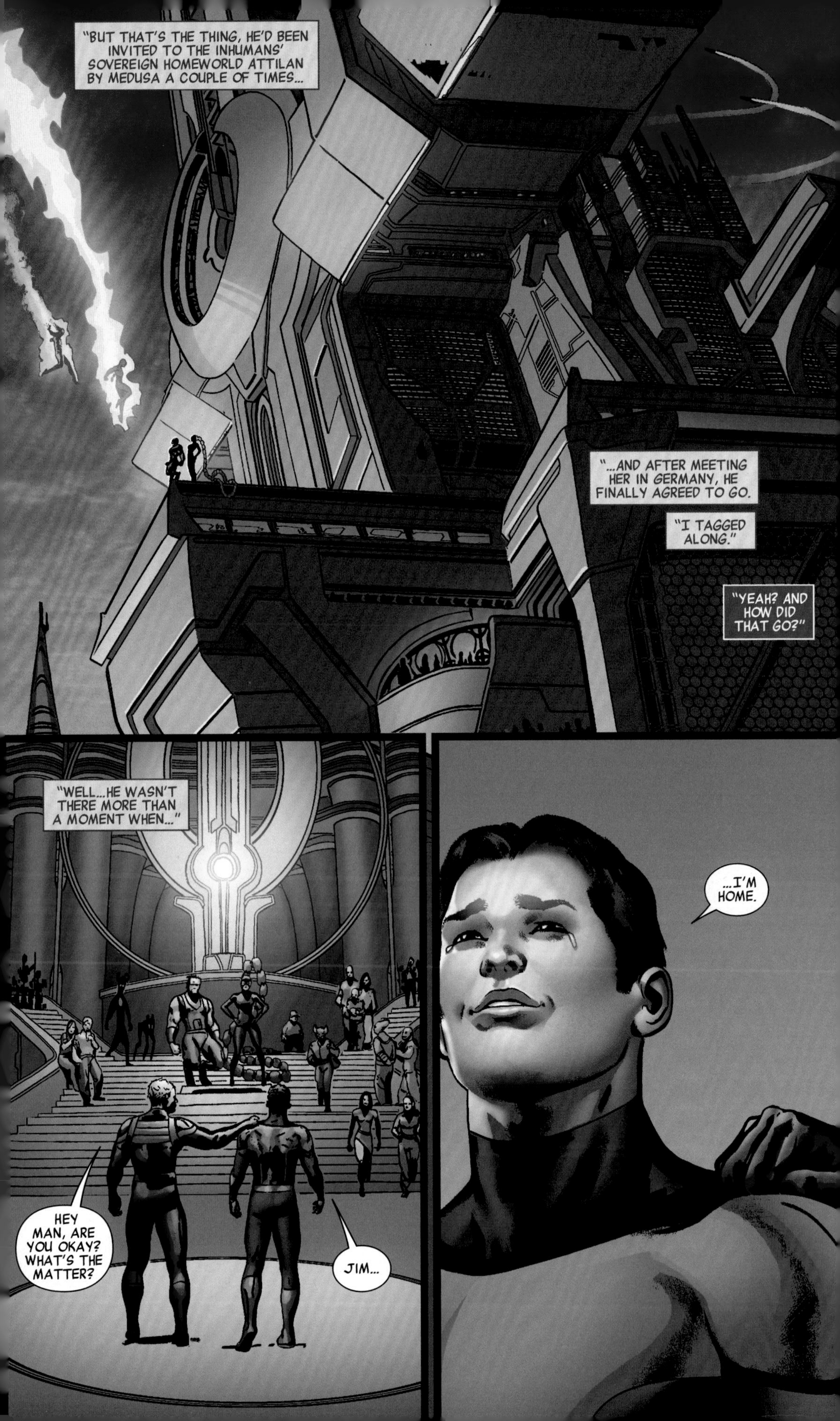
"BUT THAT'S THE THING, HE'D BEEN INVITED TO THE INHUMANS' SOVEREIGN HOMEWORLD ATTILAN BY MEDUSA A COUPLE OF TIMES...
"...AND AFTER MEETING HER IN GERMANY, HE FINALLY AGREED TO GO.
"I TAGGED ALONG."
"YEAH? AND HOW DID THAT GO?"
"WELL...HE WASN'T THERE MORE THAN A MOMENT WHEN..."
HEY MAN, ARE YOU OKAY? WHAT'S THE MATTER?
JIM...
...I'M HOME.

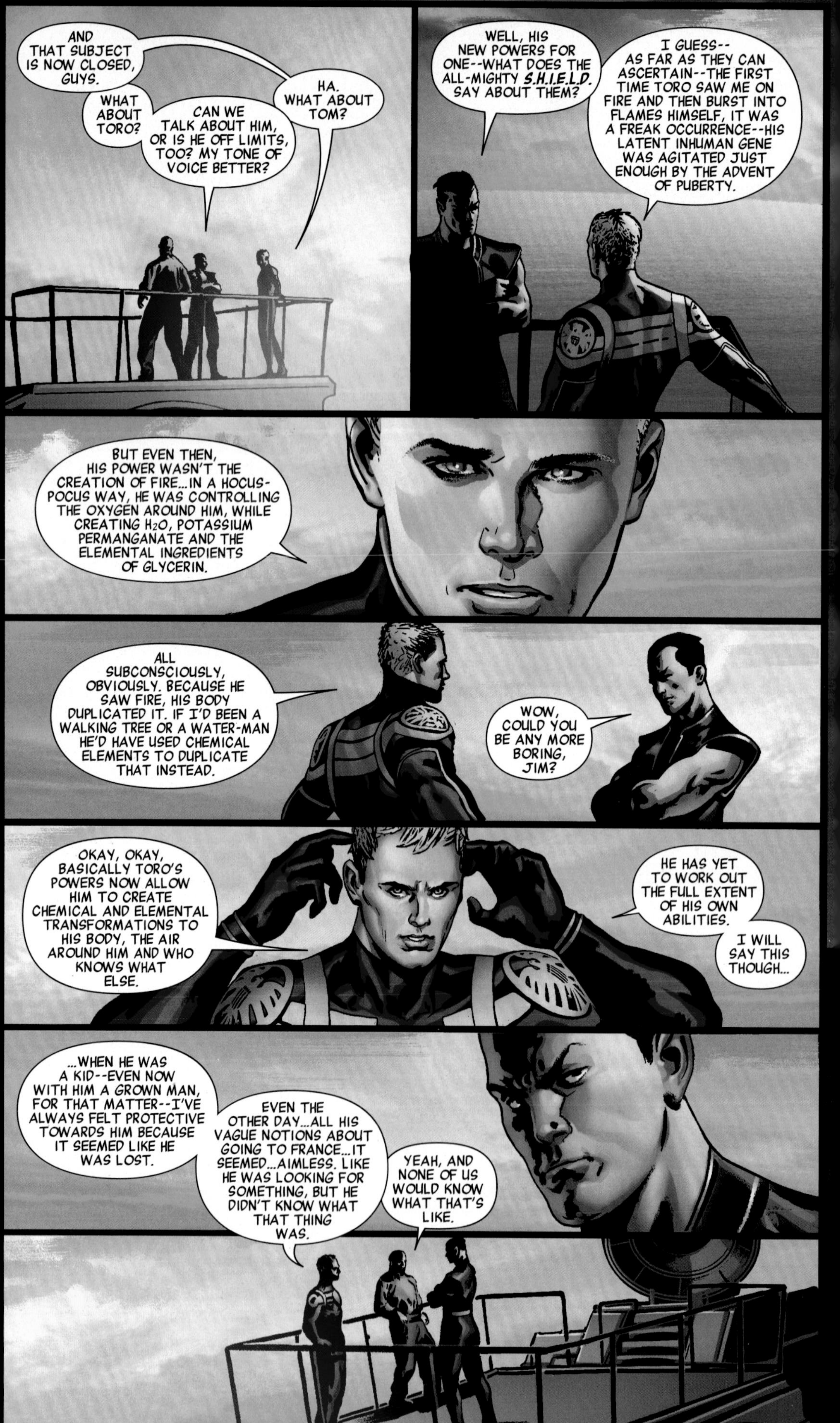
AND THAT SUBJECT IS NOW CLOSED, GUYS.
WHAT ABOUT TORO?
CAN WE TALK ABOUT HIM, OR IS HE OFF LIMITS, TOO? MY TONE OF VOICE BETTER?
HA. WHAT ABOUT TOM?
WELL, HIS NEW POWERS FOR ONE--WHAT DOES THE ALL-MIGHTY S.H.I.E.L.D. SAY ABOUT THEM?
I GUESS-- AS FAR AS THEY CAN ASCERTAIN--THE FIRST TIME TORO SAW ME ON FIRE AND THEN BURST INTO FLAMES HIMSELF, IT WAS A FREAK OCCURRENCE--HIS LATENT INHUMAN GENE WAS AGITATED JUST ENOUGH BY THE ADVENT OF PUBERTY.
BUT EVEN THEN, HIS POWER WASN'T THE CREATION OF FIRE...IN A HOCUS-POCUS WAY, HE WAS CONTROLLING THE OXYGEN AROUND HIM, WHILE CREATING H_2O, POTASSIUM PERMANGANATE AND THE ELEMENTAL INGREDIENTS OF GLYCERIN.
ALL SUBCONSCIOUSLY, OBVIOUSLY. BECAUSE HE SAW FIRE, HIS BODY DUPLICATED IT. IF I'D BEEN A WALKING TREE OR A WATER-MAN HE'D HAVE USED CHEMICAL ELEMENTS TO DUPLICATE THAT INSTEAD.
WOW, COULD YOU BE ANY MORE BORING, JIM?
OKAY, OKAY, BASICALLY TORO'S POWERS NOW ALLOW HIM TO CREATE CHEMICAL AND ELEMENTAL TRANSFORMATIONS TO HIS BODY, THE AIR AROUND HIM AND WHO KNOWS WHAT ELSE.
HE HAS YET TO WORK OUT THE FULL EXTENT OF HIS OWN ABILITIES.
I WILL SAY THIS THOUGH...
...WHEN HE WAS A KID--EVEN NOW WITH HIM A GROWN MAN, FOR THAT MATTER--I'VE ALWAYS FELT PROTECTIVE TOWARDS HIM BECAUSE IT SEEMED LIKE HE WAS LOST.
EVEN THE OTHER DAY...ALL HIS VAGUE NOTIONS ABOUT GOING TO FRANCE...IT SEEMED...AIMLESS. LIKE HE WAS LOOKING FOR SOMETHING, BUT HE DIDN'T KNOW WHAT THAT THING WAS.
YEAH, AND NONE OF US WOULD KNOW WHAT THAT'S LIKE.

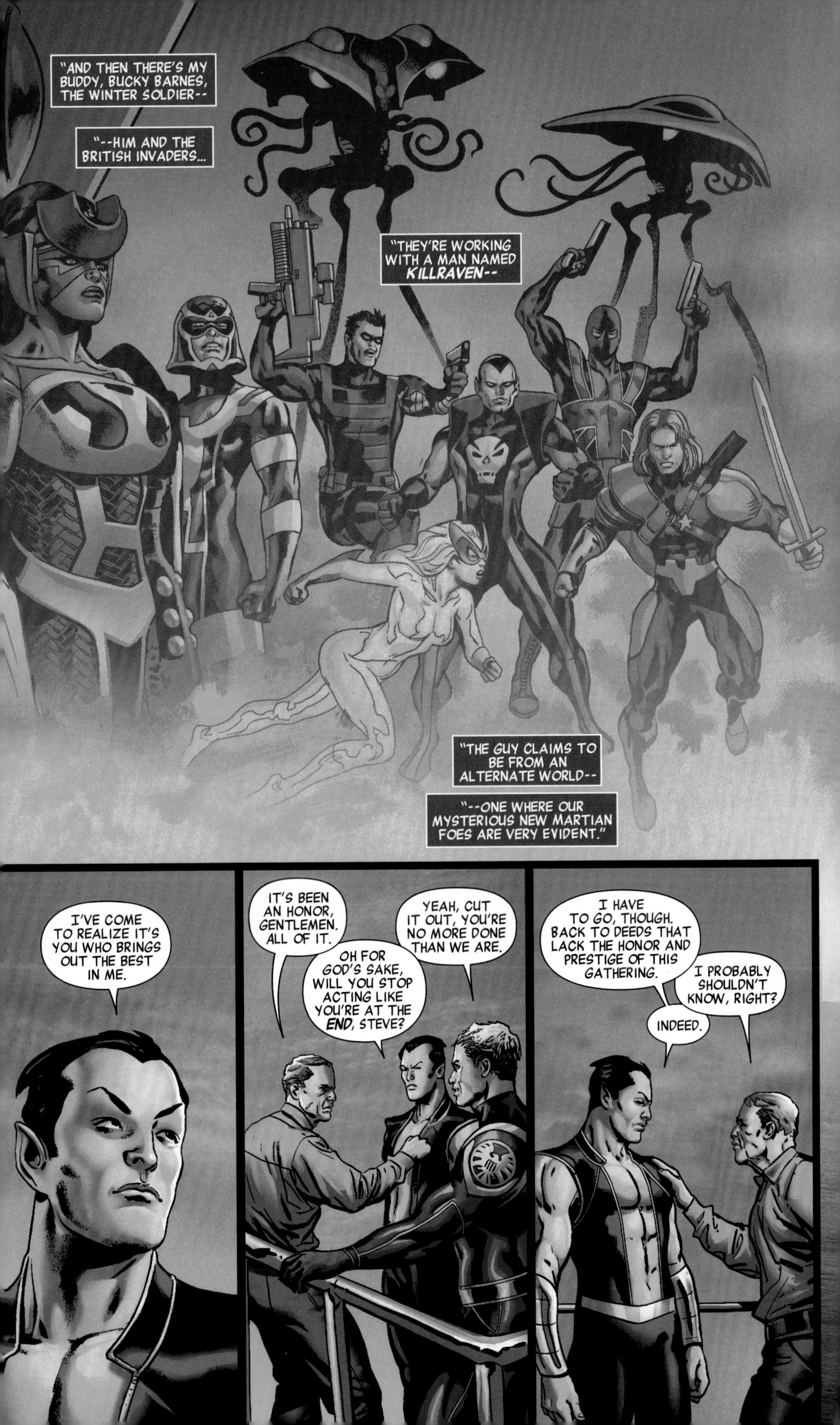
"AND THEN THERE'S MY BUDDY, BUCKY BARNES, THE WINTER SOLDIER--
"--HIM AND THE BRITISH INVADERS...
"THEY'RE WORKING WITH A MAN NAMED KILLRAVEN--
"THE GUY CLAIMS TO BE FROM AN ALTERNATE WORLD--
"--ONE WHERE OUR MYSTERIOUS NEW MARTIAN FOES ARE VERY EVIDENT."
I'VE COME TO REALIZE IT'S YOU WHO BRINGS OUT THE BEST IN ME.
IT'S BEEN AN HONOR, GENTLEMEN. ALL OF IT.
YEAH, CUT IT OUT, YOU'RE NO MORE DONE THAN WE ARE.
OH FOR GOD'S SAKE, WILL YOU STOP ACTING LIKE YOU'RE AT THE END, STEVE?
I HAVE TO GO, THOUGH. BACK TO DEEDS THAT LACK THE HONOR AND PRESTIGE OF THIS GATHERING.
I PROBABLY SHOULDN'T KNOW, RIGHT?
INDEED.

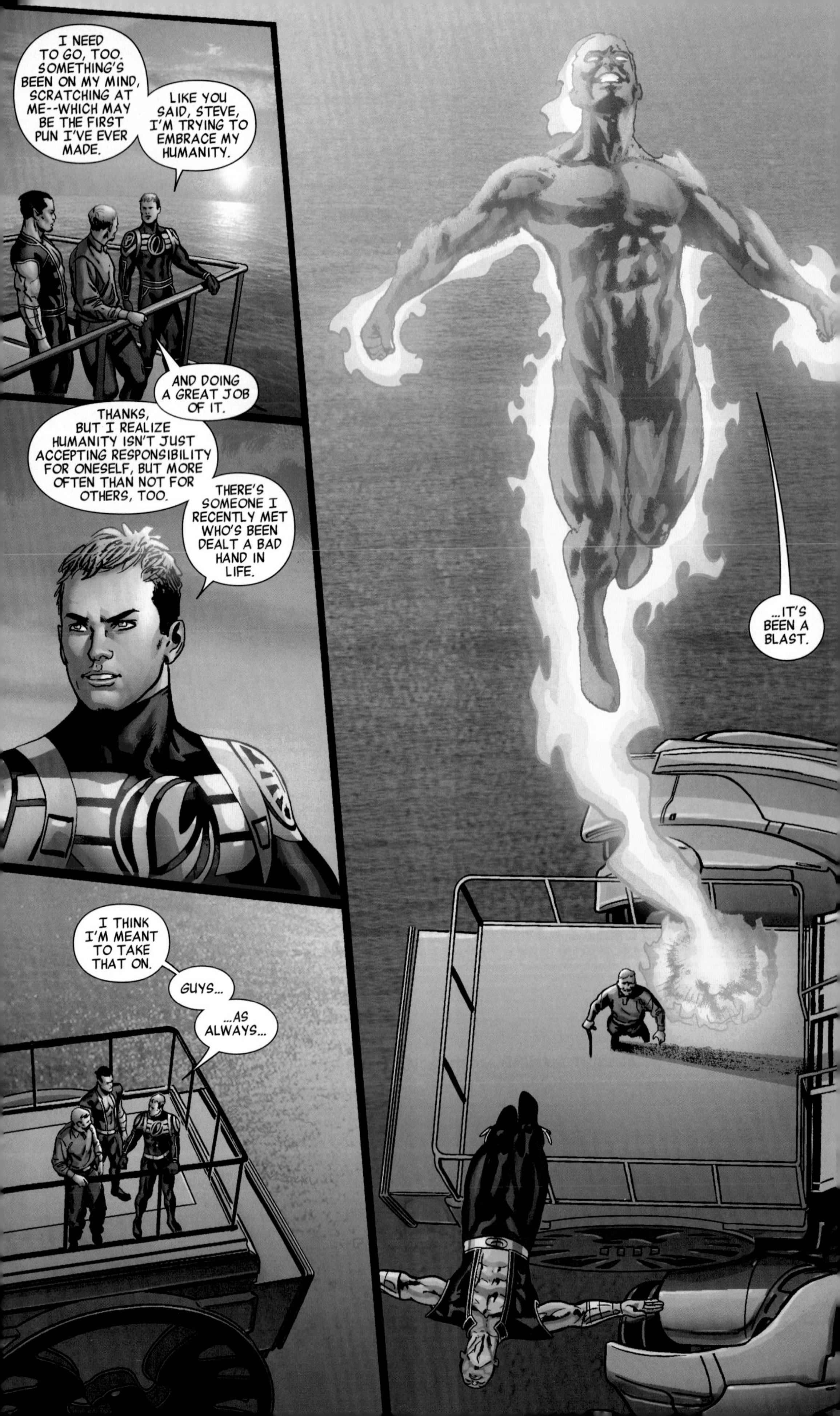
I NEED TO GO, TOO. SOMETHING'S BEEN ON MY MIND, SCRATCHING AT ME--WHICH MAY BE THE FIRST PUN I'VE EVER MADE.
LIKE YOU SAID, STEVE, I'M TRYING TO EMBRACE MY HUMANITY.
AND DOING A GREAT JOB OF IT.
THANKS, BUT I REALIZE HUMANITY ISN'T JUST ACCEPTING RESPONSIBILITY FOR ONESELF, BUT MORE OFTEN THAN NOT FOR OTHERS, TOO.
THERE'S SOMEONE I RECENTLY MET WHO'S BEEN DEALT A BAD HAND IN LIFE.
I THINK I'M MEANT TO TAKE THAT ON.
GUYS...
...AS ALWAYS...
...IT'S BEEN A BLAST.

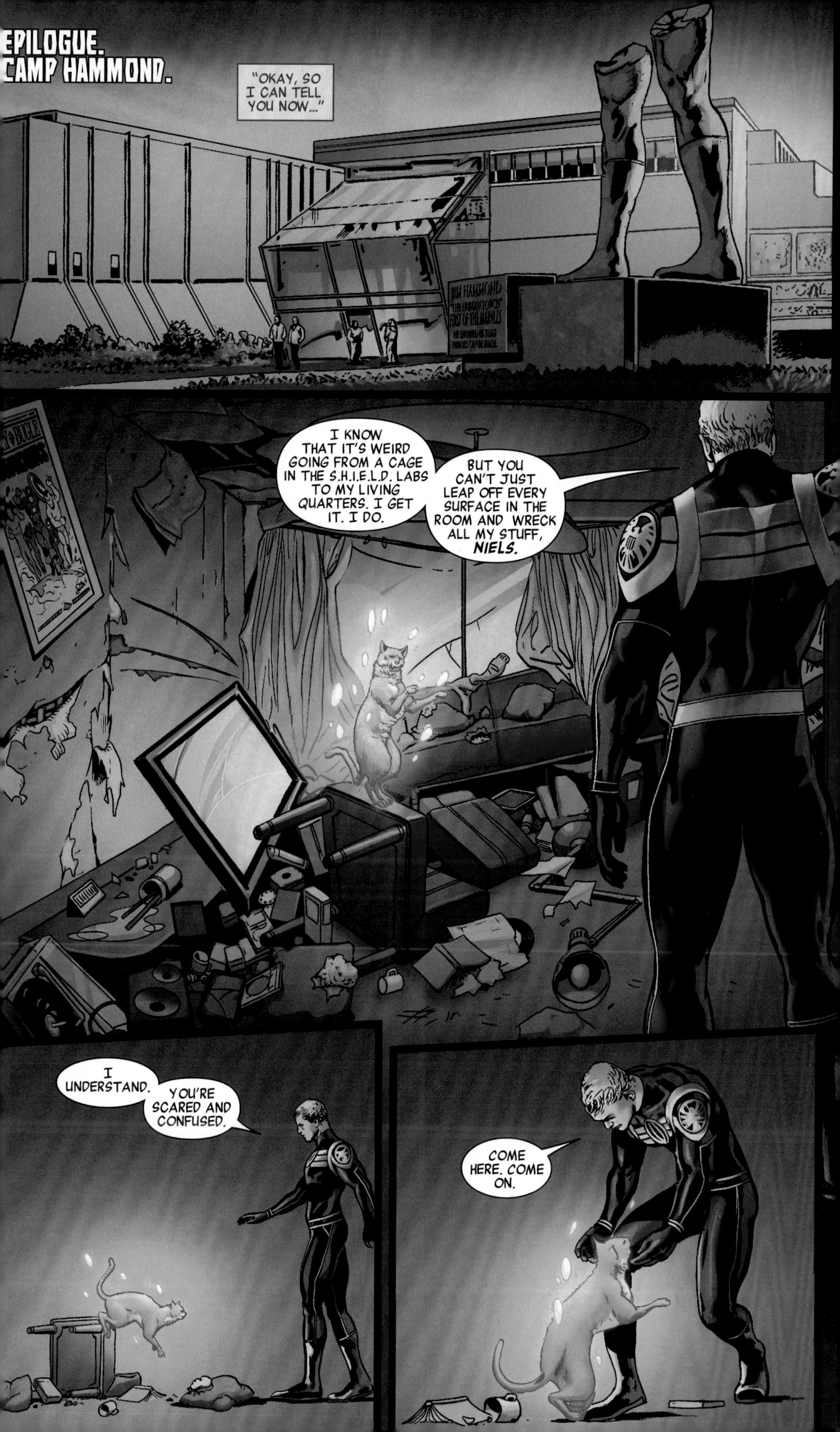
EPILOGUE.
CAMP HAMMOND.
"OKAY, SO I CAN TELL YOU NOW..."
JIM HAMMOND
I KNOW THAT IT'S WEIRD GOING FROM A CAGE IN THE S.H.I.E.L.D. LABS TO MY LIVING QUARTERS. I GET IT. I DO.
BUT YOU CAN'T JUST LEAP OFF EVERY SURFACE IN THE ROOM AND WRECK ALL MY STUFF, *NIELS.*
I UNDERSTAND.
YOU'RE SCARED AND CONFUSED.
COME HERE. COME ON.

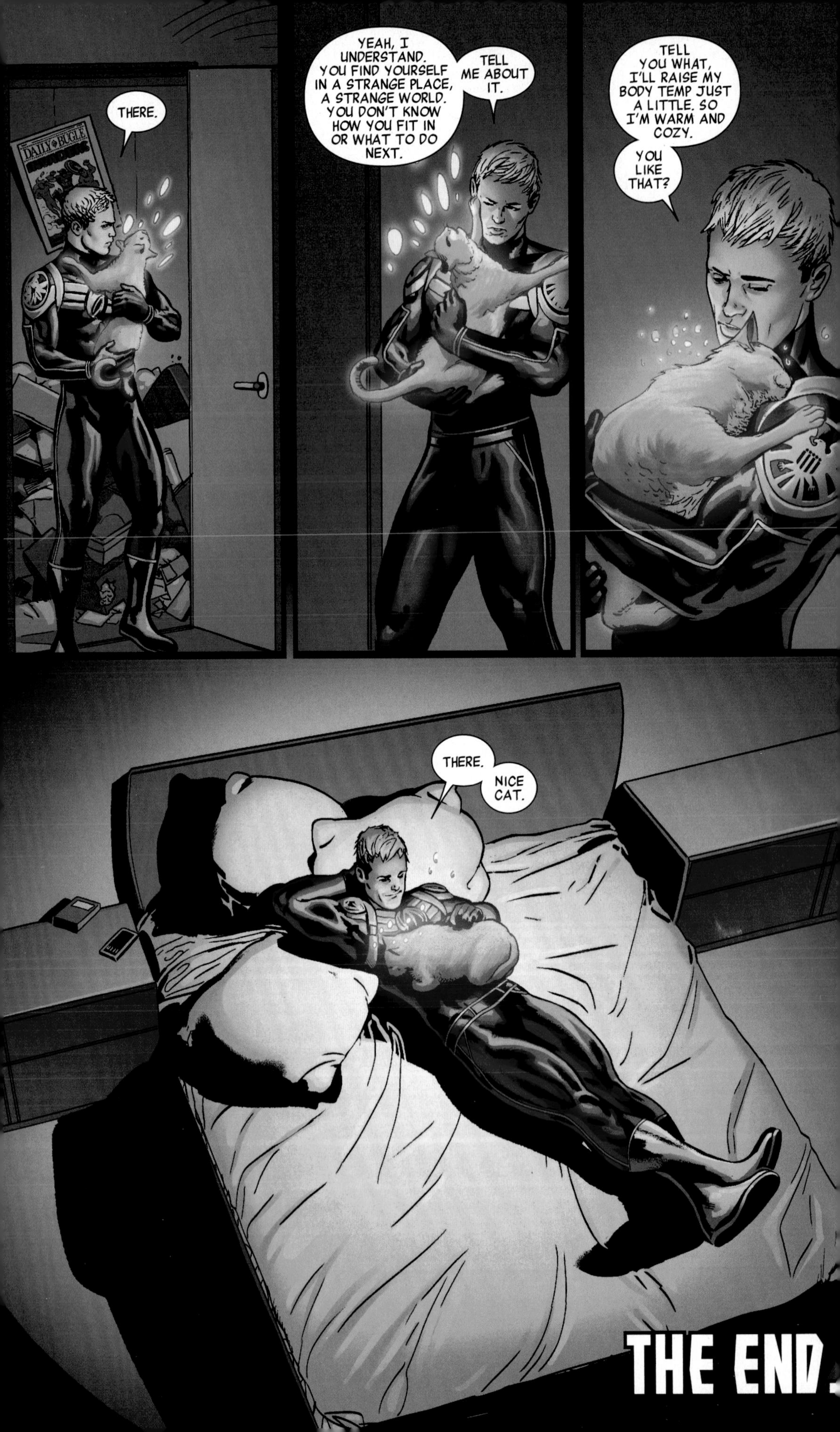
DAILY BUGLE
THERE.
YEAH, I UNDERSTAND. YOU FIND YOURSELF IN A STRANGE PLACE, A STRANGE WORLD. YOU DON'T KNOW HOW YOU FIT IN OR WHAT TO DO NEXT.
TELL ME ABOUT IT.
TELL YOU WHAT, I'LL RAISE MY BODY TEMP JUST A LITTLE. SO I'M WARM AND COZY.
YOU LIKE THAT?
THERE.
NICE CAT.
THE END.

A FAREWELL TO ARMS

THE INVADERS
MARVEL COMICS GROUP
25¢
1
AUG
02948
ALL-NEW!
THE GREATEST SUPERHEROES OF WORLD WAR TWO!
THE INVADERS
ANOTHER FRANKLY FABULOUS FIRST ISSUE!
OKAY, AXIS--HERE WE COME!!
BATTLE OVER BRITAIN!

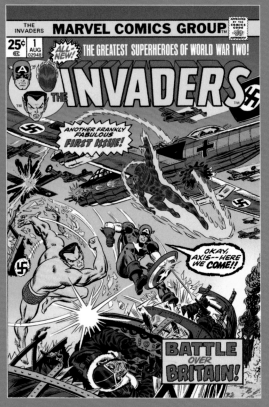

INVADERS #1 (1975) cover art by John Romita Sr. & Petra Goldberg

#1
ALL-NEW INVADERS
JAMES ROBINSON
STEVE PUGH

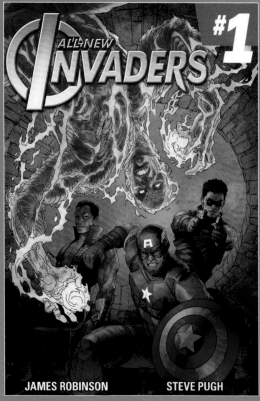

ALL-NEW INVADERS #1 (2014) cover art by Mukesh Singh

Wow, fifteen issues means fifteen months of my life writing the Invaders and loving every one of my writing experiences. I hadn't worked for Marvel in decades. My last work was a run on Cable many, many moons past. But feeling I needed to shake up my life and look in new exciting creative directions, I called up Marvel editor Mark Paniccia to see if Marvel had any interest in my working for them. (As a sidebar, Mark is someone I've known for 20+ years, beginning with my work on the Ultraverse titles. Anyone remember my series Firearm? Anyway, Mark is someone I can not see for years and then pick up a conversation with like I saw him a day prior. We always have had that kind of relationship/friendship, so reaching out to him seemed like the right move.) Mark came back to me a day later, with the offer of the Invaders. It made sense, obviously, me doing Golden Age Marvel heroes. I saw that immediately. However, when I made it clear I wanted to do something fresher -- featuring Cap, Namor, Jim Hammond, etc. but without all the usual tropes, I was gratified that Marvel agreed to let me run with my fresher take.

And was that fresh take a success? Well, you can be the judge.

While the book didn't stick around that long, at the same time, I got 15 issues of fantastic adventures with these characters I love. I especially enjoyed developing Jim Hammond and giving him some of the love and respect Marvel's first superhero deserves. (Yeah, yeah, I know there's some debate as to whether Namor was the first hero due to his appearance in the unpublished--and ever so slightly earlier Motion Picture Funnies Weekly--but that's splitting hairs. The book wasn't published. Period. And Jim Hammond the Human Torch was the first feature in Marvel Mystery Comics #1 and had the iconic first cover by pulp cover artist legend Frank R. Paul to prove it. So there.) Anyway, I'm so, so gratified to those who did check the book out and stay with it for its full run. Were there more plans? Yes, absolutely. I think it's clear from the last few pages of this issue that there is a lot to the saga I'd intended to tell, that remains as-yet untold.

Will the loose ends get tied up? Heavens, I hope so, as these are some pretty big strings. Galactus, Aarkus and the Eternals. Killraven and the Martian invaders. Not to mention smaller personal stuff like developing Iron Cross more as well as Radiance and her burgeoning relationship with Jim. Don't worry, I intend to see these plotlines through in the books I'll be doing for Marvel in the future. Yes, that's right, you haven't seen the last of me, as upcoming announcements from Marvel will confirm soon. So I'll see you then, hopefully.

I'd also like to thank Mark and his assistant editor, Emily Shaw, for all they've done. They had my back over and over again with many the creative and/or deadline crisis and always came through, giving me consideration, amazing creative input, and creative respect.

I'd also like to thank my artist, Steve Pugh, who knocked it out of the park on a monthly basis. I'm thrilled to be working with him again on one of those as-yet-to be announced projects, so it isn't the last of us together either.

Thanks to Cory Petit for the amazing lettering and GURU-eFX for the sumptuous color.

And again, thank you the reader most of all, so sticking with the book and allowing me 15 issues with some of my favorite characters. Don't worry, you'll see them pop up again before you know it.

- JAMES ROBINSON

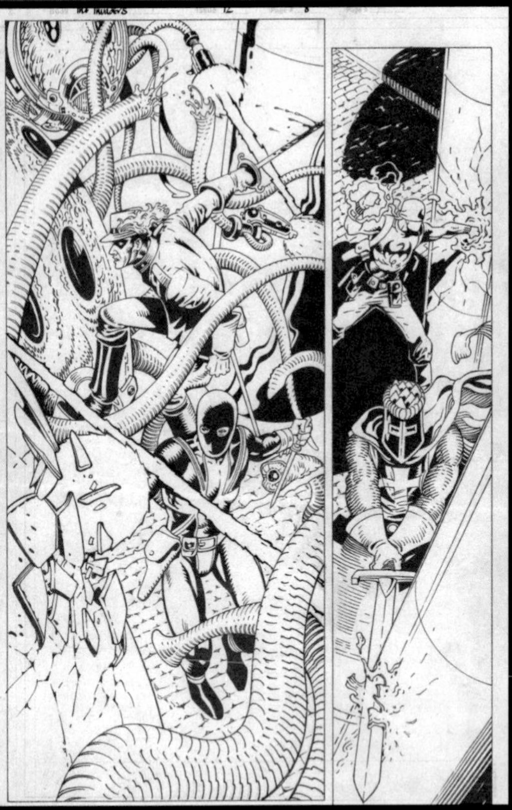

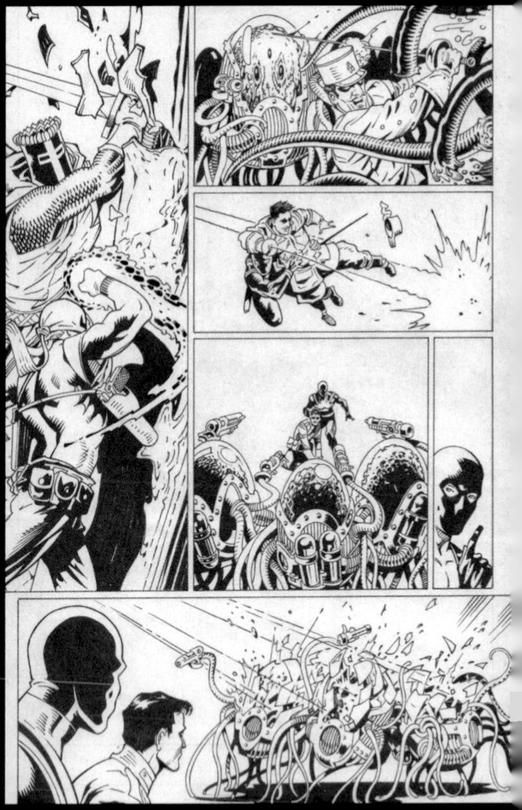

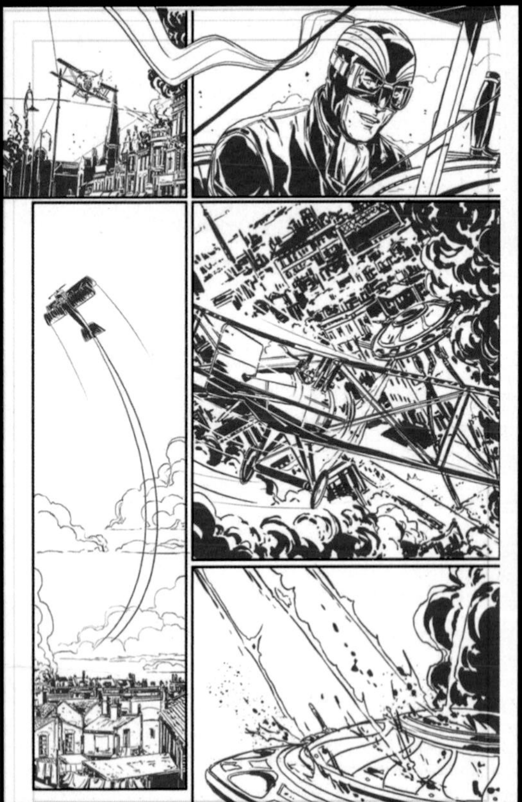

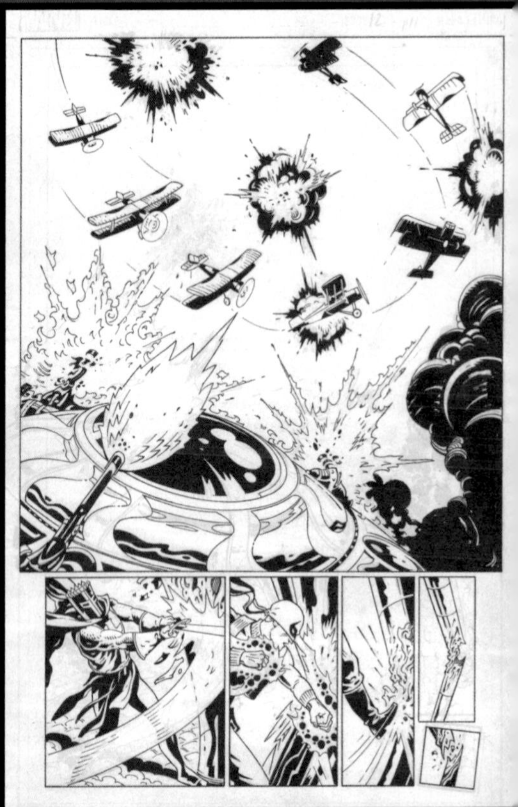

#12 pages 8-11 flashback pencils and inks by Barry Kitson, Marc Laming and P. Craig Russell

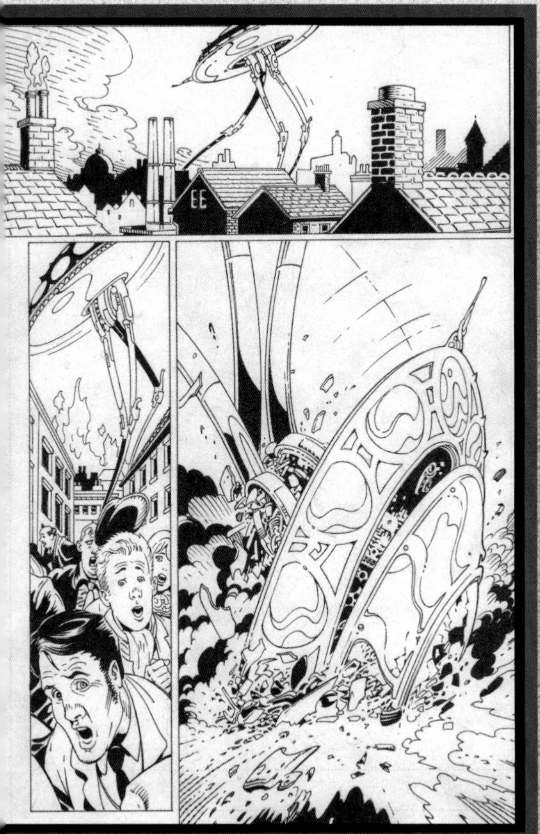

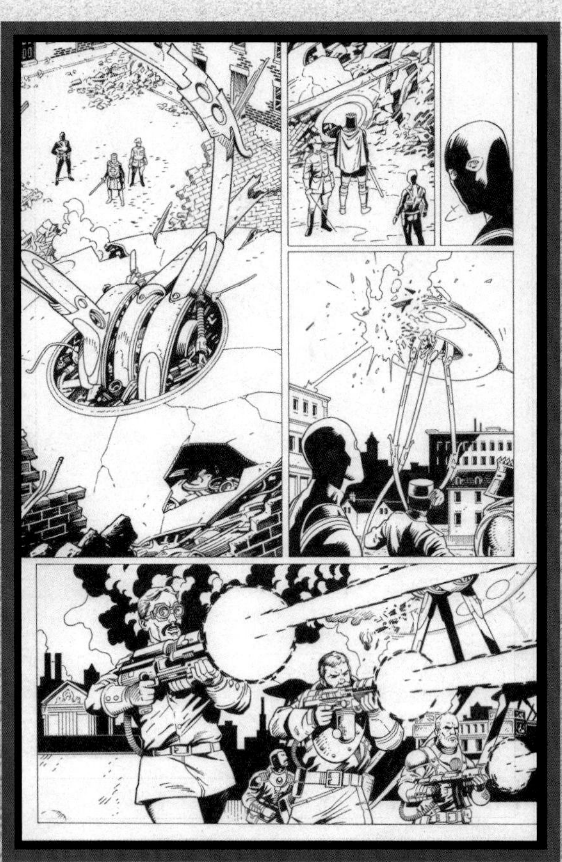

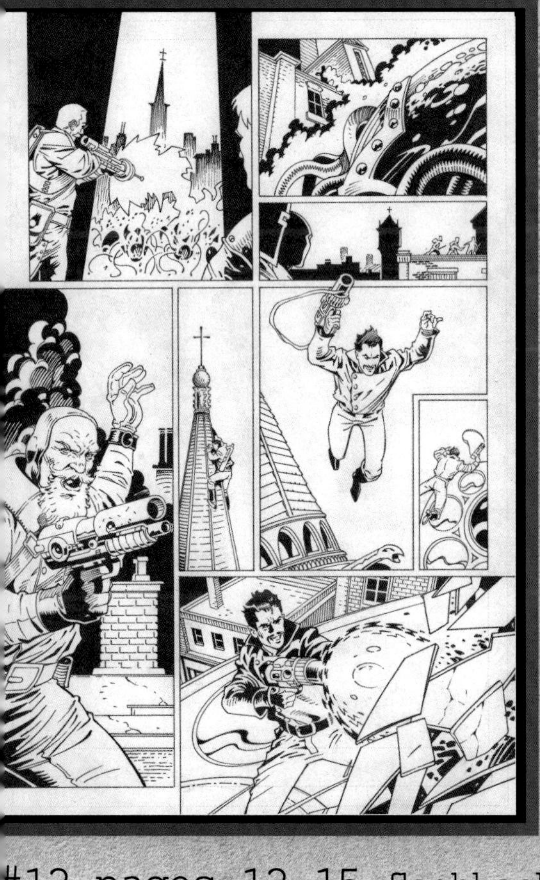

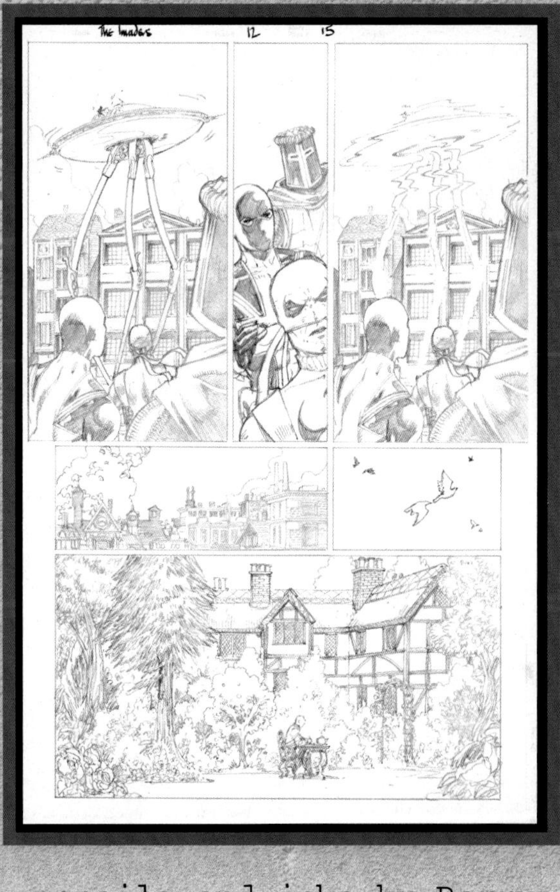
THE Invaders 12 15

#12 pages 12-15 flashback pencils and inks by Barry Kitson, Marc Laming and P. Craig Russell

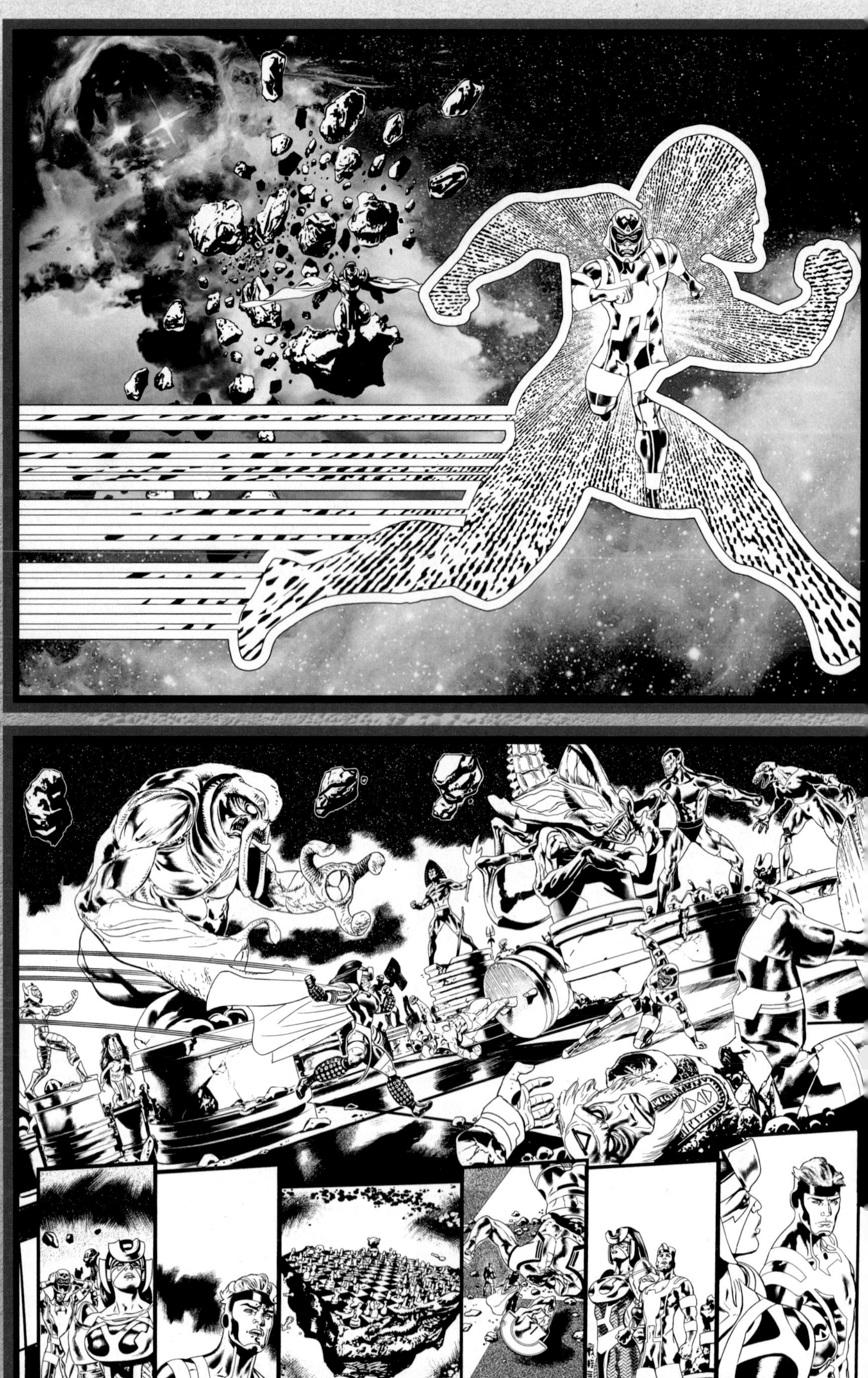

#13 pages 2-5 pencils and inks by Steve Pugh